DIVINE NATURE AND

HUMAN LANGUAGE

OTHER WORKS OF WILLIAM P. ALSTON

Epistemic Justification: Essays in the Theory of Knowledge

Philosophy of Language

Religious Belief and Philosophical Thought:
  Readings in the Philosophy of Religion (editor)

Readings in Twentieth-Century Philosophy
  (coeditor with George Nakhnikian)

The Problems of Philosophy: Introductory Readings
  (coeditor with Richard B. Brandt)

Divine Nature and Human Language

Essays in Philosophical Theology

William P. Alston

Cornell University Press

ITHACA AND LONDON

First published 1989 by Cornell University Press.

International Standard Book Number 0-8014-2258-2 (cloth)
International Standard Book Number 0-8014-9545-8 (paper)
Library of Congress Catalog Card Number 89-898
Printed in the United States of America
Librarians: Library of Congress cataloging information
appears on the last page of the book.

The paper in this book is acid-free and meets the guidelines for permanence
and durability of the Committee on Production Guidelines for Book
Longevity of the Council on Library Resources.

For Ellen and John Donnelly

Contents

Acknowledgments

I would like to thank the many people with whom I have discussed philosophical theology over the years and who have thereby contributed greatly to whatever merit these essays may possess. There is first of all my teacher, Charles Hartshorne, from whom I usually differ but from whom I have never failed to learn. Then there are my students, whose persistent and often incredulous reactions have stimulated me to think better of many of my views and, let us hope, to think better. I have been fortunate to retain close intellectual contact with many of my former graduate students, and so I have been able to continue to learn from them. I would especially like to mention in this connection Robert Audi, George Mavrodes, Nelson Pike, Alvin Plantinga, William Rowe, and William Wainwright. The participants in my two NEH Summer Seminars on Theological Predication were a great help to me in coming to what I hope are sounder views on this matter than I would otherwise have held. From that group I am especially grateful to Richard Creel, James Keller, Joseph Runzo, and Axel Steuer. The formation of the Society of Christian Philosophers in 1978 has made a tremendous difference to my intellectual life, as well as in other ways. Through meetings of the Society, through the intellectual and spiritual fellowship it has fostered among Christian philosophers, and through the stimulation it provides to turn one's energies to philosophizing about and from the Christian faith, the pattern of my life over the past decade has been very different from what it otherwise would have been. Among the members of the Society from whom I have learned much, I would like to single out, in addition to persons already named, Marilyn and Robert Adams, William Hasker, Norman

Kretzmann, Thomas Morris, Philip Quinn, James Ross, Eleonore Stump, Peter van Inwagen, Nicholas Wolterstorff, and Linda Zagzebski. Among the people not included in any of the above categories who have been extremely helpful on the topics of this book I especially think of Joshua Hoffman, William Mann, Gary Rosenkrantz, and Richard Swinburne.

Needless to say, philosophical stimulation does not come only through face-to-face contact. I have greatly profited from the writings of many persons, including many of the above. Some of those not already mentioned to whose works I find myself recurring frequently are I. M. Crombie, Austin Farrer, John Hick, and Basil Mitchell. I omit mention of great thinkers of the past, such as St. Thomas Aquinas, from whom I have perhaps learned the most.

I also want to express gratitude for the stimulation and enlightenment I have received from the many conferences in philosophical theology and allied matters in which I have participated in recent years. I have already mentioned the meetings of the Society of Christian Philosophers. The series of conferences on the philosophy of religion that have been held biennially by the Center for Philosophy of Religion at Notre Dame has been a major force in sparking work in the field and bringing together its leading figures. Essays 10 and 11 were presented at two such conferences. Participation in the Center for Christian Studies at Calvin College in 1979–80 gave an enormous boost to my work. The annual Wheaton Conference in Philosophy at Wheaton College in Wheaton, Illinois, is an important event in the philosophical community, and I owe much to involvement in those conferences. Arthur Holmes is primarily responsible for them, and the philosophical world is greatly in his debt. Essays 1 and 2 grew out of lectures presented at the 1978 Wheaton Conference. The annual meetings of the Society for Philosophy of Religion constitute a great educational experience for all involved. Members owe a debt of gratitude to Frank R. Harrison, III, Secretary-Treasurer *in perpetuo,* for his indefatigable work in the Society. Finally, the 1986 NEH Summer Institute in the Philosophy of Religion at Western Washington University was an invaluable philosophical experience for participants and staff.

I should also like to express appreciation to the students in my courses and seminars over the years who have helped me to see where I was going wrong and, sometimes, where I was going right, and who have been a great help in keeping alive the spirit of enthusiasm for the enterprise. Special thanks go to the office staff at the Syracuse University philosophy department, and especially to Sue McDougal and Lisa Mowins, for their unfailing cheerfulness in typing, photocopying, or whatever else is needed for the progress of philosophical understanding. My chairman at Syracuse, Stewart Thau, provides an ideal environment for philosophical work, and my colleague Jonathan Bennett never turns a deaf ear to requests for comments. My thanks also go to the original publishers of these essays for granting me permission to reprint them in this volume. And gratitude is due Norman Kretzmann for saving me from the title "God and Talk about God".

Last (and therefore first) my eternal love and gratitude go to my wife, Valerie, for her inextinguishable good humor, support, and love in the face of a philosopher who all too frequently gets into jams, whether from over-commitment, under-equipment, or the sheer difficulty of the subject. May she attain the crown in heaven that is her due.

WILLIAM P. ALSTON

Syracuse, New York

DIVINE NATURE AND

HUMAN LANGUAGE

Introduction

I

The essays in this volume, composed between 1979 and 1988, represent some of the fruit of my return to philosophical theology after a long absence. When I emerged from graduate school in 1949 I was hired by the University of Michigan to teach, inter alia, philosophy of religion, and a considerable part of my philosophical work in the 1950s was devoted to that subject—not, I now think, to any great effect. When I drifted away from the church in the late 50s my involvement in the philosophy of religion diminished accordingly. Unlike some of my distinguished contemporaries, I have found my philosophical interest in philosophy of religion varying directly with my religious involvement. Hence it was only after I returned to the church in the mid-70s that I turned once again to philosophical theology. I like to think that what I had learned in the intervening two decades in philosophy of language, philosophical psychology, and epistemology has put me in a position to tackle the issues of philosophical theology more effectively.

A good part of my time in recent years has been devoted to thinking about the experience or "perception" of God as a basis for beliefs about God. That interest is not represented in the present volume, largely because I am engaged in writing a treatise on the subject that will, I hope, supersede the articles I have published on the topic. The articles republished here represent the other main foci of my works in this area: the interpretation of talk about God (I steadfastly refuse to use the horrid neologism 'God-talk'), the nature of God, and God's relation to His creation. Here is a brief preview of the articles in each grouping.

Part I. Talk about God

Essay 1 explores the idea that God can be spoken of only in irreducible metaphors, metaphors that are irreducible in the strong sense that what is said by their use cannot be said, *even in part,* in literal terms. It is argued that if we can make any assertion about God definite enough to have truth-value, it will be in principle possible to say the same thing literally, at least partially, even if that requires introducing new terms (or new meanings for old terms) into the language for that purpose.

Essay 2 explores the possibility for the literal use of "P-predicates" (predicates that distinctively apply to personal agents) in application to God. More specifically, it considers the limited issue of whether such predicates can be applied to an incorporeal being. After distinguishing a "private paradigm" and a "functionalist" construal of P-predicates, I argue that there is no bar to the application of P-predicates to an incorporeal being on either view. In considering the functionalist interpretation, the discussion inevitably touches on the question of whether action concepts can be applied to an incorporeal being, i.e., whether there can be an incorporeal agent. (The answer is affirmative.) As a prelude to all this, the literal-figurative distinction is elucidated, continuing the more extended treatment of metaphor in Essay 1.

Essays 3 and 4 continue the investigation of the application of P-predicates and action predicates to God. The inquiry is broadened out beyond incorporeality to include problems posed by divine perfection and timelessness. The functionalist construal of P-predicates is in the foreground in both essays. Surprisingly enough, it turns out that functionalism offers real advantages in the search for a basic commonality in concepts of the human and divine psyche. It is not claimed that any human P-predicates can be applied to God with exactly the same meaning, but it is maintained that more abstract functional concepts can be constructed that will apply equally on both sides of the divide. In Essay 4 it is acknowledged that these concepts are quite sparse and that the univocal core of theological predication they provide has to be supplemented with figurative and symbolic discourse if the needs of religion are to be met.

Essay 5 turns from the predicate to the subject and explores the conditions for reference to God. Kripke's critique of a descriptivist view of proper name reference and his sketch of an alternative "picture" are exploited to provide a nondescriptivist view of reference to God. Reasons are given for supposing that this mode of reference to God is more basic in religion, and implications are drawn from this thesis.

Part II. The Nature of God

Essay 6 provides the blueprint for what follows in this section. Hartshorne's critique of "classical" philosophical theology is examined, and the results are mixed. On some points Hartshorne's "neoclassical" theology is awarded the palm, and on other points the classical theology of the likes of Aquinas gets the nod. The result is a mixed conception of God. With Hartshorne, God's nature is taken to involve potentiality, contingency, internal relatedness to creatures, and complexity; while with Aquinas God is taken to be absolutely perfect, (absolutely) omnipotent, incorporeal, atemporal, immutable, and to have freely chosen to created the world ex nihilo. It is argued that Hartshorne's arguments fail to shake Aquinas' position on the latter group of attributes, and that the combination of those views of Aquinas with the Hartshornean position on the first group is a coherent one.

Essay 7 argues that the "classical" attributes of omniscience and atemporality can allow for genuine divine-human dialogue and other divine-human interaction, though it acknowledges that divine "omnidetermination" (God determines every detail of His creation) would be subversive of such a possibility.

Essay 8 plunges into the continuing debate over the bearing of divine omniscience on human free will. I myself hold, with Boethius, Aquinas, and many others, that if we take God to be nontemporal in His own being, we lose even the appearance of an incompatibility. Since on this conception of God there is no *fore*knowledge (God doesn't know *in advance* what I choose to do now), God doesn't provide anything earlier in time that is incompatible with my doing something else. However, that view does not surface in this essay, which is concerned to suggest that quite different conceptions of free will are employed by various parties to the debate, with the inevitable result that they often argue past one another.

Essay 9 looks into divine cognition. Running counter to the current trend in Anglo-American philosophical theology, it argues that *beliefs* should not be attributed to God, whether or not God's knowledge is propositionally structured. The central part of the argument is that it is a mistake to think of divine knowledge as true belief + . . . ; it should rather be construed as an immediate awareness of facts (on the view that it is propositionally structured), or an immediate awareness of the whole of reality. Since beliefs would not figure in divine knowledge, there is no place for them in the divine psyche.

Part III. God and the World

The aspect of God's relation to the world that bulks largest in the religious life is His action in (toward, with respect to) the world. Essay 10 tackles the most fundamental issues involved in thinking through the concept of such activity. Thus this essay continues the concern of Essays 2 and 4 with divine activity, but at a more concrete level. Having earlier assured ourselves that actions concepts can be applied to God, we want to answer the most pressing questions that arise with respect to His activity. Is everything that happens in the world something that God does? If so, on what basis can we mark out certain events rather than others as God's doing in a special sense? Will this require us to think of God as sometimes producing effects in the world outside the course of nature? Can we recognize the possibility, and the reality, of any such "divine interventions"? How is the belief in such interventions related to the belief in the reign of natural law? The essay is rather latitudinarian on these issues, arguing that different possibilities have to be acknowledged. For example, even if universal divine agency is admitted, there will still be a point in marking out certain events as "acts of God" in some special sense. And although there are no real bars to recognizing divine action in the world outside the course of nature, there are other ways of marking out those special acts of God.

Essay 11 is devoted to one particular area of divine activity in the world, the work of the Holy Spirit in "sanctification", transforming, or contributing to the transformation of, the individual into the kind of person God has destined him/her to be. Various models of sanctification are distinguished: the "fiat" model, according to which God produces the improvements in character by just willing that it be done; the "interpersonal" model, according to which God exercises the same general modes of interpersonal influence that are open to us (though with much greater resources), and the "sharing" model, according to which there is a partial breakdown of the barriers between a human life and God's life that makes possible a (very partial) participation of the human being in the life of God. It is suggested that the last model is needed to accommodate some Christian insights into the work of the Holy Spirit. This essay, written for a volume devoted to discussions of Christian doctrine, is the most theological one in the book. It is devoted to developing the view of sanctification that best fits the "data" of the

Christian tradition and the Christian life. As a result it makes liberal use of the Bible, liturgy, and other deposits of Christian experience.

Essay 12 takes up the bearing of God on morality. It has the limited aim of determining the most defensible form of a divine command ethical theory. The contention is that the theory is best advised to think of divine commands as constitutive of moral *obligation,* rather than moral *goodness* or any other form of goodness, and to deny that any obligations attach to God. That will leave the theory free to construe divine moral goodness in some other way than as the satisfaction of obligations (and hence in some other way than as conformity to God's own commands), and it will enable the theory to hold that divine commands, as an expression of divine goodness, could not be issued arbitrarily. The essay also suggests the view that God Himself, that individual being, is the supreme criterion of goodness, moral and otherwise.

II

The essays in this volume by no means add up to a system of philosophical theology, or of any part thereof. The first section, on theological language, does exhibit more of a connected whole than the others, and I will say more about that later. But, in general, the book, like most volumes of collected essays, consists of detailed exploration of a number of particular issues, without any overall theory that assigns each its place in a system. I won't try to supply a general theory in this introduction, but readers might find some interest in the background, or general point of view, from which these treatments of specific issues have emerged. I think that the most useful thing for me to do in this connection is to make explicit my fundamental religious and philosophical orientation insofar as it is relevant to the investigations gathered here.

First, then, I am a Christian of a relatively conservative cast, by current standards outside evangelical and fundamentalist circles. I am not a fundamentalist about the Bible, and I am alive to the need of each age to rethink the substance of the faith. But I take the Christian tradition very seriously; I don't feel free to ignore it whenever it doesn't jibe with my own personal predilections. Hence the interest, displayed in these essays, in exploring, partly refashioning, and defending a fairly traditional conception of God and His work in the world, a conception that owes a great deal to medieval philosophical theology. This enterprise involves the use of much up-to-date philosophical equipment. (See, e.g., the use of functionalism in philosophical psychology in Essays 2, 3, and 4, and the use of a Kripkean theory of reference in 5.) This blend of fairly traditional Christianity, heavy borrowings from medieval philosophical theology, and the employment of contemporary analytical philosophy is typical of much recent work in philosophical theology.

The philosophical background can be most effectively set out under several headings.

(A) *Anti-positivism, anti-scientism, anti-naturalism.* (I put it in this negative way, rather than simply using the label "supernaturalism", because of various unwanted connotations of the latter.) I see no reason to limit reality, or what we can know about reality, to what can be discovered or established by the "scientific method", or to what can be known by the senses or by reasoning based on their deliverances. Still less am I disposed to accept verificationist constraints on meaningfulness, statementhood, or capacity for truth-value. This leaves me free to take seriously the possibility that religious traditions embody fundamental truths about reality, of the highest concern for human life, even if some or all of these truths are not formulated exactly right. Needless to say, this does not mean that I am disposed to accept uncritically any religious claim that comes down the pike. But it does mean that my mind is not closed to them in advance by general philosophical prejudices of the sorts just mentioned.

(B) *Realism.* I find myself at odds with most contemporary liberal theologians and religious thinkers (outside the ranks of "analytic philosophy") in accepting an uncompromisingly realistic interpretation of religious belief. I take it that when someone believes that God created the heavens and earth, then, assuming that the belief is sufficiently determinate, that belief is true or false depending on whether things are as asserted. The truth-value doesn't depend on the epistemic status of the believer, on what consensus does or doesn't exist in her social group or culture, on the inward passion involved, or on anything else of the sort. There is a truth of the matter that is independent of us, our "conceptual schemes", our social institutions and associations, our conventions and values. If the world does exist only because it is God's will that it do so, then the belief just mentioned is true; if not, it is false. And this is so whether or not we have any way of determining which it is. I note, to my dismay, that many colleagues in theology and religious studies find it unutterably quaint that serious thinkers still take this realistic stance. No doubt, it is especially difficult to render religious beliefs determinate enough to be susceptible of an objective truth-value. But that is the only bar to an objective truth-value, a truth-value that depends on how it is with what we are talking about and not on us, our society, or our culture (unless that is what we are talking about in the particular instance). I take it that religious claims, by rights, resist anti-realist reductions even more than claims about the physical environment. Even though I am a hard-nosed realist up and down the line, I can see more appeal in the idea that talk of the physical world is just talk about how *we* conceptually structure our experience than I can in analogous talk about the target of religious worship and faith. (At least that is so if the question concerns the character our discourse actually has, rather than *proposals* for its reconstruction; widespread doubt about the real existence of God undoubtedly renders nonrealist reconstructions in religion attractive to many.) It would seem to be a failing in faith, as well as in reason, to deny that God is what He is and does what He does, whatever we may think or feel about it. This is perhaps the deepest divide in current religious thought. Let the reader be forewarned that I take very seriously the idea that there is a truth about these matters, and that I am interested in getting as close to that as possible on the issues I discuss. On the other hand, I make no extravagant claims to have arrived at the final truth here. I can claim only to have presented considerations that seem to me to point in certain directions.

(C) *Multiple sources of religious knowledge.* In opposition to exclusivists of all stripes—Biblical fundamentalists, "traditionalists", rationalists—I hold that there are multiple sources of religious knowledge and/or rational (justified) belief. I take very seriously the idea that people are experientially aware of God, that God presents Himself to their experience in various ways and thereby provides them with an empirical basis for beliefs about His presence and activity. That is the topic of the book in progress I mentioned at the beginning of this Introduction. But I also take seriously the idea that God has revealed Himself, facts about His nature and character, and some of His purposes and intentions, through certain selected recipients and, more generally, through the religious community and its traditions. The traditions of the community thus serve as another avenue of religious truth, not to be taken uncritically, but not to be rejected out of hand either. Finally, I do not reject the enterprise of natural theology, the attempt to establish basic truths concerning the existence and nature of God by reasoning that does not rely in any way on data or convictions taken from the religious life. I do not think that natural theology can live up to the expectations of its more enthusiastic advocates, but nor do I take it to be worthless. I feel that all these sources have something to contribute to our understanding of God, His nature, His purposes, and His relations to us. This, no doubt, puts me in the camp of those who have lately been advocating a "cumulative case" for religious belief, though I differ with this or that cumulative case theorist on one or another particular point. But I unreservedly agree that it is a great mistake to allow one's enthusiasm for "religious experience" to lead one to ignore the tradition or the contribution of natural reason, or vice versa.

In these essays there is no discussion of religious epistemology. Nor is there any attempt to provide "arguments for the existence of God". Here I am working from within a theistic (more specifically, Christian) tradition, laying out alternative construals, providing grounds for deciding between them, elucidating concepts, laying out possibilities, tracing the interrelations of different doctrines or ways of thinking, seeking more adequate ways of construing one or another aspect. The book is a contribution to the classic project of Faith Seeking Understanding. I seek to bring rational intelligibility and order into a system of belief and thought within a religious tradition, rather than to examine the system's credentials from without. (I hope and trust that this will not make these essays without interest and relevance to thinkers who do not share my religious commitments.) Nevertheless, the multiplicity of sources mentioned above is reflected in these essays. For in carrying out my "inside job" I draw on what we have learned in the community from the experience of God, from the Bible and church tradition, and from natural theology, and bring this to bear on the task of understanding the nature of God and His relations to His creation, and on the task of understanding our talk and thought about God. Without contributions from all these sources I would not have the resources that are at my disposal.

Let me say a word about the way in which religious life and practice is taken into account in these essays. The most general point is that the conceptions, the beliefs, and the talk that set our problems are rooted in the life of theistic religions. We only have this thought and talk to philosophize about because these religions have existed as ongoing communities. This should be too obvious for notice, but I'm afraid that it is often ignored by philosophers, who not infrequently seem to think that standard issues in the philosophy of religion like the "problem of foreknowledge and freedom" are purely theoretical philosophical problems that have their ultimate roots in the course of philosophical thinking about the world and would still pose the questions they pose for philosophical reflection if there were no such thing as religion.

But this historical mode of dependence on the actual practice of religion is one that, if I am right, attaches, willy nilly, to all philosophy that is concerned with religious issues. More distinctively, religious life and practice are explicitly appealed to in these essays. Here are some examples. Essay 4 points out that the "univocal core" of talk about God that I there identify is much too sparse for worship, devotion, and spiritual direction, and that for those purposes it has to be supplemented by a liberal dose of figurative and symbolic language. Essay 5 appeals to the ways in which people learn to refer to God in religious communities, in support of the view that "direct reference" is more basic there than "descriptivist reference". Essay 7 gets its problem from the fact that divine-human dialogue bulks large in the practice of theistic religion. Essay 10 makes much of the central importance of particular divine acts in the religious life and in religious traditions, and it depends heavily on the point that even if, in some sense, everything is done by God, it is crucial to religion to mark out some events as "acts of God" in a special sense. Finally Essay 11 appeals at every point to the Christian experience of the sanctifying work of the Holy Spirit.

In this connection, let's note that philosophers of religion have, of late, been philosophizing in the light of actual religious phenomena, and, in many cases, philosophizing out of a religious commitment. The development of the Society of Christian Philosophers and of its journal, *Faith and Philosophy*, is testimony to this. The journal, according to its official statement, is "designed primarily for articles which address philosophical issues from a Christian perspective, for discussions of philosophical issues which arise within the Christian faith, and for articles from any perspective which deal critically with the philosophical credentials of the Christian faith". Such recent volumes of essays as *Rationality, Religious Belief, and Moral Commitment,* ed. Robert Audi and William J. Wainwright (Cornell University Press, 1986), and two volumes edited by Thomas V. Morris, *Philosophy and the Christian Faith* (University of Notre Dame Press, 1988) and *Divine and Human Action* (Cornell University Press, 1988), also exhibit this trend. These developments parallel the recent emphasis in the philosophy of science on philosophical questions that arise from the actual practice of science, now and in the past. In the bad old days of not so long ago, philosophers of science typically took as their main example 'All X's are Y's', or, more substantively, 'All ravens are black'. In these more enlightened times reference to what actually goes on in, e.g., relativity physics or microbiology or cognitive psychology is *de rigeur* for any serious work in philosophy of science.

III

It may also be pertinent to mention some other features of these essays that distinguish them from much work in the field.

(A) *The middle way.* Not surprisingly, it is the extreme and obscure positions in philosophical theology, and elsewhere in philosophy and in intellectual endeavor generally, that get the big press. They are exciting, provocative, annoying, sometimes even maddening, but rarely dull. Thus Hume with his absurd theories no one is even tempted to accept gets the attention, rather than the sane and balanced Reid. In our century, in Anglo-American philosophy it is Wittgenstein, with his deliberately cryptic utterances, and Quine with his paradoxical and often counterintuitive positions, that are in the limelight, rather than more sensible and judicious thinkers. The essays in this volume definitely fall on the balanced, judicious, side of this divide. The via media charted herein, in the spirit of my Anglican heritage, is evident at a number of points. The first four essays steer a middle course between pansymbolism and the view that all our serious statemental talk about God is literal, and univocal with talk of creatures. Essay 4, in particular, explicitly plumps for a "partial univocity" position that has been widely neglected in favor of more extreme views. Essay 6, with "via media" in the title, marks out an intermediate position between "classical" and "neoclassical" theology. (Is this position "neo-neoclassical" or is it perhaps "post-neoclassical"?) Essay 10 offers something to (almost) everyone, in the true Anglican spirit, by holding that we can mark out special acts as God as we do, whether or not God intervenes in the course of nature; and the latter possibility cannot be ruled out. More generally, the essays in Parts II and III mark out a middle position between crass supernaturalism and reductive naturalisms, between slavish adherence to medieval philosophical theology and the iconoclastic view that everything prior to 1950 has been superseded, and, as previously noted, between rationalism and attention to the facts of religious life.

(B) *Modesty of aims.* Along with these moderate positions goes a modest level of aspiration. In some cases, as in Essays 2, 10, and 11, I am concerned, in large part, with laying out possibilities rather than arguing for an unambiguous view as to how it is. I am often centrally concerned to argue that so-and-so does not prevent such-and-such, does not render it impossible. Thus Essay 2 in its central section is restricted to arguing that incorporeality does not prevent the application of P-predicates and action predicates to God. Essays 3 and 4, are concerned to argue that divine perfection and timelessness do not prevent the univocal application of a core of P-predicates to God and human beings. Essay 6 argues, inter alia, that divine timelessness does not prevent God from being internally related to creatures or from exhibiting potentiality and contingency in His being. Essay 7 carries this further by arguing that divine timelessness does not render divine-human dialogue impossible. In Essay 10 there is the contention that even if God does not act outside the course of nature, that does not prevent us from marking out certain events as "special acts of God".

The modesty just illustrated does not stem solely from the fact that these essays are each devoted to one little piece of the total picture. It is also due in part to a general view as to what we can expect to accomplish in philosophical theology. In my view, many thinkers in this field have much too high a level of aspiration. If we stand outside all religious traditions and seek to settle the outstanding issues on a purely nonreligious basis, abstracting from our experience of God and His dealings with us, there is little we can establish. But even when we avail ourselves of all the sources to which I have been pointing, it is unwise, I believe, to expect definitive resolution of many of the important problems. We can make considerable progress in laying out the basic nature of God, as I try to do in a sketchy way in Essay 6 (though without mobilizing there the multiple bases of support for such a conception); we can show that it is reasonable to adopt the general point of view of Christian theism (though that is not something attempted in these essays). From within, e.g., Christianity, we can bring conceptual elucidation and rational coherence to the general picture of God, His purposes, and His activity vis-à-vis the creation, though we can hardly expect to establish all this on the basis of external considerations. Nevertheless, I believe that there are many crucial points on which we must be content to remain in the dark. On the exact relation of God's action in the world to the course of nature (10), the extent to which God's actions are "basic" (2), the precise way in which the Holy Spirit goes about the work of sanctification (11), I believe that, when all is said and done, we will have to do without any secure grasp of just how it is. I take a similar position with respect to various issues not touched on in these essays. For example, in connection with the problem of evil I am not sanguine about the possibility of working out a theodicy in which we specify why God allows the particular evils He allows. But within the limits marked out by the aims I do recognize as realistic, there is much valuable work to be done, of which these essays represent only a fragment.

IV

It may be of value to sketch out some general views concerning language and speech, in religion and elsewhere, views that underlie the essays of Part I. First a general historical observation. We tend to turn our attention to talk (thought) about X at periods when things aren't going smoothly with that region of talk. So long as things are proceeding properly, we are immersed *in* the talk instead of thinking *about* it, and our attention is on X itself. Thus in our century, when the cumulative effect of the Enlightenment, the historicism of the nineteenth century, and developments in biology, psychology, and the social sciences have led to widespread disenchantment with traditional religious modes of thought and feeling, there has been a massive concentration on "religious language", with the idea that if we could understand better what it is to use such language we might see that things are not so bad after all. Or sometimes the guiding idea is, rather, that the language might be reconstructed in some way to render what is going on acceptable to contemporary sensibilities.

It is, I take it, already clear from the foregoing that I do not share the disaffection with our religious traditions that inspires this "linguistic turn". Nevertheless, I do think that it is crucially important to get as clear as we can about how religious discourse is to be understood; and apart from the religious importance of this, it is a fascinating philosophical problem in its own right. I must say, however, that I find the literature on the subject bedeviled by numerous confusions. In Essay 2 I complain about the loose use of 'literal', and in 1 there are similar complaints about the rough usage accorded 'metaphorical'. Consider, e.g., the common supposition that by pointing out that talking *to* God is more fundamental in religion than talking *about* God, we can show that religious speech is nonliteral. This ignores the point that language can be used as literally in requests and expressions of attitudes as in flat statements. But this is just the tip of the iceberg. A more fundamental confusion is that between *language* and *speech*, noted briefly in Essays 1 and 2. A language is an abstract system that is used for communication and thought. "Speech", in the technical sense in question, is the use of that system in communication (and/or thought, depending on the exact contours of the technical use of 'speech'). Most discussion of "religious language" or "theological language" has to do rather with "religious *speech*" or "religious *discourse*". It has to do with uses our language is put to in religious contexts, rather than with a distinct language. This confusion may seem innocuous, but I believe that it has had serious consequences, particularly in its false suggestions of a divide between religious discourse and other areas of discourse, and in the way it encourages us to ignore the enormous syntactical and semantic overlap between the religious and nonreligious uses of language. For if we are dealing with separate languages, why should we expect such overlap?

The main general point I want to make, however, has to do with the question of whether the "problem of religious language" is really distinctively concerned with language or speech at all. Let's think of it this way. Once one cuts through all the technicalities, it is clear that the basic aim of these inquiries is to gain a more adequate, more explicit, *understanding* of religious discourse, of our talk about God. The basic aim is to get an adequate fix on *what we are saying* when we utter such sentences as 'God created the heavens and the earth' or 'Glory be to the Father and to the Son and to the Holy Spirit'. But that means that what we are essentially concerned with is to make explicit, elucidate, drag out into the open, the *thoughts*, the *conceptions* that are expressed by that talk. (Understand 'thought' and 'conception' in a broad enough sense to include what is expressed by entreaties, by expressions of feelings and attitudes, and by performatives, as well as by statements.) If we were clear about that, we would not need to worry about the details of the ways in which these thoughts are verbally encoded. We have to refer to the linguistic vehicles of our thoughts because they are the overt expressions of those thoughts. They are publicly accessible, inter-subjectively sharable. By referring to a certain thought as "the thought expressed by 'God wills that all shall be saved'" (or, alternatively, "the thought that God wills that all shall be saved") we can more or less unambiguously pick out the thought we want to consider, the one we want to understand better. But does the linguistic vehicle have any importance other than as an aid to reference? Are we, from a religious point of view, or even from the point of view of a philosophical reflection on religion, concerned with the distinctively *linguistic* details of the ways in which these thoughts are encoded: the syntactical structure, the way the semantics operates, etc.? I can't see that we are. The "problem of religious language" is really a gigantic misnomer for the problem of making explicit the content of religious thought and conception.

Actually, discussions of "religious language" normally proceed in accordance with what I have just been saying. The concentration is on the elucidating of religious thought, more or less conducted in the guise of a concern for the meaning of words or the use of sentences, but without getting into any distinctively linguistic issues. And so it is, for the most part, in Essays 1–4, where I am content to speak with the vulgar. The one place at which the machinery begins to creak is that at which questions are raised about the analytic-synthetic distinction, about the distinction between what belongs to the meaning of a word, in contrast to contingent facts about the things denoted by the word. In Essay 4, I consider this question and rule that since we are primarily interested in our thought about God, it is not crucial how much of the thought of God as just or merciful is carried by the *meaning* of the words 'just' and 'merciful' and how much falls outside that territory. This is one point at which there are concrete disadvantages of pretending to be dealing with something other than the real focus of concern.

The main contentions concerning theological predication in Essays 1–4 are, I believe, adequately set out there, but it may be of use to put them together in a summary statement. Our thought and talk about God are derivative from our thought and talk about creatures, particularly ourselves. Just how does that derivation go? The simplest mode would be the application to God of the terms in question in just the same sense as that in which they are applied to us (straight univocity). It may be that none of the ordinary meanings of terms applied to us carry over in that simple a fashion. Nevertheless, many of our P-predicates can be fairly simply modified so as to be true of God, as construed in Essay 6, and we can construct quite abstract terms that apply univocally to God and to us (Essays 3 and 4). This gives us a "univocal core" for talk about God. Now we must not confuse 'univocal' and 'literal'. There are other possibilities for literal predication of terms to God, e.g., the construction of special technical senses for theological use. That is illustrated on a modest scale by the modification of human P-predicates just mentioned. All this literal predication nonetheless leaves us far short of what we need for the purposes of a functioning theistic religion. Thus it has to be supplemented by a liberal dose of figurative and symbolic discourse, an area on which much work remains to be done. However, since a core of literal predication of theological terms has been identified, that saves us from a morass of pansymbolism, and provides us with a firm foundation for truth claims in theology. And this core of literal predication constitutes an actualization of what, according to Essay 1, is an ever present possibility provided there are even metaphorical statements about God.

A word of explanation of the distinction between footnotes and endnotes. Footnotes are as they were in the original articles with very minor modifications, mostly updating of references. Endnotes have been added for this book. They are designed for current reflections on certain points in the essays and for interrelating the essays.

PART I

TALK
ABOUT GOD

Irreducible Metaphors
in Theology

I

My primary concern in this essay is with the possibility of irreducible metaphor in talk about God, and with the kind of significance such talk would have if possible. But before tackling those problems head on I should indicate why it seems to many that theology needs irreducible metaphors.

The impossibility of literal talk about God has become almost an article of faith for theology in this century. Of course it is not denied that one can *make* a statement in which some term, used literally, is applied to God; that is not regarded as being beyond human powers. The impossibility alleged is, rather, an impossibility of saying anything *true* about God while using terms literally. Various reasons have been given for this sweeping proscription. Perhaps the most popular in our day is the *transcendence* of God, His "wholly otherness". This appears in various forms; Tillich, e.g., holds that (a) God is not *a* being, but Being Itself, since anything that is *a* being would not be an appropriate object of religious worship, and (b) only what is *a* being can be literally characterized. Those who identify themselves with the mystical tradition emphasize the principle that God is an ineffable, undifferentiated unity. Coming from another quarter is the infamous verifiability criterion of meaning, which has been used to argue the still more sweeping thesis that no theological predication has any truth value at all.

From *Experience, Reason, and God*, ed. Eugene T. Long (Washington, D.C.: Catholic University of America Press, 1980). Reprinted by permission of Catholic University of America Press.

I myself do not regard any of these arguments as successful, but this is not the place to say why. The present point is that arguments like these have been convincing to many contemporary theologians and philosophers of religion. But many of them are not prepared to give up theological discourse. And so they must find some other way of construing what look like literal theological statements, such as,

> God created the heavens and the earth.
> God spoke to Jeremiah.
> God brought the Israelites out of Egypt.
> God sent His only begotten Son into the world.
> God forgives the sins of those who are truly repentant.
> God's purpose is that we shall all enjoy eternal life.

One popular move is to give them some noncognitive interpretation, as expressive of attitudes, feelings, or commitments,[1] or evocative of mystical experience, "insight", or "seeing X as Y".[2] But again a sizable proportion are unwilling to give up the idea that it is possible to make *true statements* about God, to articulate something that really does pertain to the divine nature, to convey in words some apprehension, however inadequate, of what God is like.

To those who find themselves in this position, metaphor can seem a promising way out. In many spheres of discourse we manage to make true statements without using terms literally. We can correctly describe what Russia did at the end of World War II by saying that she dropped an iron curtain across Europe, even though no iron curtain was literally dropped. Why can't we analogously provide some insight into the divine nature and operations by saying things like "God spoke to Jeremiah", even if none of these predicates are literally true of God? Just as the dropping of an iron curtain across a stage provides a useful "model" for thinking about what Russia did just after World War II, why can't human speech provide a useful model for thinking about God's relation to Jeremiah, and sending one's son to do a certain job provide a useful model for thinking of God's relation to the work of Jesus Christ? But of course if *no* term can be literally applied to God,

---

[1]See, e.g., George Santayana, *Reason in Religion* (New York: Scribner, 1905), and R. B. Braithwaite, *An Empiricist's View of the Nature of Religious Belief* (Cambridge: Cambridge University Press, 1955).

[2]See, e.g., W. T. Stace, *Time and Eternity* (Princeton: Princeton University Press, 1952), J. H. Randall, Jr., *The Role of Knowledge in Western Religion*, (Boston: Starr King Press, 1958), chap. 4, and John Wisdom, "Gods," *Proceedings of the Aristotelian Society*, 45 (1944–45).

our metaphorical talk about God will be *irreducible*. A metaphor is *irreducible* if what is said in the metaphorical utterance cannot be said, *even in part*, in literal terms. Obviously, if no term can be literally applied to God, we cannot do *anything* to spell out in literal terms what is said metaphorically about God. Hence theologians who go the route we have been describing will wind up construing talk about God as made up of irreducible metaphors.[3]

It may seem that very few theologians have followed what I have described as a "natural tendency"; for the term 'metaphor' does not figure heavily in twentieth-century discussions of religious language. Nevertheless I believe that in many cases in which writers speak of "analogy", "symbols", "parables", or "models", the basic linguistic mechanism involved is that of metaphor, though they may be envisaging some particular complication or elaboration of the simplest kinds of metaphors. I am unable in this paper to document this suggestion, but I would suggest that writers as diverse as Karl Barth, Rudolph Bultmann, I. M. Crombie, I. T. Ramsey, and Ian G. Barbour are in effect treating talk about God as irreducibly metaphorical, though they rarely use the term.[A]

II

We can effectively come to grips with our central question only if we have an explicit account of the nature of metaphor. To this I now turn.

---

[3]I want to emphasize that in this essay we are not asking the (silly) question as to whether it is possible to have metaphors of any sort in talk about God, nor are we asking what status our metaphorical God-talk actually has. It is obvious that much talk about God is metaphorical. For example:

The Lord is my shepherd.

His hands prepared the dry land.

The Lord is my rock and my fortress.

In thy light do we see light.

The Lord looks down from heaven.

I believe that it is commonly supposed that metaphors like these are reducible, that it is possible to say in literal terms at least part of what is being said about God metaphorically in these utterances. In saying "The Lord is my shepherd" I am saying that God will protect me and see to it that my needs are satisfied; and so on. But we are not concerned in this paper to determine whether this is so. We are concerned with a certain project—interpreting all talk about God, including the more literal-sounding statements just mentioned, as *irreducible* metaphors. We are dealing with a question that is fundamental to that project, viz., whether there can be irreducible metaphors, and if so what status they would have.

Despite the frequent occurrence of terms like 'metaphorical *meaning*' and 'metaphorical *sense*'in discussions of the subject, I believe that they reflect a confused, or at least a loose, way of thinking about metaphor. To get straight about the matter we need to keep a firm grip on the Saussurian distinction between *language* and *speech*. A (natural) language is an abstract system, a system of abstract sound types or, in principle, types of other sorts of perceptible items. The systematicity involved is both "internal" and "external". The phonology, morphology and syntax of a language constitute its "internal" system—the ways in which its elements can be combined to form larger units. The "external" system is revealed by the semantics of the language—the ways in which units of the language have the function of "representing" things in, and features of, the world.[4] A language serves as a means of communication; that is its basic raison d'être. *Speech* is the *use* of language in communication (using speech in an extended sense to cover written as well as oral communication). It is what we *do* in the course of exploiting a linguistic system for purposes of communication.[5]

Now the fact that a given word or phrase has the meaning(s) or sense(s)[6] it has is a fact about the language; it is part of the semantic constitution of the language. Thus it is a (semantic) fact about the English language that 'knit' has among its meanings:

1. To form, as a fabric, by interlacing a single yarn or thread in loops, by means of long thin bluntly pointed rods.
2. To draw together; to contract into wrinkles; as he knit his brow in thought.[7]

The fact that a word has a certain meaning is (part of) what gives it its usability for communication; it constitutes part of the linguistic resources we draw on in saying what we have to say.

---

[4]This is a very crude way of characterizing semantics, but it will have to do for now. There is no general agreement on what an adequate characterization would look like.

[5]Language and speech may also be interrelated in other and more intimate ways. Thus, in my view, language *exists* only as a set of potentialities for speech; the fact that speech is patterned in certain ways *constitutes* the reality of a natural language; if there were no speech, there would be no *actual* languages. But that is quite compatible with the existence and fundamental importance of the distinction drawn in the text.

[6]We shall not distinguish between *meaning* and *sense*.

[7]*Webster's New Collegiate Dictionary* (Springfield, Mass.: Merriam, 1959). I am far from claiming that this is the best or most adequate way to specify these meanings. Indeed it is far from clear, at this stage of development of the art, what is the most adequate way to specify meanings. But it does seem clear that 'knit' has the two meanings thus specified, however lamely and haltingly, and that its having these two meanings is (a small) part of what makes the English language what it is at the current stage of its history.

The term 'metaphor', on the other hand, stands for a certain way of *using* words, a mode of *speech* rather than a type of meaning or any other feature of *language*. More specifically, it belongs to the family of *figurative* uses of terms ("figures of *speech*", as they are appropriately called in the tradition) that stand in contrast with *literal* uses of terms. Let's make explicit the distinction between *literal* and *metaphorical* uses, restricting ourselves to the uses of predicates in subject-predicate statements, since that is the application with which we are especially concerned.

We may think of each meaning of a predicate term "correlating" the term with some (possibly very complex) property.[8] Each of the definitions of 'knit' given above specifies a (relational) property with which 'knit' is "correlated" in one of its meanings. Different theories of meaning provide different accounts of the nature of this correlation. Thus the "ideational" theory of meaning found, e.g., in Locke's *Essay*, holds that a meaning of a predicate term "correlates" it with a certain property, P, *iff* the term functions as a sign of the *idea* of P in communication. It will be convenient to speak of a predicate term "signifying" or "standing for" the correlated property.

Now when I make a literal use of a predicate term, in one of its meanings, in a subject-predicate sentence, I utter the sentence with the claim that the property signified by the predicate is possessed by the subject (the referent of the subject-term), or, if the predicate is a relational one, that the property holds between the subjects. Thus if I make a literal use of 'knit' in saying, e.g., "My wife knitted that sweater", I would be claiming that the relational property specified in the first of our two definitions holds between my wife and that sweater. And if my statement is true, if that relation does in fact hold between these terms, then we may say that 'knit' is *literally true* of these terms, or does *literally apply* to them.

But suppose I say, as Shakespeare has Macbeth say, "Sleep knits up the ravelled sleave of care". It is clear that sleep cannot possibly do to care either of the things listed as meanings of 'knit'. Nor, if we surveyed all the meanings that 'knit' has in the language, would we find any relation that literally holds between sleep and care. Hence, if I am sensible, I will not be uttering that sentence with the claim that 'knit' literally applies to sleep. Instead I will be using the term *metaphorically*. But what is it to use a term metaphorically? In presenting a brief

---

[8]I would want this supposition to be compatible with the fact that most (all?) predicate terms have meanings that are vague, have "open texture", or suffer from indeterminacy in other ways. This means that an adequate formulation would have to be considerably more complicated than the one given here.

answer to that question I shall be more or less following the admirable account given by Paul Henle in chapter 7 of *Language, Thought, and Culture.*[9]

When I use a predicate term metaphorically, or in accordance with some other figure of speech (metonomy, synecdoche, irony, hyperbole, or whatever), I am not turning my back on the meaning(s) that term has in the language. Even though I am not claiming that the term is literally true of the subject in any of those senses, I am not ignoring those senses. On the contrary, I am using the term in one of those senses, though not in the same way as in literal speech. Instead of straightforwardly applying the term in that sense to the subject, I am engaged in the following multi-stage operation. First, I envisage, and "invite" the hearer to envisage, something of the sort to which the term does literally apply. In the case under discussion this would be a person repairing a raveled piece of fabric. Let's call something to which the predicate literally applies an *exemplar.* Needless to say, we will ordinarily be dealing with *envisaged,* rather than actual exemplars. In the metaphorical statement cited earlier, "Russia has dropped an iron curtain across Europe", the exemplar is a person dropping a curtain (a rather unusual one, made of iron) in front of a stage. In "Life's a walking shadow", the exemplar is a shadow cast by a walking man (among other possibilities). Now what the metaphorical statement most basically "says" is that the exemplar can usefully be taken as a "model" of the subject. The hearer is invited to consider the exemplar *as* a model of the subject, as a way of discovering, highlighting, or rendering salient, various features of the subject.

As so far characterized, a metaphorical "statement" does not appear to be making any truth claim about the subject, other than the implicit claim that it is sufficiently like the exemplar to make the latter a useful model of the former. So long as I am simply *presenting* a model to the hearer for him to use as he sees fit, I am not myself attributing any particular feature to the subject. Now this may sometimes be a complete account of what the speaker is doing; he is simply suggesting a model that has caught his fancy, that feels right to him. But more typically the speaker is concerned to exploit the model in a particular way; he will "have in mind" one or more particular points of resemblance (between model and subject) that he intends to be attribut-

---

[9]Paul Henle, ed. (Ann Arbor: University of Michigan Press, 1958) The literature on metaphor bristles with controversy. Nevertheless, I believe that there is widespread agreement on the general lines of the following account; and the agreement would be much greater if everyone were to get straight on the language-speech distinction.

ing to the subject.[10] Thus when Churchill said "Russia has dropped an iron curtain across Europe", he wasn't just throwing the image of an iron curtain up for grabs, leaving it to his auditors to make of it what they would. He meant to be exploiting the model in a certain way—to assert that Russia has made it almost impossible to exchange information, goods, and persons between her sphere of influence and western Europe.

Thus in the typical metaphorical statement the speaker is "building on" the relevant meaning of his predicate term in two ways. First, he is presenting the sort of thing to which the term literally applies as a model of the subject. Second, he has in mind one or more resemblances between model and subject, and he extracts from these resemblances what he means to be attributing to the subject. In the Churchill quote, the resemblance is the inhibition of communication. In the "knitting" line from Macbeth the resemblance is that the agent is doing something to restore the patient to a sounder condition, one more nearly in accord with what it is "supposed" to be. And these points of resemblance are just what are being attributed to the subject(s).

Note that the speaker is doing this "on his own". Of course the semantic content of the sentence places certain constraints on him, because that is what he has to work with. But within that framework it is "up to him" *whether* he uses the predicate term metaphorically, and, if so, what features of the model he selects for attribution to the subject.[11]

---

[10]Of course, these "havings in mind" and these intentions can be of all degrees of explicitness and articulateness, just as with other thoughts and communicative intentions.

[11]Here is another way of making this last point. Let's distinguish between *sentence-meaning*—the meaning(s) that a sentence has "in the language", as a compositional function of the meanings of its constituent morphemes, and *speaker-meaning*, what the speaker means in uttering the sentence. We may identify the latter with *what the speaker is saying* (in a sense of 'saying' in which that is not equivalent to what sentence he is uttering), what "illocutionary act" he is performing. In terms of our previous distinction sentence-meaning belongs to language, while speaker-meaning belongs to speech. With this new distinction, we may say that in literal subject-predicate statements there is a complete coincidence, so far as the predicate is concerned, between sentence-meaning and speaker-meaning. Since what the speaker is *saying* is simply that the subject has the property that is determined by the relevant meaning of the predicate, *what he is saying about the subject* is fully determined by the meaning of the sentence. Whereas in a metaphorical statement about the subject what is said goes beyond sentence-meaning. What we get out of sentence-meaning, for declarative subject-predicate sentences, is the proposition that the property signified by the predicate attaches to the subject; and that is *not* what the speaker is saying in a metaphor. His speech act utilizes and builds on sentence-meaning, but it "goes beyond" that by virtue of his intentions. Hence he is saying more than, as well as less than, what the sentence means. To use a currently fashionable term, the "pragmatics" of the speech situation plays a much larger role in determining the content of metaphorical than of literal statements.

The sharp outlines of this idealized picture will have to be softened in various ways if it is to faithfully depict the often blurred reality of metaphorical speech. Let me just mention the most important qualifications. (A) 'Speaker' will have to be taken in an extended sense to include "hearers" as well. For a hearer may himself exploit the model in certain specific ways, and thus endow the statement with a propositional content not foreshadowed in the speaker's intentions; and do this without abandoning the communicative role of hearer. We can handle this by thinking of the hearer as making a metaphorical statement himself. (B) It is not true that propositional content always gets generated "from scratch" with each metaphorical utterance. There are standard, well-known metaphors with standard interpretations, or at least standard cores of interpretations to which variations may be added. Thus if I were to say "Life's a walking shadow", meaning to assert that life is spontaneous and free-swinging, not "tied down" or rigid, that would be a strange use of the sentence. I would be violating a sort of convention, even if it is not strictly a semantic rule of the language. We can handle this complexity by thinking of subsequent utterances of the sentence as simply repetitions or quotations of the utterance of some original or standard speaker, who is the source of the standard propositional content. (C) Speaker intentions can be of all degrees of explicitness. The speaker need not rehearse to himself in so many words that he intends to be asserting that. . . . In certain cases he may not even be able to say, in literal terms, what it is that he is asserting, but be asserting that nonetheless. (This might be elicited by skillful questioning.) What it finally comes down to is what the speaker would take as truth conditions of his utterance when they are presented to him. Of course, as with all such issues, questions can be raised as to whether his later responses to suggested truth conditions accurately reproduce his dispositions at the moment of utterance. But like practically all interesting concepts, the concept of *what a speaker asserted* does not come with fool-proof decision procedures attached.

One may wonder how a speaker communicates what he is asserting in a metaphorical utterance if that is determined by his intentions, since these latter are typically unannounced. Part of the answer is that he relies on contextual clues as to what similarities he most has in mind. If I say "He's a flat tire" in the context of a discussion of possible dinner guests, that is an indication that I am focusing on the lack of liveliness and bounciness of a flat tire, rather than, e.g., its bulk. But at least equally important is the fact that we rely on common tendencies, even cross-culturally, to be more struck by some similarities than others. The

24

pervasiveness of thermal (a "cold person") and kinetic ("a forceful argument") metaphors is testimony to this commonality.[12]

It may be helpful to append a few notes to this account.

(1) Talk about "metaphorical senses" is encouraged by the fact that many established senses of terms have historically resulted from what were originally metaphorical uses of the term in other senses. Thus one originally spoke metaphorically in referring to something as the "mouth" of a river, the "hood" of an automobile, a "fork" in the road, or "knitting" one's brow. However, when we now use such phrases we are applying the terms in senses they have in the language. The metaphor has "died", has "ossified", and has given rise to a new sense. It can be called a "metaphorical sense" but only by reference to its origin. Insofar as there *is* such a sense in the language, we are *not speaking* metaphorically, not using the term metaphorically, when we speak of the hood of a car.

(2) The term 'literal' has picked up a number of adventitious associations in the course of the rough treatment it has received in recent times. I think particularly of 'precise', 'univocal', 'specific', 'factual', 'empirical', and 'ordinary'. However common the conflation, it is simply a confusion to suppose that 'literal', in the historically distinctive sense just set out, implies any of the features just mentioned. Meanings that words have in a language can be more or less vague, open-textured, unspecific, and indeterminate in a variety of ways. Hence I can be using words literally and still be speaking vaguely, ambiguously, or unspecifically. Again, I can be using my words just as literally in asking questions, cursing fate, or expressing rage, as in soberly asserting that the cat is on the mat. The conflation of 'literal' with 'empirical', on the other hand, is something more than a vulgar error; it reflects a basic issue in the philosophy of language as to the conditions under which a word can acquire a meaning in the language. If this requires contact with "experience" in one or another of the ways spelled out in empiricist theories of meaning, then only terms with "empirical" meanings can be used literally, for only such terms *have* established senses. But that doesn't follow just from the meaning of the term 'literal'; it also requires an empiricist theory of meaning, and it is by no means clear that any such theory is acceptable.

(3) The other side of this last coin is that various theorists, such as Cassirer, Langer, and Wheelwright, have fallen into speaking of an

---

[12]See George Lakoff and Mark Johnson, *Metaphors We Live By* (Chicago: University of Chicago Press, 1980).

original "metaphorical" use of language that is distinguished from what Wheelwright calls the "steno" language of science by its "plurisignification", "lack of precision", etc. But this has nothing to do with the metaphorical, as contrasted with literal, use of words. Put unconfusedly, the thesis is that the further back one goes in the development of a language the less precise, specific, etc., the meanings of words are, and the less possible it is to make sharp distinctions between different meanings of a term. In asking about the possibility of irreducible metaphors in theology we will not be asking whether it is possible to speak of God imprecisely, unspecifically, etc. That, obviously, is all too possible.

III

With this background we may turn to our central problem concerning the possibility and status of irreducible metaphors in theology. A metaphor is irreducible if what it says cannot be said, even in part, in literal terms. How we answer our central question will depend, inter alia, on how we pick out *what is said* in a metaphorical utterance. So a word on this is in order.

There are, no doubt, various ways of drawing a distinction between *what* is said, *how* it is said, and other aspects of what is *done* in a speech act. Our way of drawing these distinctions is dictated by the fact that we are interested specifically in the use of metaphors to attribute properties to subjects, with an attached "truth claim", the claim that the property in question does indeed belong to the subject in question. Hence the "what-is-said" on which we will concentrate is the proposition(s) *asserted* in an utterance, those propositions the speaker is claiming to be true. When we ask whether what is said in a metaphor can be said in literal terms, we are asking whether the *propositional* content of the metaphorical statement can be literally expressed. This is by no means the whole story about a metaphorical statement. As we have seen, a speaker makes a metaphorical statement by using the literal meaning of his predicate to present a model of the subject. Now, by definition, that *way* of asserting a certain proposition cannot be reproduced in a literal utterance; any assertion done that way is, by definition, a metaphorical assertion. And any feature that attaches to a metaphorical statement by virtue of this distinctive mode of statement will likewise fail to survive transposition to the literal mode. Thus it is often pointed out that a metaphorical statement is characterized by a certain "openendedness". However definite an attribution the speaker means to be making via his model, he is also *presenting* the model as a source of hitherto unnoticed insights into the nature of the subject. And so meta-

26

phorical statements always have what might (metaphorically) be called a penumbra of inexplicit suggestions that surround whatever definite propositional content is present. Again, this cannot be captured in a literal re-statement. Even if we explicitly assert in literal terms *that* the model may be indefinitely rich in insights into the subject, that is not the same as *presenting* the model with the implied suggestion of untapped resources. Thus we are not asking whether metaphors can receive exact or exhaustive literal paraphrases, as that question has often been understood in the literature.

Moreover we are not even asking whether the propositional content can be exactly or exhaustively expressed in literal terms. It may be, e.g., that the "open-endedness" alluded to in the last paragraph affects the propositional content of a metaphorical statement. It may be that in a metaphorical statement there is no sharp line between what is being asserted and what is only more or less explicitly suggested, so that propositions asserted metaphorically possess a kind of fuzzy boundary that is not shared by propositions expressed literally. But even if that is so it would not prevent the propositional content from being partially expressed in literal terms. Remember that our concern is with the idea that, since no predicates can be literally true of God, God can be spoken of only in metaphors that are wholly irreducible. Our question is, then, whether there can be a metaphorical statement the propositional content of which cannot be expressed, even in part, in literal terms.

In tackling this question it will be useful to consider separately the two strata of truth claims we have found to be contained in metaphors. First, there is the very *unspecific* claim that the exemplar is sufficiently similar to the subject, in some way(s) or other, to make the former a useful model of the latter. (Call this M-similarity.) Second, there is, normally, some more *specific* attribution that is derived from one or more particular points of resemblance.

The first level can be handled very quickly. There is obviously no difficulty in literally applying the predicate 'M-similar' to any pair of entities whatever. Moreover this predicate will be literally true of the exemplar and subject whenever the metaphorical statement is true, or, indeed, whenever the metaphor is successful or appropriate in any way.[13] Thus the literal expressibility of that much of the propositional

[13]If the basic truth claim were only that exemplar and subject are similar in some way or other, then we could say without qualification that it could never fail to succeed. It is a priori true that any pair of objects exhibit similarity in indefinitely many respects. Just for starters, each shared nonidentity constitutes a point of similarity. But the basic presupposition has a bit more content than that; it stipulates similarity in such a way as to make the one a useful model for the other. It is not clear just what that takes. Presumably the

content unquestionably holds for any metaphorical statement whatever. This gives us a "floor" of guaranteed literal paraphrasability that
cannot be gainsaid.

The additional, *specific* propositional content is a more complicated
problem. Yet I believe there to be a simple argument that shows that
the specific content must, in principle, be expressed in literal terms.
Let's restrict ourselves to the predicative part of the propositional content, since we have just been taking for granted the reference to the
subject; and let's consider the statement "God is my rock". Let us say
that when a speaker asserts this, the property he means to be attributing to God is P. What would it take to express P in literal terms? There
must be some predicate term such that by a literal employment of that
term in the frame 'God is ____' I can attribute P to God. That is, we
need a term that signifies P, so that just by virtue of the term's meaning
what it does one can use it to attribute P to some subject. And what does
it take for that to be possible? An adequate answer to that question
would involve going into the mechanisms by which terms acquire
meaning in natural languages—a very murky subject. But at least this
much is clear. So long as it is possible for members of the linguistic
community to form a concept of P, it will be possible for P to become
the meaning of a predicate term in the language. For so long as I can
form the concept of P, it will be possible for me to associate an element
of the language with P in such a way as to use that element to attribute
P to something. How could that be impossible for me to do, so long as I
have "cognitive access" to P? And if the property is cognitively accessible to me, then, unless this is by virtue of superhuman powers, it will
be, in principle, cognitively accessible to any other human being. But if
it is conceptually accessible to the language community, there is no bar
in principle to a word's signifying the property *in the language*.

And now we are ready for the final turn of the screw. The sufficient
condition just uncovered is automatically satisfied whenever a certain
property figures in the propositional content of a metaphorical utterance. For, as we have seen, it cannot so figure unless the speaker has
that property in mind as what he means to be attributing to the subject.
And he cannot have the property in mind without having a concept of
that property. No matter in how inexplicit or inarticulate a fashion he
"has it in mind", he will be in possession of at least an equally inexplicit

---

fact that X and Y are both nonidentical with Z would not suffice by itself. But since we are
often surprised at what ingenious modelers can make of unpromising material, it is not
clear that this presupposition cuts out anything that would be allowed by the more
unqualified presupposition. Hence it may be that even this presupposition is satisfied by
any pair of objects whatever. But I do not feel confident in pushing this point.

or inarticulate concept. Therefore a statement cannot possess a propositional content unless it is, in principle, possible that a language should contain words that have the meanings required for the literal expression of that content.

There is one transition in this argument that needs further discussion, viz., the step from "it is possible for members of the linguistic community to form a concept of P" to "it is possible for P to become the meaning of a predicate term in the language". The problem is this. What if, although each member of the community can acquire the concept of P and some or all do, still there is, in principle, no way of sharing this concept, no way of telling whether what I call my concept of P is the same, even in part, as what you call your concept of P. In that case, though one could coin a term for P for one's private use, it would not be possible to introduce a term for P into a public, socially shared language, usable for interpersonal communication. Furthermore it may seem that this is a real possibility for talk about God. I might develop a certain concept on the basis of my experience of God, and so with you. But how can we compare our experiences and thereby determine the degree of overlap of our concepts?

It would be tempting, at this point, to fall back on the Wittgensteinian "private-language argument", which is designed to show that what was just presented as a possibility is not possible. From that standpoint I can linguistically express a certain concept only if it is in principle possible that other people should realize what concept I am expressing. However, since I don't regard Wittgenstein's argument as compelling, I cannot take this way out. What is needed here is an investigation of the features of religious thought, activity, and experience within religious communities that make it possible to share common theological concepts. There is no time for that here. I will take it for granted that whatever factors are generally available for disseminating socially shared meanings in religious communities are also available for establishing new meanings of terms out of originally metaphorical uses.

It may be thought that we have made our job too easy. "You have secured this conclusion only by making the standards for meaning-acquisition too loose. What if the property in question is one that is not open to our experience, or has to do with another realm of being that is radically beyond our ken, or . . . ?" But this is not to the point. Our argument assumes nothing as to what is or is not within our experience or our ken. The point is that whatever restrictions there are on meanings of predicate terms, they will follow from corresponding restrictions on concepts. If certain features of the world cannot be literally represented in language because they cannot be experienced by us, that will be because their unexperienceability prevents us from forming a conception of them. So that if P really does belong to the propositional content of a metaphorical utterance, it is *conceivable,* and hence can be semantically correlated with a predicate term. And, conversely, if it cannot, it ipso facto cannot form part of the propositional content of any utterance.

Let's be clear as to what I do and do not claim to have shown. I have argued that the propositional content of any metaphorical statement issued with a truth claim is, *in principle,* capable of literal expression, at least in part. It is important to recognize that this does not include the following claims.

(1) "Anyone who makes or understands a metaphorical statement can restate it (at least in part) in literal terms." This is *not* part of my claim. Although the unspecific presupposed claim could easily be literally expressed by any minimally articulate person, the specific content is another matter. A careful examination of our argument on that point will reveal its conclusion to be quite compatible with the possibility that one who makes or grasps the statement may not be in a position to bring off even a lame and inadequate literal version. One may have the property "in mind" in too implicit or intuitive a fashion to know whether any term in the language signifies it, or to associate it explicitly with a new term. Or perhaps the most we can come up with is a paraphrase into other metaphors. The "in principle" possibility for which I have argued may not be a real possibility for anyone at this point, or, perhaps, at any point.

(2) "Literal paraphrasability is a necessary condition of any intelligible metaphorical utterance." My conclusion extends only to metaphorical statements that make *truth claims.* My thesis does not extend to the case in which the speaker simply puts forward, e.g., kingship as a possible model for God, inviting the hearer to make of it what he can. Here the speaker is making no claim that can be evaluated as true or false, and so my argument does not apply. This may be all that is going on in some metaphorical talk.[14]

IV

The argument against irreducibly metaphorical statements has been a completely general one. Let's now apply the results to theology.

[14]One may wonder why I would bother to throw out the model if I am prepared to make no claims for it. But this is not to the present point, and in any event there are various possible answers to the question. I might issue the metaphor just because it seems apt to me. Or I might have been seized by a divine frenzy; I may be the unwitting mouthpiece of the muse of poesy; it may be a posthypnotic suggestion, or some mad scientist may be manipulating my behavior by remote control.

Of course the direct application is obvious; it is just universal instantiation. If there can be no irreducibly metaphorical statements anywhere there can be none in theology. So this way out is unavailable for one who denies the possibility of literal predication. But let us not be too hasty. The distinction between two levels of propositional content may give our quarry some room for maneuver. In particular, we might imagine an opponent of literal predication attempting to construct the following halfway house.

"Let's grant that in order to have any metaphorical truth claim at all, one must at least be presupposing that the exemplar is like the subject in some significant way(s); and your point that at least this presupposition can be literally expressed is an undeniable one. Nor is this a trivial point; it does show that the unqualified denial of literal predication cannot be sustained, if we are to talk of God even metaphorically. But that denial never was (should have been) issued in so unqualified a form. What we anti-literalists are really concerned about is not those abstract, 'structural' predicates like (*significantly*) *similar in some way or other,* but specific predicates like *wise, loving, makes, forgives, commands,* and so on. Therefore if we can make the denial of specific[15] literal predicability stick, we will have gotten what we were after. For in that case it will be impossible to say, literally, what God is like, what He has planned, done, what He would have us do, and so on. We deniers of literal predication will be only minimally shaken by having to admit that God is, literally, *significantly like a king in some way or other.* Again, we will admit that you have shown that if we issue a metaphor with some specific property 'in mind' as the one we mean to be attributing to God, then it is, in principle, possible to make that attribution in literal terms. Since we are operating within these constraints, the way out is to construe theological statements as limited to the unspecific claim, as far as 'propositional content' is concerned. So when one says 'God gave me courage to face that situation', he is to be interpreted as simply putting forward the model of one human being encouraging another, with only the unspecific claim that this is sufficiently similar to God's relation to my being encouraged to be usefully employed as a model thereof. There is no further claim of some particular point of similarity, P. The speaker is simply suggesting that we think of the matter in terms of that model. And hence the assertion need be literally paraphrasable only so far as the totally unspecific claim is concerned."

This is pretty much what I take to be I. M. Crombie's position, with

---

[15]It is incumbent on our opponent to say something by way of indicating *how* specific a predicate must be to fall under the ban. But let that pass.

the extra fillip that we accept these models on the authority of Christ, even though we are unable to interpret them ourselves.[16]

In discussing this attempt at a mediating position, I am going to (1) bring out unacceptable features, features that would be unacceptable to all or most theologians, and (2) suggest that even its proponents do not, in practice, stick to it. These points are not unrelated.

Metaphorical statements about God that are restricted to the *unspecific* truth claim will suffer from a number of disabilities that render them unfit for theological duty.

(A) Since virtually any such statement will be true, the theological attributions we like will enjoy this status only at the price of sharing it with indefinitely many statements we do not like. Perhaps we can best appreciate this point by starting from the weaker but more clearcut presupposition of *some similarity or other between exemplar and model*. As noted above, since it is a priori true that any two entities are similar in indefinitely many respects, if that were all that were being claimed in a statement about God, all such statements would be true alike; it would be just as true, true in the same way, that God is cruel as that God is merciful, just as true that God is a spider, a mud-pie, or a thief as that God is the creator of heaven and earth and that He has reconciled us to Himself. To be sure, the presupposition with which we are working is not as empty as that; it involves the more specific claim that the exemplar is *M-similar* to God, similar in some way(s) that renders it suitable to be used as a model. But since the force of this further restriction is so difficult to assess, we are in a similar position. Though I cannot claim it is a priori true that God is M-similar to anything whatever, it is difficult to be confident, with respect to any proferred exemplar, that it is not M-similar to God. The standard way of testing a putative model is by attempting to elaborate it, to spell out the respects in which it is fitted to function as a model. This enterprise is complicated, on the pan-metaphoricist approach, by the fact that all the elaboration will have to be done in metaphorical terms, each of which is subject to the same challenge. Needless to say, this makes it much more difficult to be sure that a given model *doesn't* work. But waiving that difficulty, I will just note that it seems plausible to suppose that, with sufficient ingenuity, virtually any metaphorical predicate can be elaborated in a theologically plausible way. Thus God is a spider in the sense that He weaves the web of our lives; God is an apple in that we find at the core

---

[16]See his contribution to "Theology and Falsification" in *New Essays in Philosophical Theology*, ed. Antony Flew & Alasdair MacIntyre (London: SCM Press, 1955), and his "The Possibility of Theological Statements" in *Faith and Logic*, ed. Basil Mitchell (London: Allen & Unwin, 1957).

of His nature the seeds of truth; and so on. Now what I take to be unacceptable theologically is not that God can metaphorically be said to be a spider or an apple, but that these statements are on a par with statements like "God created the heavens and the earth" and "God commanded us to love one another". Not that the position under consideration is unable to make *any* distinction between these groups of statements; it can recognize that those in the latter group are more effective in evoking desired emotional and practical responses, more in line with the ecclesiastical tradition, involve exemplars that are experienced as sacred, and so on. But what this position is debarred from claiming is that these groups of statements differ in truth-value. The members of our favored group do not correspond to the way things are any better or in any different way than do the innumerably many statements in the less favored group.

(B) The logical relations in which a theological statement stands with other statements (theological and otherwise) are determined by their propositional contents, i.e., on this position, by the unspecific presupposition. And that content fails to stand in the desired logical relations. First consider contradictoriness. For the same reasons that led us to suppose that virtually any statement about God will turn out to be true, we will also be forced to recognize that a given statement about God will be logically incompatible with virtually no other statements about God. "God is loving and merciful" does not logically exclude "God is arbitrarily cruel and bloodthirsty". For the fact that a loving and merciful human being is a suitable model for God certainly does not *logically* exclude the possibility that an arbitrarily cruel and bloodthirsty human being is a suitable model for God (in some respect or other). Not even straight contradiction works. The fact that human wisdom is a suitable model for God does not *logically* prevent the lack of wisdom (the holy fool) from being a suitable model. Thus "God is wise" is logically compatible with "God is not wise".

(C) Nor does logical entailment fare better. Consider the following apparently unexceptionable argument.

1. A perfectly loving being will forgive the sins of the truly repentant.
2. God is perfectly loving.
3. Therefore God will forgive the sins of the truly repentant.

Surprisingly enough, on the position under consideration one does not fall into contradiction by affirming the premises and denying the conclusion. For even granting the literal truth of the first premise, it is certainly *logically* possible that both a perfectly loving human being and an unforgiving human being are useful models of God, in some respect(s) or other. Thus we must abandon all hope of inferring theological propositions from other propositions, theological or otherwise, or of rejecting some theological propositions because they contradict others; in short, any hope of logically systematizing theology in any way whatever.

(D) One class of putative consequences of theology that is of particular interest to many religious people comprises predictions of the future course of the world, human life, or of this or that human life. I believe that it is universally acknowledged by thoughtful religious people in our society today that no very specific predictions can be derived from theology, in however full-blooded a way it be understood. We cannot infer from Christian theology that Joan will recover from her illness, that democracy will triumph in Africa, or that the church will greatly increase in numbers over the next fifty years. Nevertheless it is widely supposed by traditional Christians that predictions of a less specific sort can be derived—e.g., that the church will prevail on earth (some day), that Christ will return in glory (some time), that either some or all human beings will enjoy eternal blessedness in the knowledge and love of God. These consequences are supposed to follow from premises like the following:

1. It is God's purpose that. . .
2. God's purposes are unchanging.
3. God is able to carry out any purpose.

But clearly from the fact that God is M-similar to a human being that unvaryingly has a certain purpose he is able to carry out, it does not follow that this purpose *will* be carried out. For the respect(s) in which God is like such a person may not be such as to have anything to do with the actual course of events. That gap in the argument could be filled only by spelling out the points of similarity (and their being of the right sort). But this we are debarred from doing.

(E) Predictions of the future course of events are viewed as unworthy by some of our more advanced religious thinkers. However, even thinkers of this degree of advancement are likely to set great store by another class of consequences, practical consequences concerning how we ought to act and feel, or what attitudes we should have. But these fare no better. The proposition that God is M-similar to a human being who commands us to love one another or to refrain from commiting adultery, provides us absolutely no ground for loving one another or refraining from adultery, until that proposition makes more specific in what way God is like a human being who has issued such commands. Pending some clarification on that point, it is completely up in the air whether God is like the human issuer of injunctions in a way that is relevant to the question of what we ought to do.

I take it that these consequences are radically unacceptable to the "religious attitude" or, to speak less pretentiously, to the bulk of those in the mainstream of the Judeo-Christian tradition. A theology the propositions of which are logically compatible with anything else sayable of God, which can be true only in the same way virtually anything one might say of God is true, which have no determinate consequences either for theory or for practice, so eviscerated a theology is stripped of virtually all its impact for human life.

Now for a consideration of what happens when those who begin taking a tough pansymbolist or panmetaphoricist line come to the actual working out of details. My observation is that in the crunch they either give up the idea that theological statements provide a true insight into the nature of things, or they, in effect, relax the ban on literal predication, or sometimes, I am sorry to say, both. Let me document this judgment by a brief look at two cases.

The first reluctant witness for the prosecution is Paul Tillich. Tillich does not fall squarely within the scope of this paper, for his view does not represent theological statements as making truth claims about God. But Tillich does not really stick to this, and that is why he must be counted among those who inconsistently combine both of the moves just mentioned. On the one hand, the official line (to fill out Tillich's often inchoate remarks in what seems to be the most natural way) is that theological predicates get that status by virtue of the fact that they literally denote "places" in the natural world at which Being-Itself is encountered. Thus what a theological statement does is to direct us to something through which the Ultimate can be experienced. On this interpretation the theological statement tells us nothing of what the Ultimate is like or what it "does". But Tillich is not satisfied with this; he wants his theology to come closer than that to satisfying the traditional requirements of theology. Therefore he sets himself to tell us, in terms of his ontology, what religious symbols really *mean*, what is being said about the Ultimate in theology. And so we get statements like the following:

> Divine will and intellect are symbols for dynamics in all its manifestations and for form as the meaningful structure of being-itself.[17]

[17]*Systematic Theology* (London: Nisbet, 1953), vol. 1, p. 274.

35

If we call God the 'living God' we assert that He is the eternal process in which separation is posited and overcome by reunion.[18]

Providence is the divine condition which is present in every group of finite conditions and in the totality of finite conditions . . . . It is the quality of inner directedness in every situation.[19]

This sounds like just the sort of thing we are familiar with from Hegel and others, viz., using the more abstract language of ontology to say in literal terms what is said metaphorically in religious language. If this is not what is intended, I do not see what Tillich can mean by the claim that he is telling us how to "interpret" religious symbols—telling us what they mean. Thus in the attempt to give theological utterances a more determinate propositional content, Tillich, in effect, revokes his ban on literal predication.

Second, let's take a look at I. M. Crombie, a thinker who represents more unambiguously the kind of panmetaphoricism I have been discussing. Crombie is quite clear that the terms we apply to God are not literally true of Him,[20] but that we have it on authority (in central cases, the authority of Christ) that there is an underlying analogy between God and the things to which the terms literally apply,[21] though we are not in a position to say, or to know, what the analogy is.[22] Since we are assured that there is an underlying analogy, we can justifiably apply the terms to God metaphorically (Crombie does not use the term 'metaphor', but he is obviously employing the concept), and in doing so we are enunciating fundamental truths about God, though we don't know just what truths these are.[23]

Crombie's apostasy is not so blatant as Tillich's. I have not caught Crombie with his finger in the jam-pot of literal metaphysical interpretation. His lapse comes in the form of insisting on implications from theological statements, both theoretical and practical. On the one

---

[18]Ibid., p. 268.

[19]Ibid., p. 296.

[20]*New Essays*, p. 122; *Faith and Logic*, pp. 43, 70.

[21]*New Essays*, pp. 119, 122–23, 127; *Faith and Logic*, p. 70.

[22]*New Essays*, pp. 122, 127, 128; *Faith and Logic*, pp. 70, 71.

[23]Although I am reading Crombie as a panmetaphoricist, he is susceptible of an interestingly different reading according to which theological metaphors can be literally paraphrased, though not by mere mortals. That is, we might think of Christ, who, according to Crombie, guarantees that the models he provides for us are suitable models, as being able to spell out the crucial similarities in literal terms. This, then, would be an extension of the familiar situation in which a poet uses a metaphor with some definite intention in mind that he could express literally, but where none of his readers could do so, though some of them are "grasped" by the metaphor.

hand, he insists that our beliefs about God do have implications for the future course of events, albeit of a very indefinite sort. Thus he holds that "suffering which was utterly, eternally, and irredeemably point-less" would count decisively against the assertion that God is merciful,[24] which means that that assertion implies that there is no suffering that is utterly, eternally, and irredeemably pointless. He also refers in this connection to looking "for the resurrection of the dead, and the life of the world to come".[25] Again, he recognizes that theological principles function as a guide to conduct, that they mark out certain kinds of reactions as appropriate, others as inappropriate. Thus the parable of the prodigal son teaches us that "whenever we come to ourselves and return to God, he will come to meet us".[26] But clearly, for reasons of the sort I have already rehearsed, theological statements will not have implications, even of that degree of determinacy, unless their propositional content is made more specific than just—some unspecified likeness between God and the exemplar. More specifically, if Crombie takes the proposition "God is merciful" to have consequences like those just noted, he must be ascribing a more definite content to that proposition, he must be supposing himself to have some grasp of the respects in which God is similar to a merciful human being, whether or not he has *said,* or even thought explicitly, what he takes those similarities to be. And so once more we see that the burden of making a pan-metaphoricist theology function like a theology has proved too much for the theologian.

V

The main upshot of this paper is that though irreducible metaphors seem to promise a way of combining the denial of any literal predication in theology with the preservation of significant theological truth claims, this fair promise dissipates on scrutiny like mist before the morning sun. Either the panmetaphoricist abandons the aspiration to significant truth claims or he revokes the ban on literal predicability. He cannot have both. Which way he should jump depends, inter alia, on the prospects for true literal predication in theology.[27]

[24]*New Essays,* p. 124.
[25]Ibid., p. 129.
[26]Ibid., p. 127.
[27]This paper grew out of material presented in my NEH Summer Seminars on Theological Language, given in 1978 and 1979, and more directly out of a lecture delivered at the 1978 Wheaton College Philosophy Conference. I am grateful to the participants in my summer seminars and at the Wheaton Conference for many valuable reactions.

NOTES

A. Since this paper was written, metaphoricists in theology have begun to come out of the closet. See, e.g., Sallie McFague, *Metaphorical Theology* (Philadelphia: Fortress Press, 1982).

Can We Speak
Literally of God?

I

In this essay we shall be concerned with only one stretch of talk about God, but a particularly central stretch—subject-predicate statements in which the subject-term is used to refer to God. I mean this to be limited to *statements* in a strict sense, utterances that are put forward with a "truth claim". This is a crucial stretch of the territory, because any other talk that involves reference to God presupposes the truth of one or more *statements* about God. For example, if I ask God to give me courage, I am presupposing that God is the sort of being to whom requests can be sensibly addressed. Thus our more specific topic concerns whether terms can be literally predicated of God.

According to contemporary Protestant theologians of a liberal cast, it is almost an article of faith that this is impossible. Let us be somewhat more explicit than people like that generally are, as to just what is being denied. When someone says that we cannot speak literally of God, that person does not mean to deny us the capacity to form a subject-predicate sentence that contains a subject-term used to refer to God, making a literal use of the predicate term and uttering the sentence with the claim that the predicate is true of the subject. I could easily refute that denial here and now—"God has commanded us to love one another". I

From *Is God GOD?*, ed. Axel D. Steuer and James W. McClendon, Jr. (Nashville: Abingdon Press, 1981), pp. 146–77. Copyright © 1981 by Abingdon. Reprinted by permission.

have just done it. But presumably it is not that sort of ability that is in question. It is rather a question as to whether any such truth claim can succeed. What is being denied is that any predicate term, used literally, can be *truly applied* to God, or as we might say, that any predicate is *literally true* of God.

But even this is stronger than a charitable interpretation would require. Presumably, no one who thinks it possible to refer to God would deny that some negative predicates are literally true of God—for instance, incorporeal, immutable, or not-identical-with-Richard-Nixon. Nor would all extrinsic predicates be ruled out; it would be difficult to deny that 'thought of now by me' could be literally true of God. Now it is notoriously difficult to draw an exact line between positive and negative predicates; and the class of predicates I am calling "extrinsic" is hardly easier to demarcate. It is either very difficult or impossible to give a precise characterization of the class of predicates to which the deniers of literal talk should be addressing themselves. Here I shall confine myself to the following brief statement. The reason various predicates are obvious examples of "negative" or "extrinsic" predicates is that they do not "tell us anything" about the subject—about the nature or operations of the subject. Let us call predicates that do "tell us something" about such matters "intrinsic" predicates. We may then take it that an opponent of literal theological talk is denying that any *intrinsic* predicate can be literally true of God. It will be noted that "intrinsic" predicates include various *relational* predicates, such as "made the heavens and the earth" and "spoke to Moses".

Various reasons have been given for the impossibility of literal predication in theology. Among the most prominent have been the following.

1. Since God is an absolutely undifferentiated unity, and since all positive predications impute complexity to their subject, no such predications can be true of God. This line of thought is most characteristic of the mystical tradition, but something like it can be found in other theologies as well.
2. God is so "transcendent", so "wholly other", that no concepts we can form would apply to him.
3. The attempt to apply predicates literally to God inevitably leads to paradoxes.

It is the second reason that bulks largest in twentieth-century Protestant theology. It has taken several forms, one of the more fashionable being the position of Paul Tillich that (a) God is not *a* being but Being-

Itself, since anything that is *a* being would not be an appropriate object of "ultimate concern"; and (b) only what is *a* being can be literally characterized.

In my opinion, all these arguments are radically insufficient to support the sweeping denial that *any* intrinsic predicate can be literally true of God. But this is not the place to go into that. Nor will I take up the cudgel for the other side on this issue and argue that it must be possible for *some* intrinsic predicates or other to be literally true of God. Instead I will focus on a particularly important class of predicates—those I shall call "personalistic" (or, following Strawson, 'P-predicates')—and consider the more specific question, whether any P-predicates can be literally true of God. Or rather, as I shall make explicit shortly, I will consider one small part of this very large question. By "personalistic" predicates, I mean those that, as a group, apply to a being only if that being is a "personal agent"—an agent that carries out intentions, plans, or purposes in its actions, that acts in the light of knowledge or belief; a being whose actions express attitudes and are guided by standards and principles; a being capable of communicating with other such agents and entering into other forms of personal relations with them. The conception of God as a personal agent is deeply embedded in Christianity and in other theistic religions. Communication between God and man, verbal and otherwise, is at the heart of the Judaeo-Christian tradition. Equally fundamental is the thought of God as a being who lays down commands, injunctions, rules, and regulations, and who monitors compliance or noncompliance; who created the world and directs it to the attainment of certain ends; who enters into convenants; who rewards and punishes; who loves and forgives; who acts in history and in the lives of men to carry out His purposes. The last few sentences indicate some of the kinds of P-predicates that have traditionally been applied to God.

II

Before coming to grips with this problem, we must provide some clarification of the central term 'literal'. To begin on a negative note, despite the frequent occurrence of phrases such as 'literal *meaning*' and 'literal *sense*', I believe that such phrases constitute a confused or at least a loose way of thinking about the subject. To get straight about the matter, we need to keep a firm hold on the distinction between *language* and *speech*. A (natural) language is an abstract system, a system of sound types or, in principle, types of other sorts of perceptible items. The systematicity involved is both "internal" and "external". The phonology, morphology, and syntax of a language reveal its internal system—the ways its elements can be combined to form larger units. The external system is revealed by the semantics of the language—the way units of language have the function of "representing" things in the world and features of the world.[1] A language serves as a means of communication; in fact, it is plausible to look on the entire complex structure as "being there" in order to make a language an effective device for communication. Speech, on the other hand, is the *use* of language in communication (using 'speech' in an extended sense, to cover written as well as oral communication). It is what we *do* in the course of exploiting a linguistic system for purposes of communication.

Now the fact that a given word or phrase has the meaning(s) or sense(s) that it has is a fact about the language; it is part of the semantic constitution of the language.[2] Thus it is a semantic fact about English that 'player' has among its meanings:

1. an idler;
2. one who plays some (specified) game;
3. a gambler;
4. an actor.[3]

It is partly the fact that a word *has* a certain meaning in a language that gives the word its usability for communication; this fact constitutes one of the linguistic resources we draw upon in saying what we have to say.

The term 'literal', on the other hand, stands for a certain way of *using* words, phrases, and so on; it stands for a mode of *speech* rather than for a type of meaning or any other feature of *language*. As such, it stands in contrast with a family of *figurative* uses of terms—"figures of speech", as they are appropriately termed in the tradition—the most familiar of which is metaphor. Let us make explicit the difference between literal and metaphorical uses, restricting ourselves to uses of predicates in subject-predicate statements.

We may think of each meaning of a predicate term as "correlating"

---

[1]This a crude characterization of semantics, but it will have to do for now. There is no general agreement on what an adequate semantics would look like.

[2]We shall not distinguish between *meaning* and *sense*.

[3]*Webster's New Collegiate Dictionary* (Springfield, Mass.: Merriam, 1959). I am far from claiming that this is the most adequate way to specify these meanings. Indeed, it is far from clear what that way would be. But it is clear that 'player' has the meanings thus specified, however lamely and haltingly, and that its having these meanings is (a small) part of what makes the English language what it is at this stage of its history.

the term with some, possibly very complex, property.[4] Different theories of meaning provide differing accounts of the nature of this correlation. Thus the "ideational" theory of meaning, found for example in Locke's *Essay*, holds that a meaning of a predicate term correlates it with a certain property—P—*iff* the term functions as a sign of the *idea* of P in communication. Other theories provide other accounts. It will be convenient to speak of the predicate term as "signifying" or "standing for" the correlated property.

Now when I make a *literal* use of a predicate term (in one of its meanings) in a subject-predicate statement, I utter the sentence with the claim that the property signified by the predicate term is possessed by the subject (i.e., the referent of the subject-term), or holds between the subjects, if the predicate is a relational one. Thus, if I make a literal use of 'player' in saying "He's one of the players", I am claiming, let us say, that the person referred to has the property specified in the fourth definition listed above. And if my statement is true, if the person referred to really does have that property, we may say that 'player' is *literally true* of him in that sense—does *literally apply* to him in that sense.

But suppose I say, as Shakespeare has Macbeth say, "Life's . . . a poor player that struts and frets his hour upon the stage and then is heard no more". It is clear that life is not really an actor; nor, if we surveyed the other established meanings of 'player', would we find any properties signified that are exemplified by life. Hence in uttering Macbeth's sentence, I will, if I am sensible, be using the term 'player' metaphorically rather than literally. Since figurative uses appear in this paper only as a foil for literal uses, I will not be able to embark on the complex task of characterizing the figures of speech. Suffice it to say that when I use a term metaphorically, I exploit some meaning the term has in the language, but not in the straightforward way that is involved in literal usage. Rather than claiming that the property signified by the predicate does apply to the subject(s), I do something more complex, more indirect. I first, so to speak, "present" the hearer with the sort of thing to which the term literally applies (call it an exemplar) and then suggest that the exemplar can be taken as a "model" of the subject(s); I suggest that by considering the exemplar, one will thereby be put in mind of certain features of the subject(s). In the example just given, the exemplar is an (insignificant) actor who plays his part in a stage production and then disappears from the view

---

[4]I want this supposition to be compatible with the fact that most or all predicate terms have meanings that are vague, exhibit "open texture", or suffer from indeterminacy in other ways. This implies that an adequate formulation would be more complicated than the one given here.

of the audience; the suggestion is that a human life is like that in some significant respect(s).[5]

The term 'literal' has picked up a number of adventitious associations in recent times. I think particularly of 'precise', 'univocal', 'specific', 'empirical', and 'ordinary'. However common the conflation, it is simply a confusion to suppose that 'literal', in the historically distinctive sense just set out, implies any of the features just mentioned. Meanings that words have in a language can be more or less vague, open-textured, unspecific, and otherwise indeterminate. Hence I can be using words literally and still be speaking vaguely, ambiguously, or unspecifically. Again, I can be using my words just as literally when asking questions, cursing fate, or expressing rage, as when I am soberly asserting that the cat is on the mat. The conflation of 'literal' with 'empirical', however, is more than a vulgar error; it reflects a conviction as to the conditions under which a word can acquire a meaning in the language. If this requires contact with "experience" in one or another of the ways spelled out in empiricist theories of meaning, then only terms with empirical meanings can be used literally, for only such terms *have* established senses. But that does not follow merely from the meaning of 'literal'; it also requires an empiricist theory of meaning, and it is by no means clear that any such theory is acceptable.

It might be thought that after the term 'literal' has been stripped of all these interesting connotations, the question as to whether we can speak literally of God has lost its importance. Not so. To demonstrate its importance, we merely need appeal to some highly plausible principles which connect meanings and concepts. It seems clear that I can attach a certain meaning to a predicate term only if I have a concept of the property signified by the term when used with that meaning; otherwise, how can I "get at" the property so as to signify it by that term? And on the other hand, if I do have a concept of that property, it could not be impossible for me to use a term to signify that property. And if a sufficient number of members of my linguistic community share that concept, it could not be, in principle, impossible for a term to signify that property in the language. Thus it is possible for a term in a certain language to signify a certain property *iff* speakers of that language have or can have a concept of that property. Hence our language can contain terms that stand for intrinsic properties of God *iff* we can form concepts of intrinsic properties of God. And since we can make true literal predications of God *iff* our language contains terms that stand

---

[5]Metaphor is a topic of unlimited sublety and complexity, and the above formulation barely scratches the surface. For a bit more detail, see Essay 1.

for properties exemplified by God, we may say, finally, that we can speak literally of God (in the relevant sense of true literal predication) *iff* we can form concepts of intrinsic divine properties.[6] And whether this last is true is *obviously* an important issue—one that has been at the very center of metatheology from the beginning.

The question whether certain terms can be literally applied to God is often identified with the question whether those terms are literally true of God in senses they bear outside theology. Thus with respect to P-predicates, it is often supposed that God can be spoken of as literally having knowledge and intentions, as creating, commanding, and forgiving, only if those terms are literally true of God in the same senses as those in which they are literally true of human beings. The reason usually given for this supposition is that we first come to attach meaning to these terms by learning what it is for human beings to command, forgive, and so on, and that there is no other way we can proceed. We cannot begin by learning what it is for God to know, command, or forgive. I do not want to contest this claim about the necessary order of language learning, though there is much to be said on both sides. I will confine myself to pointing out that even if this claim is granted, it does *not* follow that terms can be literally applied to God only in senses in which they also are true of human beings and other creatures. For the fact that we must begin with creatures is quite compatible with the supposition that at some later stage terms take on special technical senses in theology. After all, that is what happens in science. There, too, it can be plausibly argued that we can learn theoretical terms in science only if we have already learned commonsense meanings of these and other terms—senses in which the terms are true of ordinary middle-sized objects. But even if that is true, it does not prevent such terms as 'force' and 'energy' from taking on new technical senses in the development of sophisticated theories. Why should not the same be true of theology?

Many will claim that the same cannot be true of theology, because the conditions that permit technical senses to emerge in science do not obtain in theology. For example, it may be claimed that theological systems do not have the kind of explanatory efficacy possessed by scientific theories. These are important questions, but I can sidestep them for now, because I will restrict myself here to whether (some) P-predicates can be true of God in (some of) the senses in which they are true of human beings. The only qualification I make on that is that I shall consider a simple transformation of certain human action predi-

---

[6]This argument is developed more fully in Essay 1.

cates—"simple", in that the change does not involve any radical conceptual innovation. The revised action predicates are fundamentally of the same sort as human action predicates, though different in some details.

Whether certain predicates are literally true of God depends on both parties to the transaction; it depends both on what God is like and on the content of the predicates. To carry out a proper discussion of the present issue, I would need to (a) present and defend an account of the nature of God, and (b) present and defend an analysis of such P-predicates as will be considered. That would put us in a position to make some well-grounded judgments as to whether such predicates could be literally true of God. Needless to say, I will not have time for all that; I would not have had time, even if I had cut the preliminary cackle and buckled down to the job straight away. Hence I must scale down my aspirations. Instead of trying "tell it like it is" with God, I shall simply pick one commonly recognized attribute of God—incorporeality—which has been widely thought to rule out personal agency, and I shall consider whether it does so. My main reasons for focusing on incorporeality, rather than on simplicity, infinity, timelessness, or immutability, are that it, much more than the others, is widely accepted today as a divine attribute and that it has bulked large in some recent arguments against the literal applicability of P-predicates. On the side of the predicates, I shall consider those types of analyses that are, in my judgment, the strongest contenders and ask what each of them implies as to literal applicability to an incorporeal being.[7]

This investigation is only a fragment of the total job. It is radically incomplete from both sides, and especially from the side of the divine nature. Even if we satisfy ourselves that personalistic terms can be literally true of an incorporeal being, that will by no means suffice to show that they are literally true of God. God is not just any old incorporeal being. There may well be other divine attributes that inhibit us from thinking literally of God as a personal agent—simplicity, infinity, immutability, and timelessness. But sufficient unto the day is the problem thereof.

[7]The question as to whether P-predicates could be applied to an incorporeal being presupposes that we can form a coherent notion of an incorporeal substance or other concrete subject of attributes. This has often been denied on the grounds that it is, in principle, impossible to identify, reidentify, or individuate such a being. See Antony Flew, *God and Philosophy* (London: Hutchinson, 1966), chap. 2; Terence Penelhum, *Survival and Disembodied Existence* (New York: Humanities Press, 1970), chap. 6.; Sydney Shoemaker, *Self-Knowledge and Self-Identity* (Ithaca: Cornell University Press, 1963), chaps. 4 and 5. If arguments like this were successful, as I believe they are not, our problem would not arise.

III

P-predicates may be conveniently divided into mental or psychological predicates (M-predicates) and action predicates (A-predicates).
M-predicates have to do with cognitions, feelings, emotions, attitudes,
wants, thoughts, fantasies, and other internal psychological states,
events, and processes. A-predicates have to do with what, in a broad
sense, an agent *does*. For reasons that will emerge in the course of the
discussion, it will be best to begin with theories of M-predicates. I shall
oscillate freely between speaking of the *meanings* of predicates and the
concepts those predicates express by virtue of having those meanings.

The main divide in theories of M-predicates concerns whether they
are properly defined in terms of their behavioral manifestations.[8] On
the negative side of that issue is the view that was dominant from the
seventeenth through the nineteenth century—what we may call the
Private Paradigm (PP) view. According to this position, the meaning of
an M-predicate—for example, 'feels depressed'—is given, for each
person, by certain paradigms of feelings of depression within his own
experience. By 'feels depressed' I mean a state such as X, Y, Z, . . . ,
where these are clear cases of feeling depressed that I can remember
having experienced. We might say that on this model an M-predicate
acquires meaning through "inner ostension"; I attach meaning to the
term by "associating" it with samples of the state it signifies. On the PP
view, an M-predicate is not properly defined in terms of its invariable,
normal, or typical behavioral manifestations. Even if feelings of depression are typically manifested by droopy appearance, slowness of
response, and lack of vigor, it is no part of the *meaning* of the term that
these are the typical manifestations. Our *concept* of feeling depressed is
such that it makes sense to think of a world in which feelings of depression typically manifest themselves in alert posture and vigorous reactions. Since the term simply designates certain feeling qualities, it is just
a matter of fact that feelings of depression manifest themselves in the
way they do.[9]

---

[8]Note that the issue here concerns the content (character, correct analysis) of psychological *predicates* or *concepts*, not the *nature* of the human psyche or the *nature* of human
thought, intention, etc. Obviously the divine psyche, if there be such, is radically different in nature from the human psyche. The only question is as to whether there are any
psychological *concepts* that apply to both. Hence our specific interest is in what we are
saying about a human being when we say of that person that s/he is thinking, has a certain
attitude, or whatever. Thus the classification to follow is not a classification of theories of
the nature of human mind—dualism, materialism, epiphenomenalism, etc.

[9]The PP view was espoused or presupposed by the great seventeenth- and eighteenth-
century philosophers: Descartes, Spinoza, Locke, Leibniz, Berkeley, Hume, and Reid. It

There are solid reasons for the PP view, especially for feeling and sensation terms. (1) If I have never felt depressed, then in an important sense, I do not understand the term, for I do not know *what it is like* to feel depressed; I simply do not have the concept of that sort of feeling. (2) My knowledge of my own feelings is quite independent of my knowledge of my behavior or demeanor; I do not have to watch myself in a mirror to know how I feel. Hence it seems that what I know when I know how I feel cannot consist in any behavioral manifestations or tendencies thereto. (3) It does seem an *intelligible* supposition that the kind of feeling we call a feeling of depression should be manifested in ways that are radically different from those that do in fact obtain. And the PP account allows for this.

However, the PP account has been under attack throughout this century. There are four main motives for dissatisfaction. (1) If feeling depressed is not, by definition, typically manifested in certain ways, then how can I tell what other people are feeling, on the basis of their behavior and demeanor? For I can discover a correlation between a certain kind of feeling and certain kinds of behavior only in my own case; and how can I generalize from one case? Thus the PP view has been felt to rule out knowledge of the mental states of others. (2) How can you and I have any reason to suppose that we attach the same meaning to any M-predicate, if each of us learns the meaning from nonshareable paradigms? How can I tell whether my paradigms of feeling depressed are like your paradigms? Thus the PP view has been thought to sap our conviction that we share a public language for talking about the mind. (3) On the widely influential Verifiability Theory of Meaning, the meaning of a term is given by specifying the ways in which we can tell that it applies. Since we can tell whether M-predicates apply to others by observing their demeanor and behavior, the latter must enter into the meaning of the term. (4) Wittgenstein mounted a very influential attack on the possibility of attaching meaning to terms by private ostension.[10]

These arguments against PP support the idea that mental states are identified in terms of their typical manifestations in overt behavior and demeanor. We may use the term Logical Connectionism (LC) as a

---

surfaces as an explicit dogma in Book II of Locke's *Essay Concerning Human Understanding,* throughout Hume's *Treatise of Human Nature,* and in Essay I of Reid's *Essays on the Intellectual Powers of Man.*

[10]Ludwig Wittgenstein, *Philosophical Investigations,* trans. G. E. M. Anscombe (Oxford: Basil Blackwell, 1953), nos. 258–70. In briefly indicating the main arguments for and against the PP view, I am merely trying to convey some sense of why various positions have seemed plausible. No endorsement of any particular argument is intended.

general term for views of this sort, on the ground that these views hold that there is a logical (conceptual) connection between a mental state and its manifestations.

The general concept of LC allows plenty of room for variation. The simplest form that is not wildly implausible is Logical Behaviorism (LB). LB may be formulated as the view that an M-predicate signifies a set of behavioral dispositions—dispositions to behave in a certain way, given certain conditions.[11] Thus a logical behaviorist would explain "S feels depressed" in some such way as this: If someone makes a suggestion to S, S will respond slowly and without enthusiasm; if S is presented with something S usually likes, S will not smile as S normally does in such situations, and so on.[12] LB is not nearly as prominent now as a decade or so ago, and in my opinion, there are excellent reasons for this decline. The fatal difficulty is this. The response tendencies associated with a particular case of a mental state will depend upon the total psychological field of the moment—that is, the other mental states present at the time. For example, whether a person who feels depressed will react in a characteristically depressed way depends upon whether he is sufficiently motivated to conceal his condition. If he is, the typical manifestation may well not be forthcoming. Thus any particular behavioral reaction emerges from the total contemporary psychological field and is not wholly determined by any one component thereof. This consideration should inhibit us from attempting to identify any particular M-concept with the concept of any particular set of behavioral dispositions.

Under the impact of these considerations, more subtle forms of LC have developed, for which we may use the generic term, 'Functionalism'. The general idea of Functionalism is that each M-concept is a concept of a certain functional role in the operation of the psyche. A major emphasis in this position has been the functional character of M-concepts. In attributing a certain belief, attitude, or feeling to S, we are committing ourselves to the position that a certain function is being carried out in S's psyche, or at least that S is prepared to carry it out if the need arises. We are not committing ourselves on the physical (or

---

[11]For an important statement of LB, see Rudolf Carnap, "Psychologie in physikalischer Sprache," *Erkenntnis,* Vol. 3 (1932). English translation, "Psychology in Physical Language," by George Schick in *Logical Positivism,* ed. A. J. Ayer (New York: The Free Press, 1959). Gilbert Ryle's *The Concept of Mind* (London: Hutchinson, 1949) is an influential work that is often regarded as a form of LB.

[12]In this quick survey I am ignoring many complexities. For example, the most plausible LB account of feeling depressed would involve some categorical overt manifestations, such as "looking droopy", as well as response tendencies like those cited in the text. I am also forced to omit any consideration of the relation of LB to behaviorism in psychology.

spiritual) structure or composition of whatever is performing this function; our concept is neutral as to that. M-concepts, on this position, are functional in essentially the same way as the concept of a mousetrap. A mousetrap, by definition, is a device for catching mice; the definition is neutral as to the composition and structure of devices that perform this function. That is why it is possible to build a better mousetrap.[13]

To exploit this initial insight, the functionalist will have to find a way of specifying functional roles in the psyche. It is now generally assumed by functionalists that the basic function of the psyche as a whole is the production of overt behavior. That is why Functionalism counts as a form of LC. To understand the concept of belief is, at least in part, to understand the role of beliefs in the production of behavior. But "at least in part" is crucial; it is what enables Functionalism to escape the above objections to LB. Functionalism is thoroughly systemic. The vicissitudes of LB have taught it to avoid the supposition that each distinguishable mental state is related separately to overt behavior. It has thoroughly internalized the point that a given belief, attitude, or feeling gives rise to a certain distinctive mode of behavior only in conjunction with the rest of the contemporary psychological field. Therefore in specifying the function of an enthusiasm for Mozart, for example, in the production of behavior, we must specify the way that enthusiasm combines with each of various other combinations of factors to affect behavioral output. It also recognizes that intrapsychic functions enter into M-concepts. Our concept of the *belief that it is raining now* includes (a) the way this belief will combine with others to inferentially generate other beliefs, and (b) the way it will combine with an aversion to rainy weather, to produce dismay, as well as (c) the way it will combine with an aversion to getting wet, to produce the behavior of getting out one's umbrella. Clearly, a full functionalist specification of an M-concept would be an enormously complicated affair.[14]

With an eye to putting some flesh on this skeleton, consider this attempt by R. B. Brandt and Jaegwon Kim to formulate a functionalist analysis of the ordinary concept of *want*, conceived in a broad sense as any state in which the object of the "want" has what Lewin called positive valence for the subject.[15]

---

[13]I am indebted to Jerry Fodor, *Psychological Explanation* (New York: Random House, 1968), pp. 15–16, for this felicitous analogy.

[14]The functionalist is not committed to holding that all functional relations in which a given mental state stands will enter into our ordinary concept of that state. Picking out those that do is admittedly a tricky job; but that difficulty is by no means restricted to Functionalism.

[15]I follow Brandt and Kim in taking Functionalism, as well as the other views can-

"*X* wants *p*" has the meaning it does for us because we believe roughly the following statements.

1. If, given that *x* had not been expecting *p* but now suddenly judged that *p* would be the case, *x* would feel joy, then *x* wants *p*.
2. If, given that *x* had been expecting *p* but then suddenly judged that *p* would not be the case, *x* would feel disappointment, then *x* wants *p*.
3. If daydreaming about *p* is pleasant to *x*, then *x* wants *p*.
4. If *x* wants *p*, then, under favorable conditions, if *x* judges that doing *A* will probably lead to *p* and that not doing *A* will probably lead to not *p*, *x* will feel some impulse to do *A*.
5. If *x* wants *p*, then, under favorable conditions, if *x* thinks some means *M* is a way of bringing *p* about, *x* will be more likely to notice an *M* than he would otherwise have been.
6. If *x* wants *p*, then, under favorable conditions, if *p* occurs, without the simultaneous occurrence of events *x* does not want, *x* will be pleased.[16]

In terms of our general characterization of Functionalism, we can think of each of these lawlike generalizations as specifying a *function* performed by wants. Thus a "want" is the sort of state that (a) together with unexpected fulfillment, gives rise to feelings of joy; (b) renders daydreaming about its object pleasant, and so on. (c) is the crucial connection with behavior, though in this formulation it is quite indirect, coming through a connection with an "impulse" to perform a certain action.[17] This is in contrast to PP, which would view a want for *p* as a certain kind of introspectable state, event, or process with a distinctive "feel"—for instance, a sense of the attractiveness of *p*, or a felt urge to realize *p*.[18]

Now let us turn to the way these views bear upon the applicability of M-predicates to an incorporeal being. I believe it would be generally

---

vassed, to be an account of the ordinary meanings of M-predicates. Some theorists present it as a proposal for developing psychological concepts for scientific purposes, or as an account of the *nature* of mental states.

[16]R. B. Brandt and Jaegwon Kim, "Wants as Explanations of Actions," *Journal of Philosophy*, 60 (1963), 427.

[17]Different forms of Functionalism display special features not mentioned in this brief survey. Cybernetic analogies are prominent in many versions, with psychological functions thought of on the model of the machine table of a computer. Some, like the Brandt and Kim account, find a useful model in the way in which theoretical terms in science get their meaning from the ways in which they figure in the theory.

[18]It may be doubted that 'want' is a serious candidate for theological predication. It would not be if the term were being used in a narrow sense that implies felt craving or lack of need. But I, along with many philosophers, mean to be using it in the broad sense just indicated. To indicate how the term might be applied to God in this sense, Aquinas uses the term 'appetition' more or less in the way Brandt and Kim explain 'want'; *will* for Aquinas is "intellectual appetition", and he applies 'will' to God.

supposed that our two views have opposite consequences: that on a PP view, M-predicates could be applied to an incorporeal being, but not on an LC view. However, I will contest this received position to the extent of arguing that neither position presents any conceptual bar to the literal application of M-predicates.

First, a brief word about the bearing of the PP view before turning to the debate over LC, which is my main concern in this section. Presumably, an incorporeal subject could have states of consciousness with distinctive phenomenological qualities, just as well as we could. Hence terms that signify such states of consciousness would not be inapplicable in principle to such a being. But though I believe this is correct, I do not feel that it is of much significance for theology, and this for two reasons.

First, the PP account is most plausible with respect to feelings, sensations, and other M-states which clearly have a distinctive "feel". It is much less plausible with respect to "colorless" mental states such as beliefs, attitudes, thoughts, and intentions. We cannot hold an intention or a belief "before the mind" as we can a feeling of dismay, and thereby form a conception of "what it is like". But it is M-predicates of the colorless sort that are of most interest to theology. In thinking of God as a personal agent, we think of God as possessing (and using) knowledge, purpose, intention, and the like. Feelings and sensations either are not applicable to God at all, or they are of secondary importance. Theology quite properly avoid trying to figure out what it *feels* like to be God.

Second, suppose that one defends the applicability of M-predicates on a PP basis because he considers them inapplicable on an LC construal. This latter conviction would presumably be based on an argument similar to the one to be given shortly, to the effect that M-predicates, as analyzed in LC, are inapplicable to God because, as an incorporeal being, God is incapable of overt behavior. In that case, even if our theorist succeeds in showing that PP predicates can apply, he has won, at most a Pyrrhic victory. To secure application of M-predicates at the price of abandoning the idea that God acts in the world is to doom the enterprise to irrelevance. Whatever may be the case with the gods of Aristotle and the Epicureans, the God of the Judaeo-Christian tradition is preeminently a God who *acts,* in history and in the lives of individuals, not to mention His creation and preservation of the world. Hence even if, one the PP view, M-predicates are applicable to an incorporeal being incapable of overt action, that does nothing to show that M-predicates are applicable to the Judaeo-Christian God.

Turning now to LC, let us look at a typical statement by one who is arguing from an LC position.

> What would it be like for an x to be just loving without doing anything or being capable of doing anything? . . . Surely 'to do something', 'to behave in a certain way', is to make—though this is not all that it is—certain bodily movement . . . . For it to make sense to speak of x's acting or failing to act, x must have a body. Thus if 'love' is to continue to mean anything at all near to what it normally means, it is meaningless to say that God loves mankind. Similar considerations apply to the other psychological predicates tied to the concept of God.[19]

It will help us in evaluating this argument to set it out more carefully.

1. On LC, an M-concept is, at least in part, a concept of dispositions to overt behavior (perhaps through the mediation of other mental states).[20]
2. Overt behavior requires bodily movements of the agent.
3. An incorporeal being, lacking a body, cannot move its body.
∴4. An incorporeal being cannot engage in overt behavior.
5. A being that is, in principle, incapable of overt behavior cannot have dispositions to overt behavior.
∴6. M-concepts are, in principle, inapplicable to an incorporeal being.

This argument is certainly on sound ground in claiming that, on LC, an M-predicate is applicable to S only if A-predicates are so applicable. Its Achilles' heel, I will claim, is 2, the thesis that overt behavior requires bodily movements of the agent. My attack on that thesis will occupy the next section. Let us take the upshot of this section to be that, on the most plausible account of the M-predicates that are of most interest to theology, God can literally know, purpose, and will, only if God can literally perform overt actions. This result nicely mirrors the fundamental place of divine agency in Judaeo-Christian theology.

---

[19]Kai Nielsen, *Contemporary Critiques of Religion* (London: Macmillan, 1971), p. 117. See also Paul Edwards, "Difficulties in the Idea of God," in *The Idea of God*, ed. E. H. Madden, R. Handy, and M. Farber (Springfield, Ill.: Charles Thomas, 1968), pp. 45 ff.

[20]Let us define "overt" behavior as action that essentially involves some occurrence outside the present consciousness of the agent. This will exclude, e.g., "mental" actions such as focusing one's attention on something or resolving to get out of bed. The kinds of actions that are crucial to the Judaeo-Christian concept of God—creating the world, issuing commands, and guiding and comforting individual—count as overt on this definition.

Before embarking on the discussion of A-predicates, I want to make two points.

First, there are forms of LC that do rule out the application of M-predicates to an incorporeal being. I am thinking of those views that put certain kinds of restrictions on the input, or output, of the psyche. Some forms of LB, for example, require that the behavioral output be specified in terms of bodily movements of the agent, and the input in terms of stimulations of the agent's sense receptors. Functionalist theories may also be so restricted. Clearly, M-predicates analyzed in this way are applicable only to beings capable of such inputs and outputs. But our concern in this paper is to determine whether any version of LC would allow the application of M-predicates to an incorporeal being.

Second, we should not suppose that the question of the applicability of A-predicates to an incorporeal being is prejudged by the fact that all cases of overt action with which we are most familiar involve bodily movements of the agent. A feature that is common to the familiar *denotata* of a term may not be reflected in the meaning of that term, even if this class of *denotata* is the one from which we learn the meaning of the term, and even if it contains the only *denotata* with which we are acquainted. It is doing small honor to human powers of conception to suppose that one must form one's concept of P in such a way as to be limited to the class of Ps from which the concept was learned. Surely we can think more abstractly and generically than that. Even though our concept of *animal* was formed solely from experience of land creatures, that concept might still be such that it contains only features that are equally applicable to fish. And even if that were not the case—even if the capacity to walk on legs is part of our concept of an animal—it may be that it can be easily extended to fish, merely by dropping out the feature just mentioned. The moral of the story is obvious. We cannot assume in advance that our concept of making, commanding, or forgiving includes the concept of bodily movements of the maker, commander, or forgiver. And even if it does, this may be a relatively peripheral component which can be sheared off, leaving intact a distinctive conceptual core.

IV

Let us consider, then, whether it is conceptually possible for an incorporeal being to perform overt actions. Our entrée to that discussion will be a consideration of the vulnerable premise in the argument, the thesis that overt behavior requires bodily movements.

To understand the grounds for this thesis, we must introduce the notion of a *basic action*. Roughly speaking, a basic action is one that is performed *not* by or in (simultaneously) performing some other action. Thus if I sign my name, *that* is done by moving my hand in a certain way, so the action is not basic; but if moving my hand is *not* done *by* doing something else, it will count as a basic action. Just where to locate basic human actions is philosophically controversial. If contracting muscles in my hand is something I *do* (in the intended sense of 'do'), then it seems that I move my hand *by* contracting my muscles, and moving my hand will not count as a basic action. Again, if sending neural impulses to the muscles is something I *do*, then it seems that I contract the muscles *by* sending neural impulses to them, and so the contraction of muscles will not count as a basic action. Since I do not have time to go into this issue, I shall simply follow a widespread practice and assume that all overt human basic actions consist in the movements of certain parts of the body which ordinarily would be thought to be under "voluntary control", such as the hand.

It follows from our explanation of the term 'basic action' that every nonbasic action is done *by* performing a basic action. If we are further correct in ruling that every human basic action consists in moving some part of one's body, then it follows that every human nonbasic action is built on, or presupposes, some bodily movement of the agent. The relationship differs in different cases: Sometimes the nonbasic action involves an effect of some bodily movement(s), as in the action of knocking over a vase; sometimes it involves the bodily movement's falling under a rule or convention of some kind, as in signaling a turn. But whatever the details, it follows from what has been laid down thus far that a human being cannot do anything overt without moving some part of the body. Either the action is basic, in which case it merely *consists* in moving some part of one's body; or it is not, in which case it is done *by* moving some part of one's body.

But granted that this is the way it is with human action, what does this have to do with A-*concepts*? As noted earlier, our concept of a φ never includes all the characteristics that are in fact common to φs we have experienced. So why should we suppose that our concepts of various human actions—making or commanding, for example—contain any reference to bodily movement?

Again it will be most useful to divide this question in accordance with the basic-nonbasic distinction. Our concepts of particular types of human basic actions certainly do involve specifications of bodily movements. This is because that is what such actions *are*. Their whole content is a certain kind of movement of a certain part of the body. That is

55

what distinguishes one type of human basic action from another. Hence we cannot say what kind of basic action we are talking about without mentioning some bodily movement—stretching, kicking, raising the arm, or whatever. Clearly, A-predicates such as these are not literally applicable to an incorporeal being. But this will be no loss to theology. I take it that none of us is tempted to think that it could be literally true that God stretches out His arm or activates His vocal organs.

The more relevant question concerns the status of such human non-basic A-predicates as 'makes', 'speaks', 'commands', 'forgives', 'comforts', and 'guides'. In saying of S that he commanded me to love my neighbor, am I thereby committing myself to the proposition that S moved some part of his body? Is bodily movement of the agent part of what is *meant* by commanding?

One point at least is clear. Nonbasic human A-concepts do not, in general, carry any reference to particular types of bodily movements. There is indeed wide variation in this regard. At the specific end of the continuum, we have a predicate such as 'kicks open the door', which clearly requires a certain kind of motion of a leg. But 'make a soufflé' and 'command' are more typical, in that the concept is clearly not tied to any particular *kind* of underlying bodily movement. I can issue a command orally or in writing. Indeed, in view of the fact that no limit can be placed on what can be used as a system of communication, any bodily movements whatever could, with the appropriate background, subserve the issuing of a command. In like manner, although there are normal or typical ways of moving the body for making a soufflé, we cannot suppose that these exhaust the possibilities. In this age of electronic marvels, one could presumably make a soufflé by pushing some buttons on a machine with one's toes.

Thus if any reference to bodily movement is included in such A-concepts as making and commanding, it will have to be quite unspecific. The most we could have would be along these lines:

Making a soufflé—causing a soufflé to come into being by some movements of one's body.
Commanding—producing a command by some movements of one's body.[21]

---

[21]These formulations raise questions that are not directly relevant to our concerns in this paper, e.g., how to think of a "command" in such a way that it might be "produced" by an agent. I should note, however, that the causation involved is not restricted to direct causation; intermediaries are allowed.

But can we have even this much? Is it any part of the meaning of these terms, in the sense in which they are applied to human beings, that the external effects in question are produced by movements of the agent's body? No doubt it is completely obvious to all of us that human beings cannot bring about such consequences except by moving their bodies. But to repeat the point once more, it does not follow that this fact is built into human A-concepts. Perhaps our *concept* of making a soufflé is simply that of *bringing a soufflé into existence,* the concept being neutral as to how this is done.

What we have here is one of the numerous difficulties in distinguishing between what we mean by a term and what we firmly believe to be true of the things to which the term applies—in other words, distinguishing between analytic and synthetic truths. These persistent difficulties have been among the factors leading to widespread skepticism about the viability of such distinctions. But for our purpose we need not decide the issue. Let us yield to our opponent. If we can make our case even on the position most favorable to our opponent, we can ignore the outcome of this skirmish.

Let us suppose, then, that all human A-concepts do contain a bodily movement requirement. It clearly follows that no *human* A-concepts are applicable to an incorporeal being. But that by no means shows that *no* A-concepts are applicable. Why should we suppose that the A-concepts we apply to human beings exhaust the field? We must at least explore the possibility that we can form A-concepts that are (a) distinctively and recognizably *action* concepts and (b) do not require any bodily movements of the agent.

In order to do this we must bring out the distinctive features of A-concepts that make them concepts of *actions*. Thus far in discussing human A-concepts, we have gone only as far as the thesis that every human A-concept involves some reference to bodily movement. But that by no means suffices to make them concepts of *actions*. The concept of a heart beat or of a facial tic involves reference to bodily movements, but it is not a concept of an action. What else is required?

I will continue to use human A-concepts as my point of departure for the exploration of the general field, since that is where we get our general concept of action. And I will continue to concentrate on concepts of *basic* actions; since they are relatively simple, the crucial features of A-concepts stand out more clearly there.[22] To focus the discus-

---

[22]There is another reason for this procedure. Since nonbasic actions presuppose basic actions, and not vice versa, there could conceivably be only basic actions, but it is not

sion further, I shall restrict attention to *intentional* actions—those the agent "meant" to perform.[23]

Now, as intimated above, although every human basic action consists in moving some part of the body, not just any bodily movement constitutes a basic *action*. It is possible for my arm to move without my having *moved* it, as in automatic twitches and jerks. In order for it to be the case that I performed the basic action of raising my arm, some further condition must hold, over and above the fact that my arm rose. Thus we can pose the crucial question about the constitution of human basic actions in the classic Wittgensteinian form: "What is left over if I subtract the fact that my arm goes up from the fact that I raise my arm?"[24] Or, putting it the other way round, what must be added to the fact that my arm goes up, to make it the case that I raise my arm?

The recent literature contains many attempts to answer this question, and I shall not have time for a survey. Leaving aside views that, in my opinion, do not survive critical scrutiny (such as the "ascriptive" view, according to which it is an action because we hold the agent responsible for it[25] and the view that "it all depends on context,"[26] we have two serious contenders.

1. *Psychological causation (explanation) view.* What distinguishes the action from the "mere" movement is the psychological background of the movement, what gives rise to it, or issues in it.[27]
2. *Agent causation view.* A bodily movement is an action *iff* it is caused in a certain special way—not by some other event or state, but by the agent itself.[28]

---

possible that there should be only nonbasic actions. We shall see that it is a live possibility that all God's actions are basic.

[23]Again, the basic (but not as obvious) point is that intentional actions are conceptually more basic. It seems that the analysis of action concepts is best set out by beginning with intentional actions and then defining unintentional actions as a certain derivation from that, rather than beginning by analyzing a neutral concept and then explaining *intentional* and *unintentional* as different modifications of that. On the former approach it turns out that all basic actions are intentional. See Alvin I. Goldman, *A Theory of Human Action* (Englewood Cliffs, N.J.: Prentice-Hall, 1970), chap. 3.

[24]Wittgenstein, *Philosophical Investigations*, no. 621.

[25]H. L. A. Hart, "The Ascription of Responsibility and Rights," *Proceedings of the Aristotelian Society*, 69 (1949), 171–94.

[26]A. I. Melden, *Free Action* (New York: Humanities Press, 1961).

[27]Goldman, *Theory*, chaps. 1–3; Charles Taylor, *The Explanation of Behavior* (New York: Humanities Press, 1964), chaps. 2 and 3; W. P. Alston, "Conceptual Prolegomena to a Psychological Theory of Intentional Action," in *Philosophy of Psychology*, ed. S. C. Brown (London: Macmillan, 1974), pt. 2.

[28]Roderick M. Chisholm, "The Descriptive Element in the Concept of 'Action'," *Journal of Philosophy*, 61 (1964), 613–24; Richard Taylor, *Action and Purpose* (Englewood Cliffs, N.J.: Prentice-Hall, 1966), chaps. 1–9.

The psychological causation view exists in many forms, depending on just what psychological factors are specified and just what relation to the bodily movement is required. As for the former, popular candidates have been the will, volitions, intentions, and wants-and-beliefs. On the second score, it is generally required that the movement occur "because of" the psychological factor in question, but there has been considerable controversy over whether to regard the relation as "causal". So as to have a simple form of the view to work with, let us focus on the position that what makes a case of my arm's rising into a case of my raising my arm, is that my arm rose because it was in accordance with my dominant *intentions* at the moment that it should rise.

So the model of a basic action that we get from the human case is:

1. bodily movement
2. caused by ____

To construct an analogous model for incorporeal action that will be an unmistakable model for *action,* we must (a) find a suitable replacement for bodily movements and (b) show that incorporeality is no bar to the satisfaction of a causal condition that will make the whole package into an *action*. It will prove best to begin with the second task, since that poses the more complex and difficult, as well as more controversial, issues. I shall proceed as I did with M-concepts—by considering, with respect to each of our contenders, whether that condition could be satisfied by an incorporeal being.

As for the agent causation view, the concept of agent causation may well be obscure, and it certainly runs violently counter to some deeply rooted contemporary prejudices, but at least it is clear that it does not carry a restriction to *corporeal* substances. The theory avoids, on principle, any specification of the internal machinery by which an agent exercises its causal efficacy—"on principle", since the whole thrust of the position is that when I bring about a bodily movement in performing a basic action, I am not bringing about that movement by initiating certain other events which, in turn, bring about the movement by "event causation". Rather, I directly bring about the bodily movement simply by exploiting my basic capacity to do so. Hence the agent causality interpretation is not restricted to substances possessing one kind of internal structure or equipment rather than another.

On the psychological explanation view, things are a bit more complicated. Let us recall that the "causal condition" on this view is that the bodily movement results from an intention, or the like. So our question divides into two parts. (1) Can an incorporeal being have intentions, or whatever kind of psychological cause is required by the particular version of the theory under discussion? (2) Can an intention cause whatever substitutes for bodily movement in incorporeal basic action? As for (2), it is difficult to discuss this without deciding what does play the role of bodily movement in incorporeal basic actions. Hence we will postpone this question until we specify that substitute.

That leaves us with the question as to whether an incorporeal being can have intentions and the like. And now we find ourselves in a curious position. For that is exactly the question we were asking in the previous section on M-concepts. The conclusion we reached there, on an LC position, was that these concepts are applicable to a subject only if A-concepts are applicable. And now we see that, on the psychological explanation view, A-concepts are applicable to S only if M-concepts are applicable. Where does that leave us? We obviously are in some kind of circle. But is it the vicious circle of chasing our own tail, or a virtuous circle of the sort in which the heavenly bodies were once deemed to move?

Here it is crucial to remember the task we set out to accomplish. If we were trying to *prove* that M- and A-concepts *are* applicable to an incorporeal being, we would have reached an impasse. For since each application depends on the other as a necessary condition, we would not have established either, unless we had some independent argument for the applicability of one or the other. But in fact, we set ourselves a more modest goal—to determine whether the incorporeality of a being is sufficient ground for *denying* the applicability of such concepts. We are considering whether incorporeality renders their applicability impossible. And from that standpoint, the circle is virtuous. The reciprocity we have uncovered provides no reason for *denying* the applicability of either sort of concept. Psychological concepts are applicable only if action concepts are applicable, and vice versa. As far as that consideration goes, it is quite possible that both kinds are applicable. This circle leaves standing the *possibility* that an incorporeal being is such that actions and intentions fit smoothly into the economy of its operations.

Let us now return to the first condition of human basic action concepts, to the problem of finding something that could play the same role for incorporeal basic actions that bodily movements play for corporeal basic actions. I believe that the entrée to this question is an appreciation of the difference between the general concept of a basic action and specific concepts of particular human basic actions. Although concepts of the latter sort contain concepts of particular types of bodily movements, this is not because it is required by the general concept of a basic action. That general concept, as we set it out initially, is simply the concept of an action that is not performed *by* or *in* (simultaneously) performing some other action. This general concept is quite neutral as to what kinds of actions have that status for one or another type of agent. It is just a fact about human beings (*not* a general constraint on action or basic action) that only movements of certain parts of their bodies are under their direct voluntary control and that anything else they bring off, they must accomplish *by* moving their bodies in certain ways. If *I* am to knock over a vase or make a soufflé or communicate with someone, I must do so by moving my hands, legs, vocal organs, or whatever. But that is only because of my limitations. We can conceive of agents, corporeal or otherwise, such that things other than their bodies (if any) are under their direct voluntary control. Some agents might be such that they could knock over a vase or bring a soufflé into being without doing something else in order to do so.[29]

What these considerations suggest is that it is conceptually possible for any change whatsoever to be the core of a basic action. Movements of an agent's body are only what we happen to be restricted to in the human case. Just what changes are within the basic action repertoire of a given incorporeal agent would depend upon the nature of that agent. But the main point is that since such changes are not necessarily restricted to bodily movements of the agent, a subject's bodilessness is no conceptual bar to the performance of basic actions by that subject.

I believe that the case in which we are particularly interested, divine action, can be thought of along the lines of the preceding discussion. Of course, one can think of God as creating light by saying to himself, "Let there be light", or as parting the sea of reeds by saying to himself, "Let the sea of reeds be parted". In that case the basic actions would be mental actions. But what the above discussion indicates is that we are not conceptually required to postulate this mental machinery. We could think just as well of the coming into being of light or of the parting of the sea of reeds as directly under God's voluntary control.

This further suggests that all God's actions might be basic actions. If any change whatsoever could conceivably be the core of a basic action, and if God is omnipotent, then clearly, God *could* exercise direct volun-

---

[29]Be careful to envisage this situation just as I have described it. The agent knocks over the vase not by doing anything else—even anything mental. Telekinesis is often thought of as an agent saying to himself something like "Let the vase be knocked over", and *this* causes the vase to fall over. But that does not make knocking over the vase a basic action. It is still a matter of knocking over the vase *by* doing something else, albeit something mental. In order for knocking over a vase to be a basic action, it would have to be just as immediate as is my raising my arm in the normal case, where I do this not by saying to myself "Let the arm rise", whereupon it rises; but where I just raise the arm intentionally.

tary control over every change in the world which he influences by his activity. However, I do not claim to have done more than exhibit this as a possibility. It is equally possible that God chooses to influence some situations *indirectly*. He might choose to lead or inspire Cyrus to free the Israelites, thus using Cyrus as an instrument to bring about that result. In that case, freeing the Israelites would be a nonbasic action. I am quite willing to leave the decision on this one up to God.[30]

Now let us just glance at the question I postponed—whether it is possible for intentions, and the like, to give rise directly to changes outside the agent's body (if any). I do not have much to say about this— it obviously is something outside our ordinary experience. But I can see nothing in our present understanding of the psyche and of causality that would show it to be impossible in principle. So, pending further insights into those matters, I am inclined to take a quasi-Humean line and say that what can cause what is "up for grabs". And of course, if it is an omnipotent deity that is in question, I suppose He could ordain that intentions can directly cause a parting of waters, provided this is a logical possibility.

Let me sum up these last two sections. Action concepts applicable to an incorporeal being can be constructed that would differ from human action concepts (on the most plausible accounts of the latter) only by the substitution of other changes for bodily movements of the agent in basic action concepts. Hence there is no conceptual bar to the performance of *overt* actions by incorporeal agents and hence no conceptual bar, even on an LC position, to the application of M-predicates to incorporeal beings.

As indicated earlier, this paper constitutes but a fragment of a thoroughgoing discussion of the title question. Other fragments would go into the question as to whether timelessness, immutability, and other

[30]It might be contended that if the physical universe, or any part thereof, is under God's direct voluntary control, this implies that the world is the body of God, which in turn implies that God is not an incorporeal being; that would mean that our case for *incorporeal* basic action fails. That is, the contention would be that in order to ascribe basic actions to S we have to pay the price of construing the changes in question as movements of S's body. This claim could be supported by the thesis that a sufficient condition for something to be part of my body is that it be under my direct voluntary control. So if the physical universe is under God's direct voluntary control, it is His body. Against this, I would argue that we have many different ways of picking out the body of a human being. In addition to the one just mentioned, my body is distinctive in that it is the perspective from which I perceive the world; it provides the immediate causal conditions of my consciousness; and it constitutes the phenomenological locus of my "bodily sensations". With multiple criteria there is room for maneuver. Holding the other criteria constant, we can envisage a state of affairs in which *something other than my body*, e.g., my wristwatch, is under my direct voluntary control. Thus I deny that my position requires God to have a body.

traditional attributes constitute a bar to the literal predication of one or another kind of predicate. And of course we would have to discuss whether God *is* timeless, immutable, and so on. Moreover, we would have to scrutinize the classical arguments for the denial that *any* intrinsic predicates can be literally predicated of God. But perhaps even this fragment has sufficed to show that the prospects for speaking literally about God are not as dim as is often supposed by contemporary thinkers.[31]

[31]This paper grew out of material presented in my NEH Summer Seminars on Theological Language, given in 1978 and 1979, and more directly out of a lecture delivered at the 1978 Wheaton College Philosophy Conference. I am grateful to the participants in my summer seminars and at the Wheaton Conference for many valuable reactions.

Functionalism and
Theological Language

I

Thoughtful theists have long felt a tension between the radical "otherness" of God and the fact that we speak of God in terms drawn from our talk of creatures. If God is radically other than creatures, how can we properly think and speak of Him as acting, loving, knowing, and purposing? Wouldn't that imply that God shares features with creatures and hence is not "wholly other"?

To be sure, whether there is a problem here, and if so just what problem, depends both on the precise way(s) in which God is "other", and on the way in which the creaturely terms are used. Let's take a brief look at both issues.

The respects in which God has been thought to differ from creatures can be roughly arranged in a scale of increasingly radical "otherness". Without aspiring to range over all possible creatures, including angels, let's just think of the ways in which one or another thinker has deemed God to be different from human beings:

(A) Incorporeality.
(B) Infinity. This can be divided into:
    B_1. The unlimited realization of each perfection.
    B_2. The exemplification of all perfections, everything it is better to be than not to be.
(C) Timelessness.
(D) Absolute simplicity. No composition of any sort.
(E) Not *a* being. (God is rather "Being-itself".)

From *American Philosophical Quarterly*, 22 (July 1985), 221–30. Reprinted by permission of the Editor.

Even if (D) and (E) rule out any commonality of properties between God and man, it may still be, as I shall be arguing in this paper, that (A)-(C) do not.

As for the other side of the problem, let's first note the impossibility of avoiding *all* creaturely terms in thinking and speaking of God. We can avoid the crudest anthropomorphisms, speaking of God's hands, arms, and other bodily parts. But we cannot so easily avoid psychological and agential terms ('know', 'love', 'forgive', 'make') that are taken from our talk about ourselves. Suppose that we do carry out so heroic a renunciation and restrict ourselves to speaking of God in such terms as 'being itself', 'ground of being', 'supreme unity', and the like. Even so we would not be avoiding all terms that apply to creatures, e.g., 'being' and 'unity'. The notion of a *ground* is presumably derived from the notion of *causality,* or perhaps the notion of a *necessary condition,* and both these terms apply to creatures. So long as we say anything at all, we will be using terms that apply to creatures, or terms derivative therefrom. Hence so far as the aim at avoiding creaturely language is concerned, we may as well retain the more concrete mentalistic and agential concepts that are so central to the religious life.

But of course there are various ways in which creaturely terms can be used in speaking of God; and some of these may be ruled out by a certain form of otherness, and not others. These ways include:

(1) Straight univocity. Ordinary terms are used in the same ordinary senses of God and human beings.

(2) Modified univocity. Meanings can be defined or otherwise established such that terms can be used with those meanings of both God and human beings.

(3) Special literal meanings. Terms can be given, or otherwise take on, special technical senses in which they apply to God.

(4) Analogy. Terms for creatures can be given analogical extensions so as to be applicable to God.

(5) Metaphor. Terms that apply literally to creatures can be metaphorically applied to God.

(6) Symbol. Ditto for "symbol", in one or another meaning of that term.

The most radical partisans of otherness, from Dionysius through Aquinas to Tillich, plump for something in the (4) to (6) range and explicitly reject (1). The possibility of (3) has been almost wholly ignored, and (2) has not fared much better.

I can use this background to explain what I will do in this paper. First I shall be concentrating on the psychological terms we apply to God— 'know', 'will', 'intend', 'love', and so on. I do not suppose it needs

65

stressing that these are quite central to the way God is thought of in theistic religion. As creator, governor, and redeemer of the world God acts in the light of His perfect knowledge to carry out His purposes and intentions, and as an expression of His love for His creation. As is implicit in this last sentence, the divine psychology comes into our religious dealings with God as an essential background to divine action. God impinges on our lives primarily as agent, as one Who does things—creates, guides, enjoins, punishes, redeems, and speaks. But action is an outgrowth of knowledge, purpose, and intention; unless we could credit these to God we would not be able to think of Him as acting in these ways or in any other ways.

Second, I am going to work with a conception of God that involves modes of otherness (A)-(C), but stops short of a doctrine of absolute simplicity and does not deny that God is in any sense a being. There is no opportunity here to defend that choice; I will only say that I find the arguments for (D) and (E) quite unconvincing, and that this particular packaging has been a common one. Third, I shall seek to show that these modes of otherness are compatible with a degree of univocity in divine-human predication. I shall not go so far as to defend (1), though my position will be compatible with that strong a claim. I shall be arguing that even if God differs from creatures as radically as this, we can still identify a common core of meaning in terms for human and divine psychological states, and that we can, at least, introduce terms to carry that meaning. If ordinary terms already carry just that meaning, so much the better. But whether or not that is the case, it will at least be possible to speak univocally, in an abstract fashion, of divine and human knowledge and purpose.

As my title indicates, I am going to exhibit this divine-human commonality by exploiting a functionalist account of human psychological concepts. But before getting into the details of that, I want to give a more general characterization of the sort of view of which my functionalist account is one version.

The most general idea behind the argument of this paper is that the common possession of abstract features is compatible with as great a difference as you like in the way in which these features are realized. A meeting and a train of thought can both be "orderly" even though what it is for the one to be orderly is enormously different from what it is for the other to be orderly. A new computer and a new acquaintance can both be "intriguing" in a single sense of the term, even though what makes the one intriguing is very different from what makes the other intriguing. This general point suggests the possibility that the radical otherness of God might manifest itself in the *way* in which common abstract features are realized in the divine being, rather than in the absence of common features. What it is for God to *make something* is radically different from what it is for a human being to make something; but that does not rule out an abstract feature in common, e.g., that *by the exercise of agency something comes into existence.* It is something like the way in which a man and a wasp may both be *trying to reach a goal,* even though what it is for the one to try is enormously different from what it is for the other to try. Many theistic thinkers have moved too quickly from radical otherness to the impossibility of any univocity, neglecting this possibility that the otherness may come from the way in which common features are realized.[1]

More specifically, I shall be suggesting that there are abstract common properties that underly the enormous differences between divine and human psychological states. By extricating and specifying these properties we can form terms that apply univocally to God and man.

II

The tools I shall use to exhibit this commonality are drawn from the movement in contemporary philosophy of mind called "functionalism". Functionalism has been propounded as a theory of the meaning of psychological terms in ordinary language and as a theory of the nature of psychological states and processes, whatever we mean by our ordinary terms for them.[2] Since we are concerned here with meanings of terms, I shall restrict attention to the former version. The basic idea, the source of the name, is that the concept[3] of a belief, desire, or intention is the concept of a particular *function* in the psychological economy, a particular "job" done by the psyche. A belief is a structure that performs that job, and what psychological state it is— that it is a belief and a belief with that particular content—is determined by what that job is. In saying of a subject, S, that S believes that it will rain tomorrow, what we are attributing to S is a structure that

[1]The general thrust of the preceding paragraph is reminiscent of St. Thomas' distinction between the property signified by a term and the mode of signifying (or the mode signified). Thomas says that for certain predicates that are applied both to God and man, e.g., 'good', the property signified is common but the mode of signifying is not (*Summa Theologiae,* Iae, Q. 13, art. 3; *Summa Contra Gentiles,* I, 30). That naturally suggests an elaboration in terms of underlying common abstract features that are realized in quite different ways. But neither Thomas nor the Thomistic tradition has seized this opportunity to locate an area of univocal predication.

[2]The latter version may be accompanied by proposals as to how psychological terms should be given meaning for theoretical purposes.

[3]I shall use "The concept of X is . . ." interchangeably with "The term 'X' means . . .".

performs this function. Our ordinary psychological terms carry no implications as to the intrinsic nature of the structure, its neurophysiological or soul-stuff character. No such information is imbedded in our commonsense psychological conceptual scheme. Thus, on this view, psychological concepts are functional in the same way as many concepts of artefacts, e.g., the concept of a loudspeaker. A loudspeaker is something the function of which is to convert electronic signals to sound. Its composition, its internal mechanism, and its external appearance can vary widely so long as it has that function. In thinking of something as a loudspeaker, we are thinking of it *in terms of* its function.

If this basic insight is to be exploited we will have to specify the defining functions of various kinds of psychological states. One of the guiding principles of functionalism is that the basic function of the psyche is the regulation of behavior. The point of having desires, aversions, likes and dislikes, interests and attitudes, is that they set goals for behavior; and the point of having knowledge, beliefs, memories, perceptions, is that they provide us with the information we need to get around in our environment in the pursuit of those goals. In seeking to exploit these commonplaces in the analysis of psychological concepts, functionalism is following the lead of analytical behaviorism, one of its ancestors. Analytical behaviorism sought to construe a belief or a desire as a disposition to behave in a certain way, given certain conditions. Thus a belief that it is raining might be thought of as a set of dispositions that includes, e.g., the disposition to carry an umbrella if one goes out. Behaviorism failed because it was committed to the thesis that each *individual* psychological state determines a set of dispositions to behavior. Human beings just are not wired that simply. Whether I will carry an umbrella if I go out is determined not just by whether I believe that it is raining, but rather by that in conjunction with my desire to keep dry, my preferences with respect to alternate ways of keeping dry, my beliefs about the other consequences of carrying an umbrella, and so on. Even if I believe that it is raining I might not carry an umbrella, if I am wearing a raincoat and hat and I believe that is sufficient, or if I do not object to getting wet, or if I believe that I will project an unwanted image by carrying an umbrella. What I do is not just a function of a single psychological state but rather of the total psychological "field" at the moment.

Functionalism, as an improved version of behaviorism, seeks to preserve the basic insight that the function of the psyche is the guidance of behavior, while avoiding the simpleminded idea that each psychological state determines behavioral dispositions all by itself. It tries to bring this off by thinking of a belief, e.g., as, indeed, related to potential behavior, but only through the mediation of other psychological states. A belief that it is raining is, *inter alia,* a disposition to carry an umbrella if one is going outside, provided one has such-and-such other beliefs, desires, aversions, attitudes, etc. The concept of a belief is (in part) the concept of a certain way in which a state combines with other states and processes to determine behavior.[4] And since other psychological states have to be mentioned anyway there is no bar to bringing purely intra-psychic transactions into the picture. Functionalism recognizes that a belief has the function of combining with other beliefs to inferentially produce still other beliefs, the function of combining with desires and aversions and other beliefs to produce other desires and aversions (as when my belief that I can't get a wanted object without earning money gives rise to a derivative desire to earn money), and the function of combining with desires to produce affective reactions (as when my belief that I have not been accepted to medical school combines with my desire to go to medical school to produce disappointment), as well as the function of combining with other psychological states to influence behavior. Clearly a complete analysis of a psychological concept along functionalist lines would be an enormously complicated affair and perhaps beyond human power to achieve.[5]

Most contemporary formulations of functionalism are even wider than we have yet suggested. A typical recent statement is the following. "Functionalism is the doctrine that pain (for example) is identical to a certain functional state, a state definable in terms of its causal relations to inputs, outputs, and other mental states."[6] This brings into the picture the way in which sensory inputs create or affect psychological

[4]When the matter is put in this way, in terms of the *determination* of behavior, it looks as if functionalism is committed to psychological determinism, and to the denial of free will in any sense in which it is incompatible with determinism. But the theory need not be stated in those terms. We could hold that one's current psychological state, at most renders certain lines of behavior more probable than others, and still state functionalism in terms of these probabilistic relationships.

[5]For important formulations of functionalism, see Ned Block, "Troubles with Functionalism," in *Perception and Cognition: Issues in the Foundations of Psychology,* ed. C. W. Savage, *Minnesota Studies in the Philosophy of Science,* vol. 9 (Minneapolis: University of Minnesota Press, 1978); Ned Block, "Are Absent Qualia Impossible?", *Philosophical Review,* 89 (1980), 257–74; David Lewis, "Psychophysical and Theoretical Identifications," *Australasian Journal of Philosophy,* 50 (1972), 2249–58; David Lewis, "Mad Pain and Martian Pain," in *Readings in the Philosophy of Psychology,* ed. Ned Block (Cambridge: Harvard University Press, 1980); Hilary Putnam, *Philosophical Papers,* vol. 2: *Mind, Language, and Reality* (Cambridge: Cambridge University Press, 1975), chap. 18–21; Sydney Shoemaker, "Some Varieties of Functionalism," *Philosophical Topics,* 12 (1981), 93–120; Robert van Gulick, "Functionalism, Information and Content," *Nature and System,* 2 (1980), 139–62.

[6]Block, "Are Absent Qualia Impossible?", p. 257. The reference to "inputs" and "outputs" reflects the computer orientation of functionalism, of which more below. The "output" on which we have been concentrating is behavior.

states, as well as the way the latter interact in the guidance of behavior. Because of the focus of this paper we will not be concerned about "inputs" or any other influences on the genesis of psychological states. Since we are looking for concepts that could be applied to a timeless deity (as will appear in due course), such concepts will have nothing to say about how a state originates. And even apart from timelessness, a being of perfect, unlimited knowledge, power, and goodness will not acquire His knowledge via any sort of process. He will have it just by virtue of being what He is. Hence in this essay I shall restrict even human functionalist concepts to those that specify the ways in which a given kind of psychological state combines with others to affect behavioral output and other psychological states.

Behaviorism was a reductive theory, one that aspired to show that each psychological concept could be explained in purely nonpsychological terms—physical antecedent conditions, physical behavioral response, plus the overall dispositional structure. But since functionalism does not take psychological states to individually determine behavioral dispositions, it cannot aspire to reduce or eliminate psychological concepts one by one. A functional definition of any given psychological term will include many any other psychological terms. If any such reduction is to be effected it will have to be a wholesale affair.[7] For our purposes we are not interested in functionalism as a reductive theory. For that matter, the use to which I am going to put functionalism does not even require that any (much less every) psychological concept has to do solely with functional role. Critics of functionalism have contended that a belief cannot be completely characterized in functional terms since that leaves out the distinctive "intentionality", the "aboutness", characteristic of the mind. And it has also been contended that feelings and sensations cannot be adequately characterized in terms of functional role, since that leaves out their distinctive "qualitative" or "phenomenal" character. For our purposes it doesn't matter whether those criticisms are justified; it doesn't matter whether a concept of a functional role does the whole job. As will appear in the sequel, it will be enough if our concept of a given type of psychological state is, *in part,* the concept of a functional role.

III

With this background we are in a position to bring out how functionalism can help us to reconcile a degree of univocity with the radical

[7]For a suggestion as to how this can be done, see Lewis, "Psychophysical and Theoretical Identifications."

otherness of the divine. The crucial point is one that was just now made in passing, viz., that a *functional* concept of X is noncommittal as to the intrinsic nature, character, composition or structure of X. In conceiving of a φ in functional terms we are simply thinking of a φ in terms of its function (or some of its functions), in terms of the job(s) it is fitted to do. So long as something has that function it will count as a φ, whatever sort of thing it is otherwise, whatever it is like in itself. One of the main sources of functionalism in the philosophy of mind is the attempt to use our knowledge of computers to throw light on the mind and mental functioning, and, conversely, to understand the sense in which mental terms can be used to characterize the activities of computers. Functionalism is well fitted to bring out a sense in which it might well be true that mental terms (or some of them) apply univocally to human beings and to computers. For if the concept of recalling that p or the concept of perceiving that p is a concept of a certain *function*, then this same concept might well apply to beings as different in their composition, nature, and structure as a human organism and a computer.[8] Since in saying that S recalled that p we are, on the functionalist interpretation, not committing ourselves as to whether a neurophysiological, an electronic, or a purely spiritual process was involved, the concept might apply in the same sense to systems of all those sorts. This point is often put by saying that a given functional property or state can have different, even radically different, "realizations".

The application to theological predication should be obvious, in its main lines. The same functional concept of knowledge that p, or of purpose to bring about R, could be applicable to God and to man, even though the realization of that function is radically different, even though what it is to know that p is radically different in the two cases. We can preserve the point that the divine life is wholly mysterious to us, that we can form no notion of what it is like to be God, to know or to purpose as God does, while still thinking of God in terms that we understand because they apply to us.

But of course the obviousness of the application is no guarantee that it will work. Even if functional psychological terms apply univocally to man and computer, to man and beast, and even to man and angel, there could still be Creator-creature differences that make common functions impossible. So we will have to get down to the details.

Whether any functional properties can be common to God and man,

---

[8]I am by no means endorsing the view that psychological terms apply univocally to human beings and computers. I am merely indicating one application that has been made of the feature of functional concepts under discussion.

and if so which, depends on what divine-human differences there are. It will be recalled that we are working with a conception of God as differing from human beings in three main respects: incorporeality, timelessness, and infinity. We shall consider them in turn.

Can an immaterial spiritual being perform (some of) the same psychological functions as an embodied human being? Are functional psychological concepts neutral as between physical and nonphysical realizations, as well as between different sorts of physical realizations? It would seem so.[9] If a functional concept really is noncommital as to what kind of mechanism, structure, or agency carries out the function, then it should be noncommital as to whether this is any kind of physical agency, as well as to what kind of physical agency it is if physical. To be sure, if human psychological functioning is, in large part, the guidance of behavior, then behavior guidance will figure heavily in human psychological concepts. The concept of the belief that it is raining will be, in considerable part, the concept of some state that joins with psychological states of various other kinds in certain ways to produce tendencies to behavior. If such concepts are to apply to God then God will have to be capable of behavior, and it might be thought that this is impossible without a body. If God has no body to move, how can He *do* anything, in the same sense in which an embodied human being does things? But this is not an insuperable difficulty. The core concept of human action is not *movement of one's own body*, but rather *bringing about a change in the world—directly or indirectly—by an act of will, decision, or intention.* That concept can be intelligibly applied to a purely spiritual deity. It is just that we will have to think of God as bringing about changes in the "external" world directly by an act of will—not indirectly through moving His body, as in our case.[10]

Timelessness, like immateriality, may seem to inhibit the application of functional concepts. How can an atemporal being *carry out* or *perform* a function, something that, like all activities, requires a temporal duration? This consideration does show that we shall have to abandon the term "function" in its strictest sense, but that does not mean that we shall have to give up the project of applying to God what functionalism calls "functional concepts". We have already noted that functionalists broaden out the strict notion of a function into the view that a functional concept of a state, S, is the concept of the causal relations in which S stands to inputs, outputs, and other states. Now if causality is

[9]A prominent functionalist without dualist or theological sympathies, Hilary Putnam, has stressed this conceptual possibility (*Mind, Language, and Reality*, p. 436).
[10]For a detailed exposition of this point see Essay 2.

thought to require temporal succession, such concepts too will be inapplicable to a timeless being. Rather than get into an argument over that, I will loosen the requirements one more notch and say that a functional concept of S is a concept of *lawlike connections* in which S stands with other states and with outputs.[11] Some such connections involve temporal sequence (as with causal laws of the "Lighting the fuse produces an explosion" type) and some do not. For an example of the latter type, consider: "If S wants X more than anything else and realizes that doing A is necessary for getting X, and believes that doing A is possible, then S will intend to do A." This is a "law of coexistence". It tells us what intention S has now if S's current beliefs, desires, etc., are related *now* as specified. Of course a human being would normally have arrived at these desires, beliefs, etc., by some kind of process, which would often have included some process of deliberation, but this particular lawlike statement doesn't get into any of that. It simply specifies what intention a subject will have at a given time, provided it has the other psychological states specified at that time. There is no reason why such regularities should not enter into a functional psychological concept, and a concept wholly made up of such regularities could apply to a timeless being.[A]

To be sure, commonsense concepts of human psychological states are not made up wholly of such "laws of coexistence", but also include "laws of temporal succession", such as "If S considers whether it is the case that *p,* and in the course of this consideration brings to consciousness his beliefs that *If q then p* and *q,* then S will come to believe that p". And this suffices to show that our ordinary concepts of human psychological states cannot be applied in their entirety to a timeless being. But I have already disavowed any intention to show that any of the psychological terms we commonly apply to creatures can, in precisely the same sense, be applied to God. I am seeking only to show that terms for psychological functions can be devised that apply in just the same sense to God and creature. What the above considerations show is that we could form functional psychological concepts that are made up wholly of laws of coexistence and that could apply univocally to creatures and to a timeless Creator. Or at least these considerations indicate that the timelessness of the Creator is no bar to this.

IV

In considering the infinity of God we will have to further restrict the range of functional psychological concepts that are applicable to

[11]See above for the explanation of why 'input' has been omitted.

God. We are understanding 'infinity' here as the absence of any imperfections and the possession of all perfections. Thus among the modes of divine infinity will be omnipotence, omniscience, and perfect goodness.

Let's begin by considering the sort of behavior-guidance principle that functionalists take to be partly constitutive of the concepts of beliefs and wants. Here is the most simpleminded version.

(I) If S wants that p and believes that doing A will bring it about that p, then S will do A.

This will not do. The antecedent might be true and yet S not do A, and this for a number of reasons.

(A) S may want something else more than she wants p.

(B) S may have a stronger aversion to doing A or to something she believes to be a consequence or accompaniment of p.

(C) S may believe that doing B would also lead to p and may prefer doing B to doing A.

(D) S may have scruples against doing A.

(E) S may not have the capacity or opportunity to do A.

(F) S may be prevented from carrying out an intention to do A by some emotional upset.

A natural way of taking account of these complexities is to change (I) to:

(II) If S wants that p and believes that doing A will bring about p, then S has a *tendency* to do A.

Having a tendency to do A is a state that will lead to doing A, given ability and opportunity, provided it is not opposed by stronger tendencies. At a given moment the "motivational field" will contain a number of competing tendencies, and what is actually done will depend on which of these tendencies is the strongest.[12]

Now let's consider whether this kind of lawlike connection could be partly constitutive of any divine psychological state, and, if not, what modifications would be required. The first point that may strike the

---

[12]Again this may seem to rule out free will. However, if we wish we can include the will as one source of tendencies, and hold that whenever a subject makes a strong enough effort of will, the tendency so engendered will be stronger than any other tendency. See Essay 4 for more on this.

reader is the inappropriateness of attributing wants to the deity. And so it is, if 'want' is taken to imply lack or deficiency. However, even if this is true of the most common psychological sense of the term (and I doubt that it is), it is easy to modify that sense so as to avoid that implication. What we need for our purposes, and for purposes of human psychology, is a sense in which a want is any "goal-setting" state. This sense is sufficiently characterized by (II). Anyone in whom a belief that A *will lead to p* increases the tendency to do A, thereby has a want for *p* in this sense.

In this broad sense 'want' ranges over a vast diversity of goal-setting human psychological states—aversions, likes, interests, attitudes, internalized moral standards, and so on. It is an important question for human motivation whether all "wants", in the broad sense, operate according to the same dynamic laws. But be this as it may, it is noteworthy for our present concerns that there is no such diversity in the divine psyche. God is subject to no biological cravings, rooted in the needs for survival. Since God is perfectly good He wants nothing that runs contrary to what He sees to be best, and so there is no discrepancy between what he wants and what He recognizes to be right and good. He does not pursue goals in sudden gusts of passion or uncontrollable longing. And so on. This means that a lot of the complexity of human motivation drops out. "Recognizing that it is good that *p*" would be a better term for the "goal-setting" state in the divine psyche.

Here is another simplification. In human motivation we can think of the various current action tendencies as interacting to produce a winner, an intention to do something right away. Whether this intention to do A actually issues in doing A will depend on the current state of S's abilities and on cooperation from the environment. But God's abilities are always in perfect condition and He needs no such cooperation. Therefore there can never be a gap between divine intention and action. But then is there any point in inserting intention as an intermediary between the field of tendencies and action? Can't we just say that what God sees to be best (or what He chooses between incompatible equal goods) He *does*? So it would seem.

I have been talking as if God apprehends or recognizes the comparative goodness of various possible states of affairs and acts accordingly, actualizing those that are good enough to warrant it. This presupposes that the values are independent of God's will, that He *recognizes* them to be as they are. But many theologians have protested against this on the ground that it limits God's sovereignty by assuming a realm of values that exists and is what it is independent of His creative activity. The "voluntarists" who put forward this argument think of values as themselves being created by an act of the divine will. Hence God's will is not guided by His apprehension of values, at least not primordially. I will not try to decide between these two powerful theological traditions in this paper. Instead I will point out that a functionalist account of the divine psychology can accommodate either, though the precise form taken by the account will be correspondingly different. On a voluntarist view there will either be a single primordial act of will that sets up values and standards, after which action is guided by apprehensions of the values so constituted; or else many divine decisions are constitutive of value. However, on either version there will still be many divine acts that are guided by the values so constituted. Whereas on the opposite view, "intellectualism" as we might call it, all divine volition and action is guided by divine apprehension of the inherent value-qualities of alternative possibilities. Thus the main bearing of these differences on functionalism stems from the fact that for voluntarism, but not for intellectualism, there is at least one action that is not guided by apprehensions of value. Nevertheless, the general account of the function of cognition and wants in the guidance of behavior will be the same on both views.

Turning now to the cognitive side of behavior guidance, we find problems about the application of 'belief' to God, somewhat analogous to the problems about 'want'. 'Belief' in the sense in which it is contrasted with knowledge, 'mere belief', does not apply to God. Since God is a perfect cognizer, He has no beliefs that do not count as knowledge. But even if we are thinking of a wider sense of 'belief', in which when S believes that p S may or may not know that p, the whole point of having that sense is that a subject *may* believe that p without knowing that p. Since that possibility is lacking for God, the term 'belief' loses its point in application to Him. Therefore we will speak most felicitously about the divine motivation if we simply substitute 'know' for 'believe' wherever cognition enters in.[B]

Where does this leave us with respect to the cognitive guidance of behavior in the divine psychology? To turn the question around, what behavior-guidance principles figure in concepts of divine cognitive states? First of all, as we have seen, evaluative apprehensions play a crucial role on an intellectualist construal and a lesser role on a voluntarist construal. Second, does God's knowledge of the existing situation exercise any guiding role? Here we must take account of another theological controversy, this time over whether God determines every detail of creation. Those who hold that He does will not recognize any action of God, with respect to the created world, other than His creation of that world in all its details. There is nothing else for Him to do.

We may think of God as reacting to successive stages of the world as they unfold, but that is because we are, illegitimately, thinking of God as moving through time, responding to successive phases of the world process as it unfolds. If God is timeless He decides on and constitutes the entire affair in one act of will—the beginning of the universe and all of its successive stages, including anything that looks to us like ad hoc responses of God at a particular time. From this perspective God's knowledge of how things are in the world plays no guiding role in His behavior, which wholly consists of the one complex act of determining every detail of the world. That act is not guided by an awareness of how things are in the world, since apart from the completed act there is no way in which things are. Cognitive guidance of behavior is limited to evaluative apprehension.

Suppose, on the other hand, that God does not determine every detail of creation. He voluntarily abstains from determining the choices of free agents like human beings. This means that there will be certain aspects of creation that He does not know about just by knowing His own creative acts. With respect to the choices of free agents and states of affairs affected by them, he will have to "look and see" how things came out in order to know what they are. If He is timeless he does not have to "wait and see"; all of his knowledge and activity is comprised in one "eternal now". Nevertheless His activity vis-à-vis the world is divided into (a) original creation ex nihilo, and (b) activity directed to states of affairs that, in part, are what they are independently of divine fiat. Creative activity of this latter sort *will* be guided by His knowledge of these states of affairs.

Next let's turn to another sort of regularity that enters into concepts of human cognitive states, viz., that based on inferential relations. One of the functions that makes a belief that p the state it is, is its tendency to enter with other beliefs into inferences that generate further beliefs. Thus the belief that Jim is Sam's only blood-related uncle tends to give rise to the belief that Sam's parents have only one brother between them; it also tends to combine with the beliefs that Jim is childless and that Sam has no aunt to produce the belief that Sam has no first cousins.

Now a timeless deity will not carry out inferences, since this requires a temporal duration. Indeed, an omniscient deity will not *derive* any of its knowledge from inference, or even from an atemporal analogue of inference; for any true proposition, p, such a deity will automatically know that p without needing to base it on something else He knows. So inferential regularities cannot be even partly constitutive of concepts that apply to God. But suitable analogues of such regularities may be

77

available. It will still be true that whatever God knows, he knows all the logical consequences thereof, knows that all probabilistic consequences thereof are probable, knows that all contradictories thereof are false, and so on. That is, there is a certain structure to divine knowledge that corresponds to logical relationships, and corresponds much more closely than does any body of human knowledge.

The discussion of this section indicates that the divine psyche is much simpler than the human psyche in the variety of its constituents. Assuming God to be atemporal, it involves no processes or activities, no sequences of events. There are no beliefs as distinct from knowledge, and hence no distinction of degrees of firmness of belief. Propositional knowledge is all intuitive, the simple recognition that p. There is no distinction between wants, cravings, longings, and the sense that something ought to be done. There is only one kind of goal-setting state, which could perhaps best be characterized as the recognition that something is good or right. There are no bursts of passion or emotional upsets to interfere with rational motivational processes. There is no point in distinguishing between a present intention to do A and doing A intentionally. Though God may not be as simple as St. Thomas supposed, it is true that much of the complexity of human psychological functioning drops out. The complexity of human psychology is largely due to our limitations: to the fallibility of our cognition, the internal opposition to rational decision making, the limitations of our capacities, and the relative irrationality of our intellectual processes.

V

Where do all these differences leave our project of identifying psychological commonalities in God and human beings? We have discovered a vast reduction in the number of distinct types of divine psychological states, in comparison with the human estate. But that is quite compatible with important commonalities in states of those types. How does the matter stand in that regard? Let's see how divine psychological states could be functionally construed, adopting a nonvoluntarist position for the sake of illustration. As for the cognitive side, a divine recognition that it would be good that p can be construed, in part, as a state that will give rise to the action of bringing about p unless God recognizes something logically incompatible with p as a greater or equal good.[13] On the cognitive side, God's knowledge that p can be

---

[13] If God apprehended something incompatible to be equally good He still might bring about p, but He would not necessarily do so.

construed as a state that (a) will carry with it the knowledge of everything logically entailed by p and exclude the knowledge of anything contradictory to p, and (b) gives rise to action that is appropriate to p, given what God sees to be good.[14] Do functional concepts like this apply to human beings?

They do not apply just as they stand, because of the human limitations we have just noted. A human being does not know, or believe, everything entailed by what she knows or believes, nor does she fail to believe everything logically incompatible with what she believes. A human being does not always (or even usually) do what she recognizes to be the best thing to do in the circumstances, even assuming that she correctly assesses the circumstances. But these differences do not prevent a significant commonality in functional psychological states. This commonality can best be brought out by constructing tendency-versions of the lawlike generalizations imbedded in the functional concepts just articulated, and attributing them to human beings. Thus we can ascribe to a human being a *tendency* to believe whatever is entailed by what she knows or believes, and a tendency to reject what is incompatible with what she knows or believes. And we can regard these tendencies as partly constitutive of the concepts of belief and knowledge. Likewise we can say of a human being that she will tend to do what she can to bring about what she recognizes to be best in a given situation, and we can take this tendency to be partly constitutive of the concept of recognizing something to be best. We can then formulate the divine regularities in tendency terms also. Thus it will be true of God also that if He recognizes that it is good that p He will tend to bring about p insofar as He can unless He recognizes something incompatible with p to be a greater good.[15] These tendency statements about God constitute a limiting case in which the qualifications are vacuous, since God can do anything He chooses to do and since God is not subject to nonrational interferences in carrying out what He recognizes to be good. Nevertheless they are true of God.

I take it that this brings out a significant commonality of meaning between psychological terms applicable to God and to man. Even though there is no carry-over of the complete package from one side of the divide to the other, there is a core of meaning in common. And the distinctive features on the divine side simply consist in the dropping

[14]As we saw earlier, (b) is applicable only if God does not determine every detail of the created world.

[15]The "or equal" drops out when the generalization is in terms of a tendency. God will still have a tendency to bring about p even if something incompatible is equally good and even if that other alternative is chosen.

out of creaturely limitations. Thus a functional approach to psychological concepts makes it possible to start with human psychological concepts and create psychological concepts that literally apply to God, thus generating theological statements that unproblematically possess truth-values.[16] This saves us from the morass of an unqualified pan-symbolism and makes possible a modicum of unquestionably cognitive discourse about God.[17]

NOTES

A. This account is defective by reason of implying not only that the divine psyche is subject to laws, but also that its constitution as a psyche and its functioning as such require law governedness. This cannot be. Since by common consent among theists, God freely decides what laws are operative, His psyche can hardly depend for its basic operations on laws. That would mean that it would be due to His decision that a necessary condition of His deciding anything obtains. Nor can this be avoided by rendering laws indeterministic (footnote 4); that might save His freedom, but it would not meet the difficulty just noted. However, the remedy is simple. Instead of thinking of God's mental states and processes as law governed, we will rather think of God's nature as being such that He will, e.g. have a certain intention whenever His conative and cognitive factors are such-and-such. That is, the stable dependence (of intentions on conative and cognitive factors) will be rooted in His nature rather than in laws to which He is subject. (Indeed, the uniformities in nature could also be thought of in this way rather than in terms of laws; but, of course, there is not the same motivation for this construal of natural regularities.)

B. For a development of this view see Essay 9.

[16]Or at least the predicates present no bar to the attribution of truth-values.
[17]This paper has profited from comments by Jonathan Bennett.

Divine and Human Action

I

This essay is not a direct discussion of divine action. Rather it raises questions of "second intention" concerning the kind of concepts we are able to form of divine action, and it considers the bearing of this on our situation vis-à-vis God.

What concepts are applicable to God depends, of course, on what God is like.[1] If, e.g., God is a personal agent in the same fundamental sense as ourselves, albeit one that is immaterial and unlimited in fundamental respects, many concepts applicable to human beings will be applicable to Him, perhaps with a little doctoring. I have no time in this essay to produce a reasoned position on the question of what sort of being God is. Hence I will just lay it down that God will be thought of as (a) immaterial, (b) infinitely perfect, and (c) timeless, in that His own being, His own life does not involve temporal succession. The third of these assumptions is particularly controversial, but I shall have to forgo any defense in this place.[2] I shall be considering what sort of action concepts could be truly applicable to such a being.

From *Divine and Human Action*, ed. Thomas V. Morris (Ithaca: Cornell University Press, 1988), pp. 257–80. Copyright © 1988 by Cornell University. Reprinted by permission of Cornell University Press.

[1]To establish a conclusion about the kinds of concepts applicable to God, or even to argue for such a conclusion, we have to say something about what God is like, thereby claiming to apply certain concepts to Him. Thus the enterprise is inevitably infected with a certain circularity.

[2]For an impressive exposition and defense of the doctrine, see Eleonore Stump and Norman Kretzmann, "Eternity," *Journal of Philosophy*, 78 (1981), 429–58.

It is a familiar truism that our concepts of God, at least those that go beyond such bare ontological features as self-identity, are derived from our concepts of human beings; and this would seem to be particularly obvious with respect to the topic of this essay. Our thought of God as agent is clearly modeled on our understanding of human agency. Thus a natural approach to our problem, one frequently taken, is to start with human action concepts and determine how much of them is transferable to the divine case. In traditional terms, can we speak *univocally* of divine and human action? Or, better, to what extent can we speak univocally of divine and human action? As the last formulation indicates, I am going to take seriously, indeed advocate, a position rarely taken on this issue, viz., partial univocity. The field has been dominated by, on the one hand, those who see no difficulty in a wholesale univocity, and, on the other hand, those who hold that no term can be univocally applied to God and to us. This latter group is divided into those who suppose that some irreducibly analogical relation holds between divine and human senses of terms and those who take the terms in question to be applied figuratively or "symbolically" to God. It is odd that the partial univocity possibility has not received more attention. After all, a partial overlap of meaning is an excessively familiar semantic phenomenon. Just to take the most obvious example, the terms for two species of the same genus share the generic feature and differ, tautologically, with respect to the differentia. I conjecture that partial overlap of meaning has been ignored because of the prominence of those who, like Tillich, construe the otherness of God so radically as to leave room for no commonality of meaning, leading in turn to an overreaction by those who feel that unless univocity receives a compensatory stress our talk about God will founder in a morass of pan-symbolism. In any event, it is the partial univocity thesis that I wish to explore and defend.

The univocity issue has a determinate sense, however, only to the extent that there are determinate boundaries around the meaning of a term. To go at it from the other side, insofar as what belongs to the meaning of a term, as contrasted with what is obviously true of the things to which the term applies, is not fixed, there is no determinate issue as to whether another term, or that term in another application, bears the same meaning. And it has been forcefully pointed out in recent decades by Quine and others that it is very difficult, impossible according to Quine, to discern such boundaries. Let's take an example directly relevant to the concerns of this paper. It is a basic fact about human action that one cannot perform an action the necessary conditions of which include changes in the world outside the agent, without doing so by moving one's body in certain ways. Does that mean that it is part of the *meaning* of 'S closed a door' that 'S brought it about by movements of S's body that a door was closed'? This obviously has a crucial bearing on whether human action terms can be univocally predicated of God; for if that is part of the meaning, then, since God has no body, no action term with that meaning could be truly predicated of God. In Essay 2, I argued that this is not part of the meaning, that it is a (conceptually as well as metaphysically) *contingent* fact about human beings that one can bring about changes in the external world only through movements of one's body, and that it is no part of the meaning of action terms, including those that in fact apply to human beings, that this should be the case. However, I must confess that the matter is not crystal clear. Again, is it part of the meaning of 'S succeeded in achieving his purpose that T' or 'S carried out her intention to do A' that there is some temporal separation between the initiation of the purpose or the intention, on the one hand, and the achievement of the purpose or the carrying out of the intention on the other? This will have an important bearing on whether notions of purpose and intention can be applied in the human sense to an atemporal deity. Again, I don't find this very clear. I am not for a moment suggesting that *no* line can be drawn between meaning and the facts of the world, between the dictionary and the encyclopedia. It is clearly part of the meaning of 'intention to do A' that the intender have some tendency to do A, and it is clearly not part of that meaning that intenders not infrequently fail to carry out their intentions. Nevertheless, in the most interesting cases it is often unclear where the line is to be drawn. If it is drawn so as to circumscribe meaning most narrowly, there will be much more of a chance for univocal terms across the divine-human gap; if it is drawn more generously, less will carry over to the divine case.

Even if we cannot settle all these boundary disputes to everyone's satisfaction in a clearly objective fashion, our problem will remain. It would be misguided to suppose that the question of how we should construe divine action is tied to the details of the ways in which conceptual content is encoded in the meaning of one or another linguistic item. The more fundamental issues concern how much of the *way we think of* human action can be carried over to our thought of divine action. It is of secondary importance how much of this is carried by the meaning of one or another linguistic expression.

It seems to be agreed on all hands that concepts of human intentional actions (we shall be restricting ourselves to intentional action) are to be understood in terms of the role of psychological, motivational factors like intentions, desires, attitudes, beliefs, and so on. To (intentionally) close a door is not just to make some particular sort of bodily movement. Nor does it just consist in a bodily movement of the agent's leading to a door coming to be closed. That overt pattern does not count as a case of S's intentionally closing a door unless it constitutes the carrying out of an intention to close the door in question, unless it was done because S had an interest in the door's being closed, . . . The dots indicate that there is a variety of ways in which psychological antecedents or concomitants of the overt activity are thought to enter into the concept of intentional human action. There are differences both as to what sorts of psychological factors play a crucial role, and as to how they are related to the more overt aspects of the action, e.g., causally or otherwise. Although these differences are of the first importance for the project of developing an adequate account of human action, they are peripheral to our concerns here, with an exception to be noted later. For the sake of concreteness let's adopt Donald Davidson's lingo, though not putting it to the same uses, and say that S intentionally closes a door just in case S performs the overt movements that lead to the door's being closed because S has a "pro-attitude" toward a state of affairs, A, and a belief that the door's coming to be closed either is or is likely to lead to a case of A.[3] In more informal terms, S intentionally brings about a state of affairs B only if there is a state of affairs, A, which might or might not be identical with B, for the sake of which S is doing what leads to the bringing about of B.

If something like this is along the right line, then the question of whether we can carry human action terms over to the divine case can be divided into two main parts. (1) Can psychological motivational concepts be applied to the divine case? (2) What about the bodily movements that get thus motivated and lead to the crucial external result? I will discuss these in reverse order.

II

It is clear that human beings bring about changes in the external world by moving their bodies in various ways, and so, as pointed out above, if this fact is (partly) constitutive of the meanings of human

[3]See his "Actions, Reasons, and Causes," *Journal of Philosophy*, 60 (1963), 685–700, for his version of this. In "An Action-Plan Interpretation of Purposive Explanations of Actions," *Theory and Decision*, 20 (1986), 275–99, I present reasons for objecting to the idea that the crucial psychological factors are to be thought of, as Davidson and many other theorists do, as antecedent causes. Again, these differences are not crucial for the present discussion.

action terms that will prevent these terms from being truly applied, in just the same sense, to an incorporeal agent. However, if everything else carries over we can still apply closely analogous terms. Whereas in the human case the appropriate psychological background leads to bodily movements that result in the door's being closed, we can think of the structure of a divine action of closing a door as being just like this except for the shortcircuiting of the bodily movement part. That is, in the divine case the sorts of psychological factors that led in the human case to the bodily movements that were designed to get the door closed will, in the divine case, lead directly to the "external" result, in this case the door's being closed. More exactly, this would be the pattern of God's closing the door as a "basic act", one done not by way of doing something else. Of course God could do everything He does as a basic act, but He may well choose to do some things by doing other things. Thus the Old Testament tells us that God got the Israelites out of Egypt not by directly bringing it about that they were instantaneously somewhere else instead, as He perfectly well could have done, but by altering the configuration of the water in a lake or inland sea in order to make it possible for them to cross. In any event, whatever it is that God does directly in any particular project will follow immediately on the relevant psychological antecedents. Thus the absence of bodily movements in the divine case will not prevent us from applying to Him human action concepts, or concepts that can be simply derived from them.[4]

The other part of the question concerning psychological factors will occupy us longer, indeed for most of the rest of the essay. Let's begin the discussion by looking more carefully at what we need to carry over from the human side in order to come as close as possible to univocity. The basic idea of the approach to intentional action with which we are working is that overt changes (to use a term that is neutral as to whether movements of the agent's body are involved) constitute, or constitute the overt aspect of, an intentional action only if they result from a psychological structure that involves at least a "goal-setting" state (our "pro-attitude") and a cognitive guidance state, one that provides "information" as to actual or probable connections in the world, information that is needed to determine how the goal may be reached.

---

[4]If someone were to ask at this point "How on earth can God bring about external results directly?", I would have to rule the question out of order. I am setting out to explore not the "mechanism" of divine action, if there can be any such thing, but rather its conceptualization, what sort of concept we can form of God's doing something. Whatever that concept may be, it most certainly will not contain any specification of how God manages to bring off what He does.

The category of *pro-attitude* stretches over a wide variety of conative factors—wants, desires, aversions, longings, yearnings, attitudes of various sorts, scruples, commitments, and so on. (Actually we are speaking of "con-attitudes" as well as pro-attitudes. In the sequel I shall frequently use the term 'attitude' for the general category, leaving 'pro or con' to be tacitly understood.) Different items on this list work differently, have different antecedents, manifest themselves differently in consciousness, and so on. Now it is doubtful that the divine nature provides any basis for such discriminations. God is subject to no biological cravings, rooted in the need for survival. Since He is perfectly good He wants nothing that runs contrary to what He sees to be best, and so there is no discrepancy between what He wants and what He recognizes to be right and good. He does not pursue goals in sudden gusts of passion or uncontrollable longing. For the divine case we can safely confine ourselves to the generic category. As for the cognitive guidance factor, we could ignore that, as far as the motivation of behavior is concerned (though we would still think of God as possessing perfect knowledge), if God were to do everything He does as a basic act. But since we want at least to leave open the possibility that this is not the case, we will have to make room for God using His knowledge to determine what will lead to what.[5] In the human case it seems that the appropriate generic term for this side of the matter is *belief*. For human beings choose means to attain their goals in the light of what they believe to be the case, whether or not these beliefs are correct and whether or not they count as knowledge. But God will not possess any "mere beliefs", beliefs that do not count as knowledge, since He has complete knowledge of everything knowable. Moreover, as I argue in Essay 9, the category of belief would seem not to be applicable to God

[5]These issues deserve much more discussion than is possible here. For one thing, since anything God brings about in the world will have innumerable consequences, it might be thought that God will be indirectly bringing about all those consequences, and so it is impossible that God should not do many things indirectly. But it must be remembered that we are restricting ourselves to *intentional* action, and it cannot be assumed that God intends to bring about all the consequences of everything He brings about, even though He will, of course, know about them. Second, if we were to take God to be "omnidetermining", deciding every detail of His creation, then He would have no need to guide His action by His awareness of relevant features of the world. For He would have chosen every such feature in the original act of creation, which was carried out on the basis of no knowledge of "the situation", there being none. If, on the other hand, as we are assuming, God has chosen to refrain from deciding some features Himself (e.g., free choices of human beings, together with their contributions to the way things go), leaving them up to the created agents in question, then He will have to "look and see" how those things have been constituted, where that is relevant to his decisions as to how to bring about a certain state of affairs.

at all. Thus it would seem that the cognitive side of the divine motivational structure should be restricted to knowledge.

Thus our question becomes: Can we use the same concepts of "attitudes" and "knowledge" of God and man? Let's begin with the former. In supposing that God has a pro-attitude toward my becoming sanctified am I attributing the same sort of thing to God that I am attributing to you when I suppose that you have a pro-attitude toward winning the race? Clearly there will be enormous differences between what is involved in God and in you having such an attitude. There is no question of assimilating the details of the divine psychology to human psychology. But is there a significant core that is common to divine and human attitudes? Clearly the answer to this is going to depend not only on what God and we are like but also on what is or can be meant by speaking of attitudes in either case. So let's turn to this latter issue.

This is just a particular form of the more general issue as to how to construe intentional psychological states, including but perhaps not restricted to "propositional attitudes". What we are calling 'attitudes', at least in their human realizations, would seem to belong to this latter category. To want, or to have an interest in, a chocolate fudge sundae would seem to involve a certain favorable conative attitude toward the proposition *my eating a chocolate fudge sundae,* or something of the sort. On the current scene there are two prominent approaches to the understanding of such states. On the one hand, there is the view identified with Brentano, and represented on the current American scene by Chisholm, that intentionality is a basic, unanalyzable feature of psychological states. The generic feature of being "directed onto" an object, propositional or otherwise, is a basic feature in the sense that it cannot be explicated in terms of other concepts. This view leaves it open as to whether each of the various forms taken by intentionality, e.g., believing, hoping, fearing, or desiring, is itself basic and irreducible to others, or whether some of these forms can be taken as basic and the others explained in terms of them. But at the very least the position will hold that the difference between knowing that p and having a pro-attitude toward p is unanalyzable in terms of anything else. In particular, a positive attitude toward a state of affairs—taking it to be desirable, gratifying, attractive, worth while, a good thing, or whatever—is a basic underivative feature of our mental life. No doubt such attitudes, in conjunction with other facts, have various consequences for behavior, thought, and feeling; but it would be a grave mistake to suppose that the intrinsic nature of attitudes can be specified in terms of such consequences.

On this view there would seem to be no bar to the univocal predication of some intentional concepts to God and to us. If *taking a state of affairs to be a good thing* is a basic, unanalyzable relation of an intelligent agent to a (possible) state of affairs, there is nothing in the concept to limit it to an embodied, finite, imperfect, or temporal agent. Why shouldn't God, as we are thinking of Him here, relate Himself in such a manner to possible states of affairs? There would seem to be no basis for a negative answer.

III

Many contemporary Anglo-American philosophers, however, are unhappy with the idea that concepts of intentional states are unanalyzable. We are committed to finding analyses; *c'est notre métier.* Various suggestions have been made as to how to unpack concepts of intentional states; currently the most popular one is *functionalism.* The basic idea of functionalism is that "psychological states are type individuated by their distinctive role within a complex network of states mediating the perceptual conditions and behavior of organisms or systems."[6] The concept of a belief, an attitude, or an intention, is the concept of what performs a particular *function* in the psychological economy, the concept of a particular "job" done by the psyche, just as the concept of a loudspeaker is the concept of what performs a certain function, viz., converting electronic signals to sound. Of course, the specification of psychological functions is far more difficult and complicated than the specification of audio functions. The above quote indicates the dominant approach to this by contemporary functionalists. The fundamental role of the psyche is to mediate between perceptual or other informational input and behavioral output; and a particular psychological role is a particular piece of that overall mission, a particular way in which one state interacts with other states and with informational input to influence behavior. Thus, e.g., a belief that it is now raining is a state that interacts with an intention to go outside, a desire to remain as dry as possible, and a belief that carrying an umbrella is the best way to stay as dry as possible, to elicit the behavior of carrying an umbrella. Other components of the total functional role of this belief include its interacting with the belief that it has been raining for the last six days to lead to the inference that it has been raining for a week, and its interacting with the strong desire for sunny

---

[6]Robert van Gulick, "Functionalism, Information, and Content," *Nature and System,* 2 (1980), 139.

weather to produce a feeling of despondency. Clearly a complete analysis of even a very specific psychological concept would be an enormously complicated affair and perhaps beyond our powers.

In Essays 2 and 3 I argue that psychological concepts of a functionalist sort can be applied to God.[7] No doubt, the challenge has contributed to the attractiveness of the project. Functionalism is generally associated with a physicalistic view of human beings, and computer analogies have played a large role in its development. It would be quite a coup to show that concepts derived from this milieu could be applied to a being that is incorporeal, timeless, and absolutely infinite. But there was also a positive lead. A major emphasis within functionalism has been the idea that since a certain kind of psychological state is that which carries out a certain function, whatever its intrinsic character, one and the same psychological state concept might be applied to beings of widely different inherent natures, to biological organisms (of various physical and chemical sorts), to computers, even, perhaps, to angels. Put in another way, the fact that Y is widely different in constitution from X will not in itself prevent a univocal application of psychological state concepts, provided the crucial sort of function is being performed. Analogously, X *is* a loudspeaker, provided it has the capacity to convert electronic signals to sound; so long as that is the case, its composition, internal mechanism, and external appearance can vary widely, as audio buffs can testify.

To be sure, at best there will still be large differences between the human and the divine psyche. Going back to van Gulick's summary account of functionalism, God is not an organism, though He may be a "system", depending on just how we use that term. Nor does God receive information through sense perception. And if van Gulick is thinking of "behavior" types as constituted by types of bodily movements, that part of the picture doesn't carry over either. So let's see how we can generalize the account to the divine case. First let's replace "organisms or systems" with "agents".[8] As for "perceptual conditions", the lack of sense organs is no disability for God just because God, being omniscient, has no need for any such means of acquiring information. Since the "input" drops out of the picture, the functionalist model will be simplified to the following: psychological states are type individuated by their distinctive role within a complex of states that gives rise to action.

---

[7]In Essay 2 I was dealing only with problems introduced by divine incorporeality. In Essay 3 I was thinking of God as I am here, but I believe that in this essay I do a better job of bringing functionalism to bear on the problem.

[8]The full implications of this shift will appear shortly.

Note that the functionalist interpretation of psychological concepts is, at least when we neglect input, simply the "motivational background" conception of intentional action stood on its head. An intentional action is one that stems from attitudes, beliefs, and the like in a certain way, and attitudes, beliefs, and the like are to be construed in terms of the way in which intentional action stems from them. At a later stage we shall look at the apparent circularity this introduces.

The following qualification should also be made explicit. Since I am aspiring only to exhibit a partial overlap between concepts of divine and human action, even if the overlap is solely functional in nature it need not exhaust our concepts of psychological states in either context. Thus I need only maintain that our concept of human belief, desire, or intention, is, *at least in part,* the concept of a role in the motivation of behavior, in order to have a basis for partial univocity.

I have already suggested that the divine psyche is dramatically simplified as compared with the human. I am loath to agree that it is as bare of distinction as, e.g., the Thomistic doctrine of divine simplicity would have it, but it lacks bases for many of the distinctions between different types of human attitudes, and it equally lacks our distinctions between different degrees of firmness of belief. For present purposes we can think of the divine motivational structure as made up of (a) attitudes toward various (possible) states of affairs,[9] and (b) complete knowledge. We can then think of divine action as arising from a pro-attitude toward some goal state and the knowledge that the action in question will realize that goal state (or will probably do so, in case free choices of creatures have a role here, and God lacks "middle knowledge" of how each free creature would act in each situation in which that creature might find itself). Of course, in a limiting case the action in question is just the bringing about of that goal state; this is the case in which God realizes His purpose directly. In terms of this simple model we can think of a divine pro-attitude toward G as, at least in part, the sort of state that, when combined with knowledge that doing A is the best way of achieving G, will lead to God's doing A. And, pari passu, knowledge that doing A is the best way of achieving G is the sort of state that, combined with a pro-attitude toward G, will lead to God's doing A.

---

[9]These attitudes will be construed differently depending on whether we think of values as chosen by the divine will or whether we think of God as recognizing values that are independent of His will. But we need not take sides on this controversy for purposes of this essay. See Essay 3 for more on this.

IV

This model is, however, much too simple in a number of respects. (The complications to be set out now should also be read back into the oversimplified account given earlier of the motivational background that makes an action intentional.) First, and most obviously, God presumably, and humans certainly, will have pro-attitudes toward mutually exclusive states of affairs. For example, God may have both a pro-attitude toward all human beings enjoying eternal felicity and a pro-attitude toward inveterate sinners being suitably punished for their sins. And, assuming that a suitable punishment would involve the lack of eternal felicity, even God can't have it both ways. Or God might have a pro-attitude toward Jacob being the (one and only) bearer of a certain revelation and also a pro-attitude toward Michael's having that status, in which case He will have to sacrifice at least one of the desiderata. Thus in order to allow for at least the possibility of incompatible divine goal states, we will have to introduce a tendency notion and say, instead of the above, that a pro-attitude toward G is the sort of state that, in conjunction with the knowledge that doing A is the best way to attain G, will give rise to a *tendency to* do A. How are we to explain this notion of a *tendency?* The rough idea is that a tendency to do A is a state that, in the absence of sufficient interference or blockage, will issue in doing A. It is, so to say, being prima facie prepared to do A. What interferences or blockages there can be will vary from case to case, and so that specification need not be included in the most general concept of a tendency.[10]

Second, and perhaps most important, we must construe the relation of tendencies to action in such a way as to preserve the divine freedom. Here my account in "Functionalism and Theological Language" was defective. Because of divine timelessness I gave up thinking of attitudes as causes of action, but I replaced this with the idea that "a functional concept of S is a concept of *lawlike connections* in which S stands with other states and with outputs."[11] This has the double disability of rendering God subject to natural laws and of denying God any real freedom of choice, at least if the laws in question are thought of as deterministic. As far as the first problem is concerned, one might replace the notion of law governedness with the notion of the nature of God being such that a tendency (formed by an attitude-knowledge interaction of the sort we have described) that is not successfully opposed will issue in

---

[10]If that did have to be included the definition would become circular. For the most important interference with a given tendency is other tendencies to incompatible actions.
[11]P. 73.

action. If such dependable regularities stem from God's nature they do not imply that God is *subject* to anything other than Himself.[12] But that still leaves the second problem. Are we really prepared to think of God's behavior as issuing automatically from the interplay of motivational factors? Wouldn't that make God into a mechanism, a system the output of which is determined by the interplay of its parts, rather than a supremely free agent? Wouldn't that represent God as less free than we are?

I take these considerations to be quite sound. But they show the above account not to be mistaken, but only to be incomplete. What we must do is to recognize that among the factors that can prevent a tendency from issuing in action is the divine will, as briefly suggested in note 12 to Essay 3. To say that God is supremely free implies that He has the capacity to refrain from doing A, whatever the strength of a tendency to do A that issues from His attitudes and knowledge, provided that refraining is metaphysically possible. This last qualification has to be added because if God is essentially perfectly good, then it will be metaphysically impossible for Him to act contrary to the best. Hence where doing A is *the* best thing for Him to do in a certain situation, it will not be possible for Him to decide to refrain from doing A. But in that case is there any scope for divine free will? Yes, there is, just because there will be alternatives none of which is better or worse than the others. For a trivial example consider God choosing between various large numbers of elementary particles for the physical universe. A quite untrivial, but correspondingly more controversial, example concerns the traditional Christian doctrine that God was free to create or to refrain from doing so. Many thinkers, of course, object to the attribution of essential goodness to God just on the grounds that it unduly limits His freedom of choice. I can't go into that issue here. I can only note that even if God is essentially perfectly good there will still be a place for divine free choice, though not so large a place as there would be if perfect goodness were not part of the divine essence.

Since a given attitude-knowledge combination does not by itself necessarily issue in action, either in the divine or the human case, we are led to recognize another sort of motivational factor that mediates between the field of tendencies and overt behavior, determining the character of the latter. If this mediating factor is simply determined by the relative strength of tendencies in the current field and the agent itself does not constitute a factor to be reckoned separately, we need not think of this factor as being different in kind from the various tenden-

[12]See endnote A of Essay 3.

cies. It is, as Hobbes says of the will, simply the strongest current tendency, the winner in the struggle between competing tendencies; let us call such a tendency an "executive intention". However, where the agent (as a whole, or *as* an agent) has the last word, we must recognize a quite different sort of factor, an internal act of the agent, an act of will or volition, that controls the gates to the external world (for embodied agents, the gates to bodily movement). Again, the human agent is more complex than divine. Since a temporal agent can form intentions for the future, we must distinguish an *intention to do A*, which may not issue immediately in doing A and which may dissipate before A ever gets done, and a *volition or executive intention* to do A, which issues in doing A unless the external world (external to the psyche) prevents it. Since there can be no intention for the future in a timeless agent, for God we need only recognize volitions (executive intentions) as leading from the field of tendencies to the actual thing done.

I can only hope to scratch the surface of human motivation in this essay, but there is one additional feature I had better make explicit. The bridge between the tendency field and overt action (the volition or executive intention) is not best thought of, as the above remarks would suggest, as confined in its intentional object to the action done (the state of affairs the bringing about of which constitutes the action). For one thing, the agent may, in one volition or intention, launch itself onto a complex activity, involving a number of subordinate states, each designed to lead to its successor. Thus if I form the intention to go to my office, this requires me to intend to perform a number of sequentially linked actions of arising from my chair, suitably garbing myself, unlocking my front door, etc. etc. Again, where God decides to restore the kingdom of Israel, this involves His doing a number of things to lead up to the restoration. In such a case what is formed, as the immediate psychological determinant of overt activity, is better termed an "action plan", something that involves a mental representation of the structure of the complex activity intended. And in the case of a temporal agent this action plan will monitor and control the evolving sequence of steps to the final goal.[13] Even where no such sequence of results is intended, the intentional object of the executive intention or volition will typically involve not only the defining result of the action in question but also that for the sake of which the action is entered on. Even if my intention is the simple one of opening the door, my intention will also involve an awareness of why I am doing it, e.g., to let someone in; and so even

[13]See my paper "An Action-Plan Interpretation of Purposive Explanations of Actions," *Theory and Decision*, 20 (1986), 275–99, for an elaboration of this idea.

here we have an action plan, though of limiting simplicity. In fact, the reason or purpose for which I do something, as I argue in the above mentioned article, is best construed as given by the structure of the action plan involved.

We can now read these additional complexities back into the account of intentional action. One intentionally brings about B *iff* the bringing about of B is due to (is the carrying out of) an executive intention or a volition to bring about B. That intention or volition, in turn, is to be understood, in part, in terms of the way in which it stems from a field of tendencies and, if what I have just been saying is well taken, it bears marks of this origin in the structure of its own intentional object.

Let's return to the functionalist account of intentional mental states in the light of this enriched model. Attitudes and cognitions are to be understood in terms of the way in which they interact to engender action tendencies. Tendencies, in turn, are to be understood partly in terms of this origin and partly in terms of the way they interact with each other either to determine executive intentions or to influence volitions, as the case may be. Finally, executive intentions and volitions are to be understood in terms both of their background and of the way they determine overt action. This whole functionalist contribution to our concepts of such states can be thought of as deriving from conditionals like the following.

1. If S has a pro-attitude toward G, then S will have a tendency to do whatever S takes to be a way of attaining G.
2. If S has a tendency to do A, then if this tendency is not successfully opposed by a stronger tendency or by an act of will, then S will do A, if the external world cooperates in the right way.[14]

We must be clear that we have deviated from the usual functionalist account by introducing free acts of will into the picture. This means that we are countenancing an irreducible concept of agency (currently termed "agent causality"), the concept of an agent's directly bringing something about, where this something is to be explained in terms of the agent's exercise of its powers, rather than by any sort of event or state as a cause, and where this activity on the part of the agent is not causally determined by anything, not even its own states, though it may well be influenced by them. This is not a notion that can be given a functionalist interpretation, so far as I can see, without losing its distinctive contours. What is directly engendered by agency, the volition,

[14]This last qualification becomes vacuous in the divine case.

can itself be partly construed in functionalist terms. But the concept of an agent's bringing something about, as we understand that here, resists any such explication.

The attentive reader will not have missed a certain circularity in this functionalist treatment of the divine psyche. Divine intentional action is what issues from a certain motivational background, and the elements of that background are in turn construed in terms of the way in which they lead to action. If all divine action issues from divine acts of will, it might be thought that we could ignore the business about pro-attitudes, tendencies, and so on in explaining divine action, thereby avoiding the circularity. But that only makes the circle smaller. It is an essential part of this program to construe volitions functionally too. If we leave out of account the way in which volitions are influenced by attitudes and the like, the only way to say what a volition is, is to say that it is an internal act of the agent that determines overt action (in the case of finite agents, within the limits of bodily capacity and external opportunity).

I'm afraid that I see no alternative to biting the bullet and admitting the circularity. Intentional action and conative psychological factors are to be understood in terms of their interrelations. For the human case, unlike the divine case, one might try to get out of the circle by construing the behavioral output in terms of bodily movements rather than full-blooded action. But this would require us to construe at least some of the attitudes and beliefs as taking bodily movements as intentional objects; and it seems to be the exception rather than the rule that human action is guided by beliefs, etc., that have to do with specific bodily movement types, rather than the results or significance of bodily movements. When we speak, e.g., the relevant purposes, beliefs, and intentions have to do with what we are saying rather than with what we are doing with our vocal organs to get it said. Even in the human case we are saddled with the circle. The way out is to recognize that functionalism cannot be a reduction of intentionalistic concepts (of actions and psychological states) to nonintentionalistic concepts, physicalistic or otherwise. It must be construed as a partial interpretation, exhibiting the conceptual interrelations of actions and intentional psychological states, thereby shedding considerable light on their nature.

The functionalist treatment of divine knowledge has thus far been restricted to the knowledge of means-ends connections, hardly even the tip of the iceberg. Even the cognitive guidance of behavior extends far beyond these narrow bounds. Depending on features of the particular case, bits of information other than means-ends connections will be relevant to one or another divine project. Thus, e.g., God will want

95

to know the details of the Israelites' observance or nonobservance of the covenant in deciding how to deal with the threat from Assyria. But unless we want to assume that everything God knows is relevant to some decision He makes or might make, that will still leave much knowledge without a functionalist interpretation. For humans the account can be eked out by reference to sources of informational input. Knowledge (belief) varies in lawful ways with sensory input, as well as interacting with conative factors to guide behavior. We have noted that this maneuver is not available for the divine case. Nevertheless, there is a divine analogue of input to which we may appeal. Since God is essentially omniscient, He knows that p for every true p. Therefore, as we might say, the facts of the world constitute "input" for the divine psyche. Knowledge is the aspect of the divine psyche that varies lawfully, indeed with logical necessity, with the facts. It is that divine psychological state that takes all and only facts (true propositions) as its intentional objects. It is thereby distinguished from all other divine psychological states.[15]

Let's take stock. I have indicated how one can give a functionalist construal of psychological and action concepts that enables us to give at least a partial account of such concepts in their divine application and thereby to articulate some commonality between our thought of human and divine action and motivation. In both cases an action can be thought of as a change that is brought about by a volition or intention, where that is formed against the background of action tendencies that are formed by the interaction of attitudes with cognition. I am not claiming that concepts of divine and human actions, conative factors, etc., are exactly the same, even in their functionalist component. On the contrary, there are many differences, some of which follow from points already made in this essay. For one thing, the form of the interactions may be different. Perhaps there is a relation of event or state causality between attitudes and cognitions on the one hand and action tendencies on the other in the human but not in the divine case. And most obviously, attitudes and beliefs are typically related by temporal succession to the action tendencies they determine in the human case; the action is "generated" or "given rise to" by the attitudes and beliefs in a temporally literal sense of these terms. This is especially obvious where there is a process of conscious deliberation as to what to do, but there are also unconscious and noncentrally directed temporal pro-

---

[15]Note that if we were to take God to be what I called "omnidetermining", we would not be able to distinguish knowledge in this way. For in that case the divine will would also have every fact as its intentional object.

cesses of tendency formation. Whereas there can be no such internal *processes* of tendency formation for a timeless agent. Moreover, if a functionalist concept of a psychological state type, P, is spelled out by the way in which states of that type interact with others in the motivation of behavior, then any differences in the total motivational field will be reflected, to some extent, in the concept of each type of state. And we have noted several such differences. Human intentions or volitions lead to the corresponding action only if the external world, including the agent's body, cooperates in certain ways, but no such qualification is needed for divine motivation. Human beings exhibit a great variety of cognitive and conative states that is not matched by the divine psyche; and at least some of these differences make a difference in the way the total motivational structure issues in behavior. For example, biological cravings influence action tendencies differently from the way in which internalized general moral principles do. Again in the human case, different degrees of firmness of belief will make a difference to the strength of tendencies formed, a difference quite inapplicable to the divine case. For another difference on the cognitive side, God, being omniscient, will know everything entailed by a given piece of knowledge, so that, assuming that the inferential interrelations of cognitions enter into a functionalist account of cognitive states, this will work out somewhat differently on the two sides of the divide. But despite all these differences there is a basic commonality in the way in which attitudes combine with cognitions to determine action tendencies, and the way in which action tendencies are related to the final active volition or executive intention. There will be crucial conditionals in common, of the sort listed earlier. In both cases, e.g., if the agent has a pro-attitude toward G and a cognition that doing A is a way to realize G, then the agent will have a tendency to do A.[16]

Since it may still be doubted that any functionally construed psychological concepts can apply to a timeless being, I should say a word about

---

[16]One might suppose that if it is possible to give a (partial) functionalist account of divine action and motivational concepts along the lines we have been suggesting, it is not so important to show a basic commonality between these concepts and their analogues in our thought about ourselves. For the search for univocity has been fueled largely by the fear that without it we will not be able to apply terms and concepts to God directly, literally, and straightforwardly, that we will at best be able to speak of Him metaphorically or symbolically. But if my suggestions in this essay are on the right track we can forge concepts that apply to God, whether or not they overlap with concepts that apply to human beings. I think this reaction is justified as far as it goes; but I think it is also true that unless our understanding of divine purpose, intention, and will had at least as much commonality with human motivational concepts as I have been alleging, we would, justifiably, doubt that the divine states in question deserve to be called 'purpose', 'intention', and so on.

that. We can assure ourselves of the intelligibility of this conception by taking as our model a physical system—mechanical, electromagnetic, or thermal—in which the values of some variables at a given time are a determinate function of the values of other variables at that same time. This gives us the idea of *simultaneous* "subjunctive" or "counterfactual" dependence, in contrast to the dependence of states on those that precede them in time. To be sure, there are other features of these systems that do not carry over to our timeless divine agent. For one thing, the value of a given variable at a particular time will have resulted from temporal processes of interaction within the system; for another, the relations of contemporaneous dependence reflect the subjection of the system to laws, and we don't want to think of God as subject to laws. Nevertheless, it seems clear that it is not a conceptual or otherwise necessary truth that relations of contemporaneous dependence are dependent on these other features. Hence we are able to form the conception of a being (a "system") in which some factors depend on their relations to others for being what they are, even though there are no temporally successive processes of formation nor any subjection to laws. More specifically, we are to think of God as realizing a complex structure of attitudes, knowledge, tendencies, executive intentions, and volitions in the "eternal now", a structure that involves the kinds of dependence we have been talking about. Thus, let us say, it is true eternally of God that He wills that the church will be inspired by the Holy Spirit to develop the doctrine of the Trinity because He has a pro-attitude toward the church's making explicit the most fundamental truths about Himself (at least those suitable for our condition), and He knows that this development is necessary for that. Note that although there is no temporal succession within the divine life there is temporal succession between the things brought about by God in the world, the external aspects of His activity. Thus although His *will* to choose Israel and His *will* to become incarnate are all embraced without temporal succession in the eternal now, it does not follow that the results brought about in the world by these volitions are simultaneous.[17]

V

That's the good news; now for the bad news. The concepts I have been adumbrating are very thin, to say the least. All we have are con-

[17]For more on this point see Stump and Kretzmann, "Eternity," and Essay 7 in this volume.

cepts of positions in a structure of mutual dependence, "counterfactual dependence", to use a currently fashionable phrase. God's being favorably disposed toward G and God's doing A are the sorts of things that are related to each other, and to other states and activities, in the ways we have been laying out. God's having a "pro-attitude" toward the rejuvenation of Israel is the sort of state that is such that if God knows that giving a certain commission to Ezekiel is the best way to bring this about, then God will have a tendency to give that commission to Ezekiel. And that tendency is the sort of state that is such that an agent that has it will give that commission to Ezekiel unless sufficient interferences are present. Among such interferences is a divine decision not to give that commission to Ezekiel. And what is a divine decision (not) to do A? It is a state such that. . . . And so it goes. We have laid out a certain structure of what depends on what in what way, but as to what it is that stands in these relations of dependence we have said virtually nothing. There are only two places at which this system of mutual dependencies gets anchored in something outside it. (1) For any proposition, p, p entails that God knows that p, as well as vice versa. (2) For any p, God's willing that p entails that p, but not vice versa. But this makes little contribution to our grasp of the nature of the internal states that stand in the specified functional relations.[18]

Of course we have said that the functionalist account claims only to be a partial account. But that's just the rub. How do we fill in what it leaves out? In the human case we have a lot to go on that is lacking in the divine case. First, and most obviously, we have our own first-person sense of what it is like to want something, to be afraid of something, to believe that something will occur, to hope for something, to feel that one ought to do something, to intend to do something, and so on. But we can hardly pretend to any such insight into what it is like to be God, or even to have purposes, intentions, and the like in the way God does. Thomas Nagel has gained fame (or at least significantly added to it) by pointing out we don't have much idea of what it is like to be a bat. How much less are we in a position to know what it is like to be God. Moreover, we can see how our concepts of human motivational factors are enriched by aspects that must be absent if God is as we have been

---

[18]Indeed there is some question as to whether our account even entails that the system constitutes a distinctively *personal* agent. See Ned Block, "Troubles with Functionalism," in *Perception and Cognition: Issues in the Foundations of Psychology*, ed. C. W. Savage, *Minnesota Studies in the Philosophy of Science*, vol. 9 (Minneapolis: University of Minnesota Press, 1978), for some doubts along this line. To be sure, since we have opted to construe the "output" of the system in rich, intentionalistic *action* terms, that may suffice to dispel the doubts.

supposing Him to be. Just consider temporality. Our conception of human purposes and intentions is partly constituted by our under-standing of the way in which the purpose or intention holds fast through a variety of changing circumstances, providing a basis for changing our approach to the goal as we encounter unforeseen diffi-culties and complications. And our conception of the relation between an intention to bring about G and actually bringing about G is partly constituted by our realization that one can have the intention even though G is not yet brought about. Again, our understanding of what it is to make a decision or form an intention is partly constituted by our sense of how a decision is the terminus of a *process* of deliberation. But none of this is applicable to a timeless deity. Again consider God's supreme perfection. This prevents our making use of any analogue of the way in which our understanding of human acts of will is enriched by our awareness of effort of will in struggles against temptation. In the human but not in the divine case, our ability to distinguish between willing, intending, or deciding to do A, on the one hand, and doing A, on the other, is partly dependent on the fact that the former will not issue in the latter unless one receives the right sort of cooperation from the external environment. Finally, consider the point that even if God is temporal, He will, since supremely perfect, have at any moment a perfect knowledge of whatever is the case at any time. Hence He will know just what situation He will be reacting to at any point in the future *and what His reaction will be.* And that means, in effect, that His decision as to what to do in that situation has already been made; He will never decide on the spot how to react. Again, even though God be temporal, He cannot go through any genuine process of deliberation as to what to do at *t*, or any process of genuine *formation* of an intention to do something at *t*, since at every previous moment He will already know what He will do at *t*. These contributions to our understanding of our own motivational structure are unavailable in the divine case, not only because of timelessness but also because of omniscience.

Thus the account we have offered of concepts of the divine psyche and divine activity leaves them quite sparse. Even if we help ourselves to an unanalyzed conception of personal agency, we are still left with only a tenuous conception of the knowledge, attitudes, and volitions of the divine agent. Is this enough? "Enough for what?" I would suppose that we do not need more for theoretical purposes, just because we have no right to expect a satisfactory theoretical grasp of the divine nature and doings. That is, we would need more to attain a satisfactory theoretical grasp, but such is, by common consent, unsuited to our condition. However, there are more practical needs to be considered as well. There is the need for guidance, direction, inspiration, assistance in attaining salvation, in leading the kind of life and becoming the kind of person God intends us to. For these purposes do we need more of a grasp of the divine psyche and activity than is provided by my austere conditionals?

Whether or not it would be possible for people to receive adequate guidance in the religious life while deploying only the meager conceptual resources I have allowed, it is clear that this is not the way it goes in actual theistic religions. If you think of the Bible and, more generally, of practically oriented religious literature, it is at once apparent that God is represented as deliberating, forming purposes and intentions in the light of developing events as they occur, acquiring knowledge of events as they transpire, exhibiting features that attach only to temporal, imperfect agents. It may be said that those who write, and read with approval, such writings simply do not share the conception of God with which I have been working. I have been dealing with the "God of the philosophers", while theirs is the "God of the Bible" or the "God of simple believers". But this reaction fails to take account of the point that those who explicitly advocate the conception I was using typically take the Bible as authoritative, and also speak and write in these terms themselves when their purpose is homiletical, pastoral, or edificatory. Thus there seems to be a deeply felt need to represent God and His doings in a much more concrete way than I have provided in this essay. Moreover, I think we can see why this should be the case. For the practice of the religious life we need to think of ourselves in genuine personal interaction with God: in prayer, in the action of the Holy Spirit within us, in God's providence for our needs, in seeking enlightenment from Him, and so on. But the conception I have offered of a timeless "personal system" of functionally interrelated psychological states simply does not present anything with which we can coherently conceive ourselves to be in dynamic personal relations of dialogue, support, love, or instruction.[19]

Thus it seems to be a practical necessity of the religious life to represent God as much more like a created, imperfect temporal agent than a sound theology will allow. We must, for devotional and edificatory purposes, think of God as finding out what happens as it occurs and forming intentions to deal with developing situations as they develop, even though an omniscient being, whether timeless or not, would know everything about the future at any given point in time.

I would like to consider what bearing this has on the central concerns

[19]The considerations of Essay 7 are not designed to overthrow this judgment, but only to show that dialogue with an atemporal supremely perfect personal agent is not impossible. That thesis has no implications as to how such interaction, or the divine agent involved, is to be represented.

of this essay, even though I cannot hope to enter onto a proper discussion. One reaction to the points I have just been making would be to abandon the view that God is timeless and that He eternally possesses complete knowledge of the future; many religious thinkers have taken this line. But here I want to stay within the previously announced constraints and consider what moves are open. Clearly, given those constraints, this more concrete picture cannot literally apply to God. Thus with respect to whatever in the picture goes beyond my austere functional account, we will be thrown back on the familiar array of alternatives that are open, with respect to the total meaning of theological predicates, to those who deny that any terms (concepts) we can form can be literally applied to God: the alternatives of analogy, metaphor, symbolism, etc. The problem is not quite as urgent for me as for them, just because I recognize that there is an abstract core of predicates that are literally true of God. But given the ineluctability of the more concrete characterizations, it is a genuine problem. The answer would seem to lie somewhere in the general territory of metaphor and symbol, but I cannot pursue the matter further here.

I hope that I have said enough to indicate both that there is a hard literal core to our talk about divine action and that, for the religious life, we need to go beyond that in ways that launch us into the still not sufficiently charted seas of the figurative and the symbolic.

Referring to God

I

It is commonly supposed that one succeeds in referring to God only if one employs, or at least has in reserve, a description that uniquely picks out God, e.g., 'the absolutely perfect being', 'creator of the universe'. As the above disjunction indicates, the view might be that S refers to X only if S "has" a description true only of X, or it might be, more strongly, that S refers to X only if the description S is *employing* to pick out a referent is true only of X. It is the latter, stronger, view we shall be concentrating on, and that I shall call "descriptivism". On this view, if the operative description is uniquely true of X, then X is the referent; if it is not uniquely true of anything, then nothing has been referred to.

As against descriptivism, I shall be defending two theses. (1) There are other ways of referring, ways that do not require one to be using a description to fix the referent. I do not deny that reference can be carried out in the descriptivist way, but I do deny that it is the only way. (2) The other way I shall be describing, "direct reference", is more fundamental than descriptivist reference in respects I shall bring out. Though my particular interest is in reference to God, I believe that issue to present basically the same problems as any case of reference. Hence I shall oscillate freely between more general and more particu-

From *International Journal for Philosophy of Religion*, 24 (November 1988) 113–28. Copyright © 1988 by Martinus Nijhoff Publishers. Reprinted by permission of Kluwer Academic Publishers.

lar considerations. Again, although I believe that these issues concern singular reference carried out by any device, I shall, for the sake of focus, limit consideration to proper names.

Before turning to what I regard as the most serious difficulties with descriptivism, let me mention a couple of problems one encounters in trying to work it out. First, it is often difficult, or impossible, to decide just what the crucial description is, the one on which the success of the reference and the identity of the referent hangs, especially when the referring device is a proper name. In many cases the subject can easily formulate a number of descriptions he believes to be uniquely satisfied by his referent, as I can when I refer to my wife as 'Valerie'. But which of these is such that I have succeeded in referring to my wife if and only if she uniquely satisfies that predicate? I wouldn't know how to pick out just one predicate that has that status. No doubt, some of these descriptions are more central than others; 'my wife' is much more central than 'the person who bought this jacket yesterday'. Nevertheless, there are many other descriptions that are just as central as 'my wife', referentially if not uxoriously; and how can we determine just which of these it is that I am using to determine my referent? A similar point can be made about referring to God; again one typically has a number of putatively identifying descriptions among which there is no obvious choice of a *primus inter pares*. There *could* be a practice of reference in which the psychological processes of speakers are so structured that exactly one putatively identifying description plays a central role in the process, and in such a way that this central description stands out in consciousness. But our referential practice is not of this sort.

John Searle developed a well-known account of proper names that is designed to allow one to hang onto a form of descriptivism in the face of this point.[1] Contact with the referent is said to be carried by a *set* of descriptions, the ones S would be prepared to list if asked something like "To what were you referring?", rather than by one governing description. And, according to this more democratic descriptivism, S has referred to X *iff* "a sufficient number" of these descriptions are uniquely true of X. Now we can say, more plausibly, that when I say "Valerie is coming to pick me up" I have referred to whatever "a sufficient number" of my "Valerie-descriptions" are uniquely true of. I shall henceforth be thinking of this Searlean variant of descriptivism.

Second, there is the problem of just how the description(s) are supposed to function to secure reference. Whether we think in terms of a

---

[1] "Proper Names," *Mind*, 67, no. 266 (1958), 166–73.

single master description·or in terms of a large set thereof, none of this
is typically consciously appealed to by the subject in the heat of reference. Then by virtue of what do *these* descriptions determine the reference, rather than many other descriptions that S "possesses" and to
which she is not appealing at the moment? In formulating Searle's view
we have spoken of S's readiness to list the descriptions in the set in
answer to some such question as: "To what were you referring?" But
how does this readiness enable the speaker to refer to what uniquely
satisfies most of *those* descriptions? Little light is thrown on this by
descriptivists. But I will not pursue this point, partly because a satisfactory account of the mechanism of reference has not been worked out
for any mode of reference. In this essay I shall speak of the descriptions that, according to descriptivism, fix the reference as the "associated" descriptions.

Now let me remind you of Saul Kripke's main objections to a descriptivist account of proper name reference in "Naming and Necessity"[2].
But first I want to note Kripke's useful distinction between two sorts of
descriptivist views about proper names: (i) definite descriptions "give
the meaning" of, or are synonymous with, proper names, and (ii) definite descriptions "fix the reference" of proper names. It is the latter
view I am considering here, and so I will be concerned only with
Kripke's objections to that position. But note that we are taking (ii) to
claim not just that this is one way of reference-fixing for proper names,
but that it is the only way.

Kripke's principal objections are the following. (1) There are cases of
successful reference to X in which S does not have (in her mental
storage), and does not suppose herself to have, any description that
uniquely applies to X. Here the reference is clearly not fixed by a
description or set of descriptions. Thus Kripke suggests that many
people use 'Aristotle' to refer to the famous ancient Greek philosopher
of that name without being able to specify anything more nearly
uniquely identifying than, e.g., 'a philosopher that lived a long time
ago' or 'an ancient Greek philosopher'. (2) Even where S does have one
or more associated descriptions that she takes to fix the reference, they
don't always do so. These cases are divided up into (a) those in which
nothing uniquely satisfies the description(s), but S nevertheless succeeds in referring to X, and (b) those cases in which the description(s)
are uniquely true of Y, but S is referring to X. Kripke illustrates (a) with
the case of Jonah, on the assumption that none of the putatively

[2]In *Semantics of Natural Language*, ed. Donald Davidson and Gilbert Harman (Dor-
drecht: D. Reidel, 1972).

uniquely true predicates from the story are uniquely true of the prophet about whom the legend grew up or of anyone else; and he illustrates (b) with his famous fantasy that someone other than Gödel proved the incompleteness of arithmetic (where the speaker's only putatively identifying description associated with 'Gödel' is 'the man who proved the incompleteness of arithmetic').

I believe that all these criticisms can be successfully urged against the application of descriptivism to reference to God. To be sure, the first criticism is less important here just because the ways in which God is unique are much more widely advertised than is the case for any creature. Nevertheless, there may be persons who are incapable of forming putatively identifying descriptions, or of considering them as such, whether by reason of tender years or otherwise; and such persons may nevertheless succeed in referring to God by nondescriptivist means of the sorts I shall be describing shortly. Kripke's second criticism, however, seems to me much more crucial here. In defending my second thesis I shall illustrate this by presenting religious cases in which the associated descriptions fail to fix the reference.

But first I want to look at the other side of the picture. How is reference secured if not through descriptions? Kripke provides what he calls an alternative "picture," and this is as essential a part of his attack on descriptivism as his negative point that the referent is not always fixed by descriptions. Here are two of his statements.

> Someone, let's say, a baby is born; his parents call him by a certain name. They talk about him to their friends. Other people meet him. Through various sorts of talk the name is spread from link to link as if by a chain. A speaker who is on the far end of this chain, who has heard about, say Richard Feynman, in the market place or elsewhere, may be referring to Richard Feynman even though he can't remember from whom he first heard of Feynman or from whom he ever heard of Feynman. He knows that Feynman was a famous physicist. A certain passage of communication reaching ultimately to the man himself does reach the speaker. He then is referring to Feynman even though he can't identify him uniquely.[3]

> A rough statement of a theory might be the following: An initial baptism takes place. Here the object may be named by ostension, or the reference of the name may be fixed by a description. When the name is "passed from link to link", the receiver of the name must, I think, intend when he learns it to use it with the same reference as the man from whom he heard it.[4]

[3]Ibid., pp. 298–99.
[4]Ibid., p. 302.

This account is often termed a "causal theory of reference". The basis for the appellation is simply that when reference is thus secured, it is by virtue of some real (causal?) connection with the referent. However, I shall not be stressing whatever distinctively causal aspect there may be. I shall, rather, use the term 'direct reference' for my version of Kripkean reference.

But is this mode of reference really an alternative to descriptivist reference, or is it just a particular form of that mode? One who takes the latter alternative may claim that Kripke has only pointed to the important role of descriptions that are different from those usually stressed by descriptivists. On the initial baptism end of the chain he explicitly allows that the reference may be fixed by a description; but his other alternative (by ostension) can be construed descriptively too. When a person fixes a reference by labeling an ostended object, he is, in effect, fixing the reference by the description 'the item I am currently ostending', or some such. And at subsequent stages, users of the name fix the reference by the description 'what the person from whom I got this name uses it to refer to'.

Now Kripke considers the latter part of this descriptivist counterargument. He points out that the person who picks up the name 'George Washington' may have forgotten from whom she acquired it, or she may have a thoroughly mistaken idea on this point, and even so be using the name to refer to the famous person commonly so called. Even the unique satisfaction of this kind of description is not required for successful reference. Of course, S may employ a less specific description like 'the object referred to by this name by the person from whom I acquired the name, whoever that was'. Or perhaps 'the person most commonly called by this name in such-and-such a social group'. But these descriptions too may fail to be satisfied by S's referent. No doubt, the descriptivist can keep modifying his suggestions to meet any given counterexample. Suppose that he finally comes up with an absolutely fail-safe description like 'the object this name is used to refer to by the people involved in the referential practice by contact with which I have acquired this use of the name'. Since that description is modeled directly on Kripke's picture of how reference is secured, it is guaranteed to fit whatever Kripke's account would pick out as the referent. Even so the following point will remain. A descriptivist account will apply in these cases only where such a specially tailored description is employed by S to fix the reference. And surely it is obvious that in most cases no such description is operative. Our wily descriptivist has succeeded only in showing that reference *could* always take place via a description. He has failed to show that it always does.

The same point is to be made about the descriptivist's suggestion that when the name is bestowed ostensively, the object will fall under some such uniquely identifying description as 'the object I am currently ostending'. This only shows that a description *could* play a crucial role; it fails to show that a description must be employed. The subject can just attach the name to the object and form the intention to use the name for that; whereupon she has acquired what it takes to refer to the object with that name.

II

Now I want to indicate how I am thinking of direct reference to God. I want to concentrate on the most radical alternative to descriptivist reference, the alternative in which not only derivative reference along the chain of social transmission, but also the initial "baptism" (to reverse the theological order of priority) is secured otherwise than by the unique satisfaction of some predicate. We will think of a non-derivative reference to God as secured by labeling something presented in experience. This presupposes, of course, that God can be presented to one's experience in such a way that one can make a name the name of God just by using that name to label an object of experience. This is controversial, and I am prepared to argue for it, but this is not the place.[5] Note that I am making something explicit that was implicit in Kripke's formulations, that when one ostensively indicates X as the referent, one is perceiving X. Ostension, in the literal sense, is not available for fixing a reference to God, and so I am thinking of an initiator of a reference chain here as first fixing the reference for himself by focusing attention on a perceived entity. To be sure, if that referential practice is to be shared by others, there must be some way of communicating to others what entity it is to which the initiator was referring with 'God'. I shall take it that the communal worship, and other practices, of religious communities provide resources for this, though I shall not be able to go into the matter in this essay. (See the next paragraph for some hints.) Given such resources, we will think of members of religious communities as picking up this referential practice much as Kripke suggests, though many more details need to be filled in before we have a full-blown view.

Let me say why I think direct reference to God is not only an actualized possibility but is prominent in the religious life. First, it is obvious

[5]For a defense of the presupposition, see "The Perception of God," *Philosophical Topics,* 14 (Fall 1988).

that we, at least most of us, acquire our religion, including our practices of talking to and about God, from a community. We did not think it all up ourselves; nor were most of us privileged with special revelations from God. (Those who have been so privileged have themselves typically received this privilege in the context of a functioning religious community.) To be sure, this point does not by itself dispose of descriptivism, for it leaves open the possibility that the community initiates us into this referential practice precisely by providing us with identifying descriptions. No doubt, we do acquire such descriptions in the course of normal religious training. But initially we learn to refer to God (in praying to God, praising God, etc.) by being exposed to the practice of worship, prayer, confession, reception of the sacraments, and so on; we were given instructions as to how to engage in them; we were encouraged to do so. As a result of all this we were "drawn into" these practices; we learned, by doing, what it was like to come into contact or communion with God. By being initiated into the practice, we picked up the sub-practice of referring to God, of referring to the object of worship our predecessors in the community had been referring to. And, if things go right, we also attain some firsthand experiential acquaintance with God to provide still another start for chains of transmission.

Let's take it that direct reference mechanisms are operative in reference to God. I now want to explain and defend my second thesis, that direct reference is more fundamental than descriptivist reference.

III

I think of direct reference as more fundamental in more than one respect. First, genetically. I am not going to say much about this, but it does seem to me that descriptivist reference always, or virtually always, presupposes prior references. I will mention two indications of this. First, and less crucial, almost all uniquely identifying predicates themselves contain one or more singular referring expressions ('the teacher of Alexander', 'the author of Waverly', 'my cousin'). We can rarely identify something by purely qualitative predicates. And it seems very unlikely that a person could make enough references with purely qualitative descriptions to furnish an adequate foundation for our further descriptions that contain singular terms. Second, and more crucial, the use of a description to pick out a referent presupposes the mastery of a referential apparatus. For I refer descriptively by taking myself to be speaking of whatever uniquely satisfies certain predicates.

And how could I understand that notion of *something's* satisfying a predicate without already having made some singular references, or at least having acquired the ability to do so? If any use of a description to pick out a referent presupposes the mastery of a referential apparatus, that presupposed referential capacity must be a capacity to refer in some other way. However, I shall not pursue these difficult matters in this essay.

Instead I shall focus on a different sort of basicality. Where both descriptivist and direct reference are available, and even where they are both employed, it is direct reference that determines the referent. The crucial test of this claim will be a discrepancy between the indications of the two mechanisms; either one yields a referent and the other does not, or the two yield different referents. Since these are the two kinds of situations envisaged by Kripke's second argument against the pretensions of exclusivist descriptivism, in exploring such cases we will be applying these Kripkean arguments to the case of referring to God. I will mostly be concerned with the second sort of case, that in which the mechanisms indicate different referents.

First, suppose that an impostor—the devil, one's internalized father figure, or whatever—represents himself as God. We are to imagine someone who, like the Old Testament prophets, takes himself to be addressed by God, to be given commissions by God, and so on. But, unlike the Old Testament prophets, as they have traditionally been regarded, our chap is really being addressed by Satan; or else some internalized figure from his past is responsible for the "messages". To make this the kind of case we want, we must suppose that this impostor represents himself as the true God, creator of heaven and earth, righteous judge, merciful redeemer, and so on. Thus most of the operative descriptions (even if there are some Kripkean descriptions like 'He who addressed me at t' in the set) are uniquely true of God, while the direct referential contact is with, say, Satan. I think the right thing to say here is that our dupe is really speaking of Satan when he says 'God told me to put all unbelievers to the sword'. It is just that he has a lot of false beliefs about Satan; but one thing he does truly believe of Satan is that Satan addressed him at t. Moreover, if a community grows up on the basis of these revelations and epiphanies, and the practice develops in that community of using 'God' to refer to the focus of the worship of the community, we will have a Satan-worshiping community in which the members use the name 'God' for Satan.

If one is unconvinced by my reading of this case, I would commend to him the following reflections. In the Judaeo-Christian community we take ourselves to be worshiping, and otherwise referring to "the God of

Abraham, Isaac, and Israel", i.e., the being who appeared to such worthies of our tradition, revealed Himself to them, made covenants with them, and so on. If it should turn out that it was actually Satan, rather than the creator of the heavens and the earth, with whom they were in effective contact, would we not have to admit that our religion, including the referential practices involved, is built on sand or worse (muck, slime), and that we are a Satan-worshiping community, for all our bandying about of descriptions that fit the only true God? One may protest that even if, in that case, we would be referring to Satan in our worship and prayers, there are still more detached, more theoretical contexts in which the reference is determined by our descriptions; and this may be so. But with respect to the more fundamental undergirding substance of religious activity, thought, talk, and feeling, the diagnosis stands as given. It would be Satan we are addressing.[6]

Now let's consider the opposite possibility, that our descriptions (or most of them) pick out something else, but that we are still referring to God. Here the mechanisms of direct reference place our talk in the right sort of effective contact with God, but we radically misconstrue His nature, in such a way that most of our descriptions are true of something else. Consider the possibility that all religions are initiated by some experiential contact with the one true God, but that in most religions (and perhaps in all to varying extents) God's nature, doings, and purposes are misconstrued. God seeks to reveal Himself to people everywhere, but often, or always, the message gets more or less garbled in the transmission. Perhaps our sinfulness prevents us from getting it straight. Now in those cases in which the distortion is so great that most of the descriptions are not true of God it is likely that most of the descriptions are not true of anything, and so they would fail to pick out anything. But in a particular religion the descriptions might be mostly true of something other than God, some created supernatural being, let's say. In either case, assuming that the religion originated from some real contact with God and is sustained by continued experiential encounters with God, I think we would have to say that the people are referring to, addressing prayers to, worshiping, *God*, but, unfortunately, are radically misinformed about His nature and purposes.

Another variant concerns philosophers who attempt naturalistic reconstructions of theistic religion. Consider Henry Nelson Wieman, who thought of God as some complex of natural processes that is

[6]There can also be mixed cases. Perhaps some of the founders of the religion were in touch with God and others were not. Or perhaps the founders were in touch with Satan, but in the practice of the religion so founded some believers achieve real contact with God.

responsible for the realization of value in the world; or Julian Huxley, with his naturalistic trinity of the basic forces of nature (God the Father), the possibilities for the realization of value (God the Son), and human life that utilizes the first in order to realize the second (God the Spirit). What is it that they are referring to when they think about, or address, their naturalistically conceived God-surrogates? Well, if their descriptions are the only determiners of reference, they are referring to what uniquely satisfies those descriptions, if anything. But suppose, as may be the case for one or another of these souls, the person is in effective experiential contact with the only true God, but his naturalistic predilections lead him to this radically false construal of what he is experiencing. Or perhaps, as may be the case with Wieman, he intends to be referring to whatever it is that people in the Christian community are referring to as 'God'. If that's the way it goes, then, once again, I would say that these people hold wildly heterodox views about God, rather than that they hold views about some being other than God. Since they mean their views to be about what they have encountered in certain stretches of their experience, and/or what is generally referred to as 'God' in a certain community, that is what their views are about, provided there is something that fills the slot in question.

"But wait a minute. Haven't you admitted that one can fix one's reference by what uniquely satisfies a certain description? And what if the people you have been talking about were doing that? What if Wieman said (thought) what he said (thought) as true of what uniquely satisfies the description, 'that complex of natural processes that is responsible for the creation of value, whatever that may otherwise be'? Then he wouldn't have been referring to God, contrary to your ruling. And what if your dupe had resolved to refer to what satisfies the description 'the creator of heaven and earth'? Then he would have been referring to God, contrary to your diagnosis of the situation." I can't deny this. If these people had gone through these maneuvers, they would have been in touch with a referent other than what I specified. But I was assuming that they hadn't; I was assuming that these were normal cases. Let me spell out my assumptions a bit more. I am supposing that direct reference is fundamental in still a third way, viz., that where the direct reference mechanisms are in place they will determine reference unless the subject makes special efforts to counteract this, e.g., resolutions of the sort just mentioned. That is, I take it that direct reference is the natural, baseline mode of reference; it takes place "automatically" without the need for any deliberate intervention. Whereas descriptivist reference requires more active involvement on the part of the subject. It does not strictly require anything as explicit as a consciously formed resolution, but it at least requires some implicit version of that. Since most of us most of the time take the path of least resistance, most of us most of the time will be making direct reference to what we are talking about. It is only in rather unusual and special circumstances that the descriptive mode will win a contest for referent-determination.

IV

I suspect that the main resistance to the contentions of this essay will come from the recognition that 'God' involves more descriptive meaning than the usual proper name. Though this meaning will vary from group to group, and even from person to person, still for a given person or group there will be certain descriptive constraints on its use. Let's say that you and I would not be willing to refer to any being as 'God' unless we were convinced that that being were perfectly good, all-knowing, and the source of existence of all things other than itself. In fact, reflection on these points has led many to deny that 'God' is, strictly speaking, a proper name, and to regard it rather as a title. This being the case, and however it is with proper names of creatures, how can it be maintained that the referent of 'God' is fixed primarily by mechanisms of direct reference rather than by associated descriptions? To be sure, so far we have only pointed out that people commonly take the possession of certain divine-making characteristics to be necessary for being God, and purely descriptive reference requires characteristics that are *sufficient* for the individuation of the referent, i.e., uniquely exemplified characteristics. But let's concede that as well; one will not be prepared to refer to X by the use of 'God' unless one takes X to *uniquely* exemplify the properties listed above. Where that is the case, won't reference to God inevitably be descriptivist?

No. The points just brought out imply that one would not use 'God' to refer to X unless one firmly believed that X alone had certain characteristics. But that falls short of showing that it is the possession of those characteristics that makes X the referent. The arguments for the primacy of direct reference remain in full force. All of our above scenarios could be rewritten with the inclusion of the above points about the descriptive meaning of 'God'. Our dupes of Satan might have a firm resolution to use 'God' to refer only a being that is absolutely perfect; but, mistakenly supposing the being with whom they are in contact to be absolutely perfect, they are using 'God' to refer to an imperfect being nonetheless. Wieman may have as a firm a disposition as you please to use 'God' to refer to X only if X is the unique constellation of natural forces that make for goodness. But, mistakenly supposing the being with whom he is in dynamic contact in the Christian community to exemplify that feature, he is using 'God', nonetheless, to refer to the eternal creator of nature. No doubt, if either of these come to realize the true nature of the situation they will stop using 'God' to refer to the being in question (provided the meaning they attach to 'God' remains constant); but that doesn't alter the point that when they are making a referential use of the name, it is the mechanisms of direct reference that are determining the referent.[7]

An analogy to Donnellan on the referential use of definite descriptions may help one to appreciate this point. In his famous article on the subject[8] he points out that one may use 'the man in the corner drinking a martini' to refer to a man who is drinking water from a martini glass, since one may have some other way of picking out the referent than *that entity that uniquely satisfies the description.* Here too it could well be the case that one would not use that description to refer to X unless one believed that X uniquely satisfies the description; but the referent is determined otherwise nonetheless.

V

What difference does it make what determines reference in religion? That is, what practical religious or theological difference does it make, what difference does it make to the religious life? (Obviously it makes a difference to the theory of language, more particularly to the theory of religious language.)

A negative point is well brought out by Richard B. Miller in his article

---

[7]One might try to save descriptivism by giving it a subjectivist twist. The referent is, not the X if any that actually uniquely exemplifies the properties in question, but the X if any that is believed by the subject to uniquely exemplify the properties in question. This construal is proof against the argument of the last paragraph. For, by my lights, the referent in the first case is the being S believes to be absolutely perfect, and in the second case the referent is the being S believes to be a certain unique constellation of natural forces. But this cannot be the basic account of what determines reference in these cases, since it presupposes that reference has already been secured. One can't form the belief in question about X without thereby referring to X, at least mentally. And what determines that reference? There seems to be no alternative to direct reference as what plays that role.

[8]"Reference and Definite Descriptions," *Philosophical Review,* 75, no. 3 (1966), 281–304.

"The Reference of 'God'",[9] the only extended published attempt known to me to apply recent ideas of direct reference to the religious case. There Miller points out that if Kripke is right about reference this drastically alters the status of genetic arguments against theism. Attempts by the likes of Freud and Marx to discredit theism by providing naturalistic accounts of the origins of theistic religion are often dismissed by philosophers as irrelevant to the truth of theism. But if our claims, as Christians, Jews, or Moslems, to be referring to the creator of heaven and earth rest on the supposition that these referential attempts stem from some actual experiential contact with such a creator, then anything that strikes against that supposition will strike against the foundations of our faith. If Moses, Isaiah, Jesus, Paul, and John, not to mention Augustine, Francis, and ourselves, were in experiential contact not with God but rather with their own superegos, then our faith is in vain and we are, of all men, the most miserable. This would still not *disprove* theism, as Freud was careful to point out, and one might still succeed in referring to God by way of descriptions. But theistic faith would not have the status deemed essential to it in all theistic religions.

There are also more positive implications. I will mention two. First, the primacy of direct reference provides a reassurance that God can be successfully referred to by the weak and foolish as well as by the wise and the proud. One doesn't need fancy theological descriptions for the purpose. Tying onto one's experience, or the referential practice and the experience of others, will do the trick. Communion with God, including verbal communion, is not just for philosophers and theologians. Second, the prospects for taking radically different religious traditions to all be referring to and worshiping the same God are greatly increased. If one's referent in religious worship and discourse is determined by what one takes God to be like, then we, the Hindus, and the ancient Greeks and Romans cannot be credited with worshiping the same being. But if reference is determined rather by the real contacts from which a referential practice stems, then there may indeed be a common referent, in case these traditions, including their referential traditions, all stemmed from experiential contacts with the one God. For that matter, direct reference increases the chances of a common referent across major differences within a single religion like Christianity. There are theological differences within Christianity that threaten religious community, referentially as well as otherwise, on a descriptivist account of reference. But if reference is direct, then persons even as diverse theologically as Tillichians and fundamentalists

[9]*Faith and Philosophy*, 3 (January 1986), 3–15.

might all be worshiping the one true God, in spite of their radically different ways of thinking of Him.

I should also mention an implication I don't know whether to classify as positive or negative. Let me call it "neutral". The whole enterprise of theology looks different on our two conceptions of reference to God. On descriptivism the basic subject matter of theology is provided by certain concepts, the ones that uniquely pick out God. That means that we start with certain divine attributes that are not up for grabs; nothing not uniquely possessing those attributes would be what we are talking about in theology. The question, then, is as to how we can extend the account, by reasoning from the initial set, by revelation, by experience of God, and so on. But on the direct reference view we start with a being presented in individual and communal experience, not with a set of attributes. The question is, then, as to what *this* being is like. No particular characterization is sacrosanct *by reason of our starting point,* though of course it may be rendered so by other considerations. It follows right away from this that natural theology has a more fundamental and a more important role to play on the first conception than on the second. On the direct reference approach we are pretty much exclusively thrown back on our experience of God, including His messages to us, to determine what God is like, at least initially, though we can, of course, proceed to reason from that.

Let me close by quoting Kripke's caricature of descriptivist reference.

> The picture which leads to the cluster-of descriptions theory is something like this: One is isolated in a room; the entire community of other speakers, everything else, could disappear; and one determines the reference for himself by saying—'By "Gödel" I shall mean the man, whoever he is, who proved the incompleteness of arithmetic'. Now you can do this if you want to. There's nothing really preventing it. You can just stick to that determination. If that's what you do, then if Schmidt discovered the incompleteness of arithmetic you *do* refer to him when you say 'Gödel did such and such'. But that's not what most of us do.[10]

Add to this his amusing remark that "it is a tribute to the education of philosophers that they have held this thesis (descriptivism) for such a long time".[11] The point of this last remark is that philosophers are in possession of many more characteristics uniquely satisfied by historically famous personages than are most people who refer to those

[10]"Naming and Necessity," p. 298.
[11]Ibid., p. 291.

personages. Transposing all this to our present concerns, we might say that it is a tribute to the education, though not to the piety, of philosophers that they so readily assume that the unique satisfaction of descriptions is what enables them to refer to God, that referring to God is like going into a room by oneself, relying on ones own resources, without essential dependence on an environing and sustaining community of faith, articulating a theological predicate, and then saying to oneself, "God is the being that uniquely satisfies that predicate".[12]

[12]An earlier version of this paper was presented to a meeting of the Society for the Philosophy of Religion. I wish to thank the participants in that session, and especially my commentator, William Hasker, for many useful suggestions.

PART II

THE NATURE
OF GOD

Hartshorne and Aquinas:
A Via Media

I

The Hartshornean conception of God has exercised a profound influence on contemporary theology and philosophy. It is recognized as a major alternative to more familiar conceptions, and its merits and demerits are vigorously debated. The conception has a number of sources, but not least among them is Hartshorne's criticism of the way of thinking about God that was brought to classic expression by St. Thomas Aquinas. In what still remains the most extended systematic presentation of his position, *Man's Vision of God,* Hartshorne develops his conception as an attempt to remedy the defects he finds in the Thomistic view. And throughout his subsequent writings this foil is there, sometimes in the foreground, sometimes in the background, but always exercising a dominant influence. It is the Thomistic conception, or the general ways of thinking about God given definitive shape by Thomas, that Hartshorne takes as his chief rival, and he takes one of the basic recommendations of his position to be that it succeeds at those points where Thomas fails.

In contrasting his view with that of Thomas, Hartshorne presents us with a choice between two complete packages. No picking and choosing

From *Existence and Actuality,* ed. John G. Cobb, Jr., and Franklin I. Gamwell (Chicago: University of Chicago Press, 1984), pp. 78–98. Copyright © 1984 by the University of Chicago. Reprinted by permission.

of individual items is allowed. And the secondary literature has, for the most part, followed him in this. Nor is this mere sloth or heedlessness on Hartshorne's part. He explicitly propounds the view that the various elements of the Thomistic system are so tightly bound to each other that we cannot pick one or two without thereby becoming committed to the whole:

> they all belong logically together, so that there is little use in judging any of them in isolation. Either we accept them one and all, or we reject them one and all, or we merely bungle the matter. Here is the explanation of the failure of many attempts at reconstruction in theology; they sought to pick and choose among ideas which are really inseparable aspects of one idea. Here also is seen the genius of the great theologians of the past, that they really saw the logical interrelations between a large number of affirmations (they are really and admittedly denials, negations) about God.[1]

And he often imputes an equally tight coherence to his own system. In opposition to this picture of the situation, I shall be arguing in this essay that the Thomistic theses rejected by Hartshorne are by any means so tightly bound to each other as he supposes, and that one can, consistently and coherently, reject some and retain the rest. More specifically, I shall contend that Hartshorne's arguments against the Thomistic denials of internal relatedness, potentiality, complexity, and contingency (of some properties), arguments that I take to be wholly successful, do not, as Hartshorne seems to suppose, suffice also to dispose of the Thomistic doctrines of omnipotence, immutability, nontemporality, creation ex nihilo, and unsurpassability even by self. Nor do I find any other cogent arguments in Hartshorne against the attributes of the second group, though I will not be able to argue this last point in detail. Thus I shall be contending that the Hartshornean corpus leaves standing the possibility that a coherent, plausible, religiously adequate, and even true conception of God can be formed that combines the Hartshornean position on the attributes of the first group

---

[1]Charles Hartshorne, *Man's Vision of God* (1941; rpt. Hamden, Conn.: Archon Books, 1964; henceforth cited as *MVG*), p. 95. This view sorts ill with Hartshorne's frequent assertion that the position contains internal contradictions. If each of the basic theses of the Thomistic theology entails all the rest, and if the whole set is contradictory, then each of the theses individually is contradictory, a most implausible conclusion.

We should also note that Hartshorne must be very careful as to just what set of propositions he alleges to have this tight logical interconnection. Otherwise he will be saddled with the unwelcome conclusion that one cannot attribute knowledge to God without accepting the whole Thomistic system.

with a Thomistic, or at least something closer to a Thomistic, position on the attributes of the second group.

Here is a tabular presentation of the oppositions between what Hartshorne calls the "classical" position, paradigmatically represented by Aquinas, and his own, "neoclassical", position.

	Classical	Neoclassical

Group 1 Attributes

	Classical	Neoclassical
1.	Absoluteness (absence of internal relatedness).	Relativity. God is internally related to creatures by way of His knowledge of them and His actions toward them.
2.	Pure actuality. There is no potentiality in God for anything He is not.	Potentiality. God does not actualize everything that is possible for Him.
3.	Total necessity. Every truth about God is necessarily true.	Necessity *and* contingency. God *exists* necessarily, but various things are true of God (e.g., His knowledge of what is contingent) that are contingently true of Him.
4.	Absolute simplicity.	Complexity.

Group 2 Attributes

	Classical	Neoclassical
5.	Creation ex nihilo by a free act of will. God could have refrained from creating anything. It is a contingent fact that anything exists other than God.	Both God and the world of creatures exist necessarily, though the details are contingent.
6.	Omnipotence. God has the power to do anything (logically consistent) He wills to do.	God has all the power any one agent could have, but there are metaphysical limitations on this.
7.	Incorporeality.	Corporeality. The world is the body of God.
8.	Nontemporality. God does not live through a series of temporal moments.	Temporality. God lives through temporal succession, but everlastingly.
9.	Immutability. This follows from 8. God cannot change since there is no temporal succession in His being.	Mutability. God is continually attaining richer syntheses of experience.

10. Absolute perfection. God is, eternally, that than which no more perfect can be conceived.	Relative perfection. At any moment God is more perfect than any other individual, but He is surpassable by Himself at a later stage of development.

I shall go about my task as follows. I shall examine Hartshorne's arguments against the Thomistic attributes in the first group (absoluteness, simplicity, etc.), and show that they cut no ice against the Thomistic attributes in the second group. In order to carry this through, I will have to show that the classical attributes in the latter group are in fact consistent with the neoclassical features in the first group. In discussing the classical attributes in the second group, I shall cast a cursory glance at Hartshorne's other arguments against those attributes and suggest that they lack cogency. I would like to go on to argue for the religious adequacy of my "mixed" conception, but for that I will have to wait for another occasion.

Before starting on this task let me make explicit what I will not be challenging in the Hartshornean theology. First I readily and unreservedly grant that Hartshorne has made a powerful positive case for his conception of God as one that (a) is internally coherent, (b) has philosophical merit, (c) has important roots in the practice of theistic religion, and (d) nicely handles some nasty problems. Thus I allow that the full Hartshornean conception is an important alternative that must be seriously considered by contemporary theology, even though it is not my preferred alternative. Second, I acknowledge that theological thought during most of its history has been seriously hampered by the fact that the Hartshornean alternative has been almost totally ignored. Hartshorne has repeatedly shown how this neglect of an important alternative has led to bad reasoning. Finally, I grant that Hartshorne has shown the classical conception not to be required by the practice of theistic religions.

II

I now turn to a short sketch of what I take to be Hartshorne's most important arguments against the classical attributes in Group 1. Let us begin with absoluteness (in the sense of lack of internal relatedness), which is the key to the whole thing. Here I will distinguish between a very general line of argument that I do not regard as successful, and a more specific line of argument that seems to me to be completely successful.

The first argument hangs on some very general points about relations. For a given term in a relationship, the relation may be either internal or external to that term.[2] A relation is internal to a term if that term would not be exactly as it is if it were not in that relationship, if, to some extent, the term depends on the relationship for its being what it is; otherwise it is external.[3]

> But external relations are subject to two conditions. . . . First, every relation is internal to *something*, either to one at least of its terms or to some entity additional to these. Second, the entity to which the relation is internal is a *concrete* whole of which the externally related entities are *abstract* aspects. (*MVG*, 235)

The second point can be restated as: "The entity to which a relation is internal contains the relation and its relata as parts". We will find that this plays a major role in Hartshorne's theology.

To continue the argument:

> If the relation of the absolute to the world really fell wholly outside the absolute, then this relation would necessarily fall within some further and genuinely single entity which embraced both the absolute and the world and the relations between them—in other words within an entity greater than the absolute. Or else the world itself would possess as its property the relation-to-God, and since this relation is nothing without God, the world, in possessing it, would possess God as integral part of its own property, and thus the world would itself be the entity inclusive of itself and the absolute. On any showing, something will be *more* than an immutable absolute which excludes its own relations to the mutable. (*MVG*, 238–39)

Thus on pain of admitting something greater or more inclusive than God, we must embrace the remaining alternative, which is that the term to which the God-creature relation is internal is none other than God.

I do not find this argument impressive. Grant that every relation must be internal to something. Why should we hold that the term to which a relation is internal "contains" the relation and the relata? Or,

---

[2]*MVG*, 235; Charles Hartshorne, *The Divine Reality* (New Haven: Yale University Press, 1948; henceforth cited as *DR*), pp. 6–8.
[3]*DR*, 6–7.

more basically, what is meant by this thesis? In just what way does the one term "contain" the others, or in just what way, as Hartshorne says in the passage quoted above, are the relata "aspects" of that term? To focus the issue, let us consider why the second alternative in the last-quoted passage, that a God-world relation be internal to the world, is unacceptable. The reason given is that the world would "include" itself and the absolute in that case, and so would be "more" than the absolute. This reasoning shows that Hartshorne is reading more into his "containment" principle than he is entitled to. So far as I can see, the only sense in which one is entitled to say, in general, that the entity to which a relation is internal *contains* the terms, is that we have to refer to these other terms in describing that entity; that a reference to those terms *enters into* a description of that entity. But it doesn't follow from this that those terms are contained in that entity as marbles in a box, or as thoughts in a mind, or as theorems in a set of axioms, or as you and I in the universe, or as the properties in the substance of which they are properties. Thus we are not constrained to hold that the entity in question is "greater" or "more inclusive" than those entities. And obvious counterexamples to this claim are not far to seek. On Hartshornean principles, and apart from those principles, when I think about God that relationship is internal to me. Does it follow that I am "more" than God, since, on the "containment" principle, I include God as an abstract aspect?[4] Once we see the innocuousness of the "containment" that is implied by internal relatedness, the second alternative (the relation being internal to the creature) loses its repugnance, and the argument fails.

But Hartshorne also deploys a more specific argument for the same conclusion, one that depends on the character of a particular sort of relation, a relation in which God, by common consent, stands to the world. This is the cognitive relation. Hartshorne argues effectively that, in any case of knowledge, the knowledge relation is internal to the subject, external to the object,[5] and, indeed, that cognitive relations are *more* constitutive of the subject, the more certain, comprehensive, and adequate the knowledge.[6] Whenever I know something, the fact that I know it goes toward making me the concrete being I am. If at this

[4]Hartshorne will reply that I am aware of God only in a dim, inadequate, incomplete, and abstract way when I think of Him, whereas God's awareness of me is quite the opposite in these respects. I grant the point. The fact remains that when I am aware of God in any way, I am thereby related to God in a certain manner, and apart from that relationship I would not be exactly as I am. (You may substitute the solar system for God without affecting the argument.)

[5]*DR*, 7; 17.

[6]*DR*, 8–10.

moment I see a tree across the street, I would not be just the *concrete* being I am at this moment (though I might be the same enduring individual or substance, according to standard criteria of identity for such beings) if I were not seeing that tree in just the way I am. I would be different from what I am in a significant respect. But the tree would still be just what it is if I did not see it.

This being the case, how can we both maintain that God has complete and perfect knowledge of everything knowable, including beings other than Himself, and still hold that God is not qualified to any degree by relations to other beings? I wholeheartedly agree with Hartshorne that we cannot. Classical theology has typically responded to this difficulty by alleging that, since all things other than God depend on God for their existence, their relations to the divine knower are constitutive of them rather than of God. The usual order of dependence is reversed. But Hartshorne effectively replies that, even if finite beings depend for their existence on the creative activity of God, it still remains true that if God had created a different world then He would have been somewhat different from the way He actually is by virtue of the fact that His perfect knowledge would have been of that world rather than of this world; and so the point still holds that divine cognitive relations to the creatures are partially constitutive of God.[7]

Now for the other traditional attributes in the first group. On reflection we can see that the above argument for the internal relatedness of God as cognitive subject *presupposes* that there are alternative possibilities for God, at least with respect to what creatures, or what states of creatures, He has as objects of knowledge. For if, as both Thomas and Hartshorne hold, it is necessary that God know perfectly whatever there is to know, and if there were no alternative possibilities as to what there is to know (whether by way of alternative possibilities for divine creativity or otherwise), then there would be no possible alternatives to the actual state of knowledge. And in that case the question as to whether God would be in any way different if He did not know what He does know would not arise. It would be like asking whether God would be different if *He* were not God, or like asking if the number 6 would be different if *it* were not 3 × 2. But if there are alternative possibilities for divine knowledge, then this implies both that there are unrealized potentialities for God, e.g., knowing some world (as actual) that He might have created but did not, and that some of the things

---

[7]*DR*, 11. The matter is further complicated by the Thomistic principle that there is no distinction between God's knowing and willing. However, even if that extraordinary claim were accepted, it is not clear that it would negate the point that God would be different from what He is, in his concrete reality, if He did not know what He knows.

true of God are true of Him contingently, e.g., that He knows what He knows about creatures. Hartshorne's denial of absoluteness really presupposes the denial of pure actuality and of total necessity.

Thus there is an intimate connection between these three oppositions to the classical scheme. But in showing this we have also been exhibiting a vulnerability in the argument for relativity. For unless we are justified in the attribution of potentiality and contingency to God, the argument for relativity is lacking in cogency. Fortunately Hartshorne can, and does, argue independently for divine potentiality and contingency. Again he proceeds from premises admitted by his opponents, namely, that the world is contingent and that God freely creates the world He creates (and, therefore, could have created some other world instead).[8] From the first premise we have the following argument.[9]

1. (A) *God knows that W exists* entails (B) *W exists.*
2. If (A) were necessary, (B) would be necessary.
3. But (B) is contingent.
4. Hence (A) is contingent.

In other words, if what God, or any other subject, knows might not have existed, then God, or the subject in question, might not have had that knowledge. For if the object had not existed, it would not have been known. Hence God's knowledge of the contingent is itself contingent. Therefore we can totally exclude contingency from God only by denying of God any knowledge of anything contingent, a step none of the classical theologians were willing to take.

From the thesis that God could have created some other world it follows that there are unrealized potentialities for God, namely, His creating worlds that He does not create.[10] Thomas' distinction between active and passive potentialities[11] does nothing to invalidate this point. Of course unrealized potentialities also follow from the first argument, and contingency from the second; for these notions are strictly correlative. If it is contingent that I am in state S, then I might have been in some other state or had some other property instead (at a minimum,

---

[8]And, as the classical theologian would add, could have refrained from creating any world at all. Hartshorne does not accept this addition; I will deal with that issue below. For now I am exploring implications of the common ground—that God could have created a world different from the one He did create.

[9]*DR*, 13ff.

[10]*DR*, 118; Charles Hartshorne, *The Logic of Perfection* (LaSalle, Ill.: Open Court, 1962; henceforth cited as *LP*), p. 37; *MVG*, 108.

[11]*Summa Theologiae*, Iae, Q. 45, art. 1.

state non-S); that is, there are potentialities for me that I did not realize. And if there are potentialities that I might have realized but did not, then my not realizing them, and my realizing some alternative, is a contingent fact about me; it is one that might not have obtained.

Thus, starting from points insisted on by classical theology, Hartshorne has effectively shown that these points require the theologian to give up the classical attributes of nonrelativity, pure actuality, and total necessity. The final member of this group, simplicity, falls as well, since its main support was the absence of any unrealized potentialities in God.

III

Now let us turn to the classical attributes in Group 2, which I do not take Hartshorne to have succeeded in discrediting. I shall start with creation ex nihilo, since this is a fundamentally important element in classical theology, one I take to have deep roots in religious experience and practice. On this point there is a clear and sharp issue between Hartshorne and the classical tradition. For the latter not only is it the case, as Hartshorne would agree, that every finite individual owes its existence to the free creative activity of God, in the sense that apart from that creative activity *that* individual would not exist; in addition, it is wholly due to the free creative activity of God that anything other than Himself exists: it is contingent, and contingent on the will of God, that any created world at all exists. Whereas, for Hartshorne, it is a metaphysical necessity that there be a world of finite creatures, though not that there be just the one we have. This constitutes a significant difference in the area allotted to divine voluntary choice over against the area fenced round by impersonal metaphysical necessities.

Is the position of each party on this point in any tied up with its position on the attributes of the first group? I cannot see that it is.[12] Why should we suppose that a deity with unrealized potentialities and contingent properties, and qualified by His cognitive relations with contingent objects, *must* be in relation with some world of entities other than Himself? Why should it not be one of His contingent properties that He has created beings other than Himself? Why should the fact that He *is* qualified by his relations to other beings imply the *impossibility*

---

[12]A crucial part of my support for this is contained in the next section, where I argue that temporality is not required by relativity, potentiality, etc. For if God is temporal, creation ex nihilo is difficult to maintain.

of there being no other beings to which He is related and thereby qualified? I cannot see that the neoclassical properties in our first group are incompatible with the correctness of the suggestions just broached. In fact, it seems that the traditional doctrine of creation is much more attractive, plausible, and coherent in Hartshornean than in Thomistic garb. When decked out in the medieval fashion, it is saddled with just those difficulties exposed so effectively by Hartshorne in the arguments canvassed in Section II. It has to struggle to combine creation by a free act of will with the absence of alternative possibilities for God, and to combine the contingency of the world with the necessity of God's act of creation and with the necessity of God's knowledge of that world. Freed from those stultifying bonds it can display its charms to best advantage. It can mean what it says by "free act of will", by "contingency", by "knowledge", and so on. I would say that in exposing the internal contradictions of classical theology Hartshorne has done it a great service and rendered its doctrine of creation much more defensible.

Indeed, to the best of my knowledge Hartshorne does not explicitly link his position on creation with his position on relativity, contingency, and potentiality, as he does link the latter with his position on temporality.[13] On the other hand, he does present other arguments against the traditional position, none of which seem to me to have any substance. For one thing, he takes that position to be committed to a temporal beginning of the world, a bringing the world into existence at some moment of time. Against this he argues that a beginning of time is self-contradictory.[14] Be this last point as it may, the doctrine need not be so construed. Classical theologians have repeatedly pointed out that creation ex nihilo does not necessarily involve a temporal beginning of the universe; though, of course, many of them believe that in fact there was such a beginning. It only requires the principle that there would be no universe at all but for the creative activity of God. This could be the case even if the universe is temporally infinite, with no beginning and no end. Whether "creation ex nihilo" is the best term for such a doctrine is not the basic issue. What is crucial is that we can combine the theses that (a) God's not having done what is required in order that there be anything other than Himself is (was) a real possibility, and (b) the universe is temporally infinite.[15]

---

[13]See below.

[14]*MVG*, 233.

[15]This may be contested on the grounds that an act of will must take place at a time and, hence, that a temporally infinite universe could not depend for its existence on an act of will. For whenever that act of will took place, the universe was already in existence. But acts of will *must* take place in time only if the Creator is in time.

Hartshorne also argues that if God is thought of as absolutely perfect just in Himself, apart from a created world and His relations thereto, as classical theology would have it, then there can have been no point in creation.[16] But even if this argument is sound, it does not show that the classical doctrine of creation is incompatible with the neoclassical position on relativity, contingency, and potentiality. It merely shows that in order to retain the former we must modify the classical position on perfection. And is the argument sound? Why is it not intelligible to think of God as acting purely altruistically, rather than to increase his own perfection or bliss? In response to this Hartshorne makes two points. (1) Altruism involves participation in the good or evil of another, which is incompatible with the classical doctrine of impassibility.[17] But this argument is ineffective against the position that the classical doctrine of creation is compatible with regarding God as internally related to creatures through His awareness of them and hence passible. (2) If God cannot be benefited by the creation, we cannot serve Him or contribute to Him in any way.[18] But even if God is purely altruistic vis-à-vis creation, we can serve Him precisely by furthering those altruistic purposes.

Hartshorne connects his opposition to the classical doctrine of omnipotence with his rejection of the classical doctrine of creation.[19] To be sure, one might embrace creation ex nihilo while recognizing some limits to divine power (other than logical contradiction). Nevertheless it is true that Hartshorne's position on creation, according to which it is metaphysically necessary that there be contingent finite beings, entails that it is not within divine power to bring it about that nothing exists other than God. And so Hartshorne is required by his position on creation to deny the classical doctrine of omnipotence. But does he have any independent arguments against that doctrine? There is at least one: since being is power, every being has some power just by virtue of being; but then it is metaphysically impossible that God should have all the power.[20] Or to make this an internal argument against the classical doctrine, the conclusion could be softened to read: "If there is anything other than God, God does not have all the power there is." But even thus softened the conclusion does not cut against the classical doctrine, which maintains not that God has all the power there is, but rather that God has *unlimited* power, power to do anything He wills to do. This is quite compatible with God willing to bring

[16]*MVG*, 115–20; *DR*, 19.
[17]*MVG*, 115–17.
[18]*MVG*, 117–20.
[19]*MVG*, 105–9.
[20]*MVG*, 14.

creatures into existence with a power suitable to their status. That is, it is quite compatible with His delegating power to creatures. And this is the way that classical theology has construed the matter, although I would admit that Thomas, for example, can be criticized for the way in which he works out the details. The basic point is that the doctrine of unlimited power that goes with the classical doctrine of creation does not imply that no being other than God has any power.

Finally, the issue over incorporeality is tied up with the issue over creation. In chapter 5 of *MVG*, "The Theological Analogies and the Cosmic Organism," Hartshorne argues effectively that God is related to the world in two crucial respects as a human mind is related to its body: (1) God is aware, with maximum immediacy, of what goes on in the world, and (2) God can directly affect what happens in the world. On the principle that what a mind (1) is most immediately aware of and (2) has under its direct voluntary control *is* its body, Hartshorne concludes that the world is God's body, and hence that God is not incorporeal. But this analogy can be pushed through all the way only if, as Hartshorne holds, the world (some world or other) exists by metaphysical necessity, independent of God's will. Otherwise God will not be corporeal in the strongest sense—essentially corporeal. Of course even if God brings it about by a free act of will that the world exists, we might still, in a sense, regard the world as God's body. But in that case it would be a body that He had freely provided for Himself, one that He could just as well have existed without. He would not be corporeal in the way a human being is; He would not be essentially corporeal. If we understand corporeality in this stronger sense, and Hartshorne does espouse it in this sense, it is clear that it stands or falls along with Hartshorne's position on creation. If the classical doctrine of creation is retained, one can deny essential corporeality, while still agreeing with Hartshorne on relativity, contingency, and potentiality.

IV

In the foregoing section I allowed that the classical doctrine of creation *is* in trouble if we take God to be temporal. If God is temporal we have to think of Him as infinitely extended in time. If he began to exist some finite period of time ago, that would call for some explanation outside Himself; He would not be a fundamentally underived being. His ceasing to exist is impossible for the same reason. And if the fact that there is a physical universe is due to an act of divine will, that act, if God is temporal, would have to take place at some time. But then at whatever time it takes place God would have already existed for an infinite period of time; and we would be faced with the Augustinian question of why God chose to create the universe at that time rather than at some other. Thus if we think of God as temporal the most reasonable picture is the Hartshornean one of God and the world confronting one another throughout time as equally basic metaphysically, with God's creative activity confined to bringing it about, so far as possible, that the world is in accordance with His aims. And conversely, if we are to defend the classical doctrine of creation we must think of God as nontemporal. Hence in order to hold that the classical doctrine of creation is compatible with the neoclassical doctrines of relativity, contingency, etc., I must also show that the latter are compatible with the nontemporality of God. And, indeed, apart from this necessity of doing so, I am interested in defending that position.

Now for temporality and mutability. I shall take it that these stand or fall together. God undergoes change *iff* he is in time. The possibility of existing completely unchanged through a succession of temporal moments I shall dismiss as idle. Divergence in the other direction—change, in some sense, without temporal succession—deserves more of a hearing, and I shall accord it that shortly. However, since Hartshorne is clearly thinking of the sort of change that consists of first being in one state, and then at some temporally latter moment being in a different state, I shall use the term in that way. Hence I shall be taking temporality and mutability to be coextensive.

It is a striking fact that Hartshorne considers the tie between relativity or contingency, and temporality or mutability, to be so obvious that he freely conjoins them, and treats them as equivalent, without seeming to feel any necessity for justifying the stance. Thus the conclusion of the argument for internal relatedness in God on pp. 238–39 of *MVG*, quoted above, is put in terms of mutability as well as relativity.

> On any showing, something will be *more* than an *immutable* absolute which excludes its own relations to the mutable. It is therefore necessary to distinguish between the *immutable* and the absolute, if by absolute is meant the "most real," inclusive, or concrete being. The *immutable* can only be an abstract aspect of God, who as a concrete whole must contain both this aspect and its relations to the novel and contingent. (Emphasis mine)

Thus Hartshorne takes the argument, which was explicitly an argument for internal relatedness, to demonstrate mutability as well. Again, in the preface to *DR* (p. ix) Hartshorne states the basic thesis of the book in such a way as to indicate clearly his assumption of the equivalence of relativity and mutability.

> The main thesis, called Surrelativism, also Panentheism, is that the "relative" *or changeable,* that which depends upon and varies with varying relationships, includes within itself and in value exceeds the nonrelative, *immutable,* independent, or "absolute". . . . From this doctrine . . . it follows that God, as supremely excellent and concrete, must be conceived not as wholly absolute *or immutable,* but rather as supremely relative, "surrelative," although, or because of this superior relativity, containing an abstract character or essence in respect to which, but only in respect to which, he is indeed strictly absolute *and immutable.* (Emphasis mine)

We also get immutability assimilated to necessity. "It seems almost self-evident that a wholly necessary *and immutable* being cannot know the contingent and changing" (*MVG,* 242).

Although for the most part Hartshorne seems to take it as immediately evident that the relative and contingent would be mutable and temporal, there are occasional flashes of argument. At one place he simply asserts that a perfect being must change if relations to a changing world are internal to it.[21] This line of thought may indeed be the source of the impression of self-evidence. Let us try to spell it out a bit. If God is what He is partly because of the way He is related to the world, and if the world is in different states at different times, thereby entering into different relations with God at different times, it follows that God must be in different states at different times. For at one time God will have one set of relations to the world; at another time another set. Hence, if these relations are internal to God, the total concrete nature of God at the one time will be partly constituted by the relations He has to the world at that time; and so with another time. Since these relations will be different at the two times, the total concrete nature of God will be correspondingly different.

This argument involves a *petitio principii.* Of course *if* God is temporal, then He will have different relations to the changing world at different times and so will undergo change. But that is just the question. We are all prepared to grant that God changes *iff* he is temporal. We do not need the intermediate premise about relations to a changing world to derive mutability from temporality. On the other hand, if we do not *assume* divine temporality, the argument fails. If God is not in time, then the fact that relations to a changing world are internal to

----

[21]*DR,* 19.

Him does not show that He changes. If He is not in time He is not susceptible of change. The relations in which He stands to the world as it is at various moments will qualify Him "all at once", without temporal succession between different qualifications. It will be said that this is unintelligible. I will deal with that charge below.

Hartshorne also hints at an argument for the move from contingency to temporality.

> Thus there is God in his essential, and God in his accidental functions. The only way such distinctions can be made conceivable is in terms of time; the essential being the purely eternal, and the accidental being the temporal, or changing, aspects of the divine. (*MVG*, 234)

I cannot see that contingency (in the sense of that which is not necessary, that the opposite of which is possible) is intelligible only for a temporal being that successively realizes various possibilities. It is true that a nontemporal being has no "open future" before it; once it exists then whatever is true of it is fixed, in a way in which that need not be the case for a temporal being. The latter can exist at a certain time, while it is yet undetermined which of various possibilities for its future will be realized. At least this is true if, as Hartshorne supposes, what is future is not yet determined. Nevertheless it can be true of a nontemporal being that although it is R it might not have been R; that, to put it in currently fashionable terms, there is a possible world in which it is not R. This is sufficient to make the fact that it is R a contingent fact. Moreover this sense or kind of contingency, there being some possible world in which it is not the case, is the basic one. Alternative possibilities for an as yet undetermined future constitute a particular subsense or subtype. Its being contingent at this moment whether I shall finish writing this essay this week, is just a special case of the phenomenon of alternative states of affairs holding in different possible worlds. The additional feature in this case is that at this moment it is not yet determined which of these possible worlds is the actual world.

One who is indisposed to accept contingency without an open future should consider whether one could say that the past of a temporal being could be contingent in any respect. Is it now a contingent or a necessary truth that I went to bed at 10:15 P.M. last evening? In whatever sense we can recognize that to be a contingent truth we can also recognize various truths concerning a nontemporal being to be contingent.

Finally, let me point out that this "not true in all possible worlds" sense of contingency is the only one in which Hartshorne has given reason for supposing God to exhibit contingency without presupposing that God is temporal. Without that presupposition his argument simply amounts to the following. "The existence of the created world (or, less question-beggingly, things other than God) and any part thereof is contingent. Therefore it (they) might have been otherwise. Therefore any relation in which God stands to the world, e.g., creating it or knowing it, might have been otherwise, and so is contingent." The conclusion of this argument is simply that any relation in which God stands to the world *might have been otherwise*. There is no license for drawing the further conclusion that God exists at a succession of temporal standpoints relative to each of which there is an open future.

But, it will be said, we are still faced with the apparent unintelligibility of a nontemporal being qualified by its relations to temporal beings. Is it possible to make sense of this? As far as knowledge is concerned, it seems to me that the psychological concept of the specious present provides an intelligible model for a nontemporal knowledge of a temporal world. In using the concept of the specious present to think about human perception, one thinks of a human being as perceiving some temporally extended stretch of a process in one temporally indivisible act. If my specious present lasts for, e.g., one-twentieth of a second, then I perceive a full one-twentieth of a second of, e.g., the flight of a bee "all at once". I don't *first* perceive the first half of that stretch of the flight, *and then* perceive the second. My perception, though not its object, is without temporal succession. It does not unfold successively. It is a single unified act. Now just expand the specious present to cover all of time, and you have a model for God's awareness of the world. Even though I perceive one-twentieth of a second all at once, I, and my awareness, are still in time, because my specious present is of only finite duration, and, in fact, of much shorter duration than I. A number of such acts of awareness succeed each other in time. But a being with an infinite specious present would not, so far as his awareness is concerned, be subject to temporal succession at all. There would be no further awareness to succeed the awareness in question. *Everything* would be grasped in one temporally unextended awareness.

In presenting this model, I have said nothing about internal relatedness, but I cannot see that the intelligibility of the model depends on excluding that. Let us say that God would not be exactly what He is if the objects of His awareness were different. How does that make the concept of an infinite specious present less intelligible?

Volitional relations to the world can be handled in the same way. If we are strictly Thomistic and hold that God determines every detail of the world, then we can simply think of a single act of will that handles the whole thing and does not require temporal successiveness. But suppose we hold that God has endowed some or all of His creatures with the capacity to choose between alternative possibilities left open by the divine will. In that case many of God's volitions and actions will be responses to choices by creatures the exact character of which God did not determine. Even so, if within a specious present we can have non-successive awareness of a succession, why should we not have nonsuccessive responses to stages of that succession?[22]

The concept of nonsuccessive responses to stages of a temporal succession of events may seem too much to swallow, even to those who are prepared to admit the intelligibility of the specious present for cognitive phenomena. At this point we can get help from Whitehead. The crucial Whiteheadian concept for this purpose is that of the *concrescence* of an actual entity, the process by which an actual entity comes to be. Let us first see how Whitehead develops this notion for finite actual entities, and then look at the application to God.

An actual entity consists of the process by which it comes to be.[23] Without trying to go into the details of this, let us note that the process is one of developing and unifying a set of initial "prehensions"[24] into a more or less satisfying experiential whole. The particular feature of concrescence that we are interested in at this moment is the fact that it does not involve temporal succession. Whitehead was convinced by Zeno-like paradoxes that process must be made up of indivisible units, "drops" or "bits" of becoming that do not themselves consist of earlier and later becomings.[25] These quanta of becoming are called "actual entities". A finite actual entity occupies a certain position in the spatio-temporal matrix. It prehends the world from a certain perspective, one that can be determined from the relative fullness with which it objectifies the other actual entities it takes as its data. This position will involve temporal as well as spatial extension.[26] But though it occupies a temporal duration, it does not come into being by *successively* occupying the parts of this duration. It happens "all at once".

---

[22]See Essay 7 for more on this.

[23]"How an actual entity *becomes* constitutes *what* that actual entity is. . . . Its 'being' is constituted by its 'becoming'": Alfred North Whitehead, *Process and Reality* (New York: Macmillan, 1929; hereafter cited as *PR*), pp. 34–35.

[24]A "prehension" is an apprehension without the "ap", that is, an awareness that may or may not be conscious.

[25]*PR*, 105–7; Alfred North Whitehead, *Science and the Modern World* (New York: Macmillan, 1925; hereafter cited as *SMW*), pp. 183–85.

[26]The spatial dimension can be determined by tracing out simultaneity relations between actual entities.

In every act of becoming there is the becoming of something with temporal extension; but the act itself is not extensive, in the sense that it is divisible into earlier and later acts of becoming which correspond to the extensive divisibility of what has become. (*PR*, 107)

There is a becoming of continuity, but no continuity of becoming. (*PR*, 53)

The epochal duration is not realized via its successive divisible parts, but is given with its parts. (*SMW*, 183)

Hence all the parts of an actual entity are present to each other in a felt immediacy. The goal of the process, the final unity of feeling, is present throughout the process, shaping its course toward itself. Using the term 'superject' for the final upshot of the concrescence, that which will be taken as datum for later concrescences, Whitehead writes: "Thus the superject is also present as a condition, determining how each feeling conducts its own process" (*PR*, 341). Again: "The ideal, itself felt, defines what 'self' shall arise from the datum; and the ideal is also an element in the self which arises" (*PR*, 228).

In expounding this doctrine Whitehead appeals to James's concept of the specious present, but it is clear that he is going beyond that concept. The psychological concept of the specious present is intended to embody the possibility that one might be aware of a process without successively being aware of its temporal parts. But this does not imply that the awareness itself is *a process* without succession. The concept of the specious present provides for process in the object and lack of succession in the awareness; it does not provide for the joint exemplification of these by the same entity. But that is just what Whitehead is claiming. Not only is an actual entity nonsuccessively *aware of* a process; it *undergoes* the process of its own development nonsuccessively.[27] Thus the Whiteheadian notion of concrescence is more radical, more paradoxical than James's notion of the specious present. It is not entirely clear to me whether we can form an intelligible conception of process without temporal succession. This will obviously depend on our conception of time, and it is clear that the intelligibility of Whiteheadian concrescence hangs on the intelligibility of an atomic or "epochal" conception of time, one that is very different from our usual way

[27]This Whiteheadian concept of concrescence may help to flesh out the notion of an "atemporal duration" employed by Eleonore Stump and Norman Kretzmann in their essay "Eternity," *Journal of Philosophy*, 78 (1981), 429–58; even though they deny that their duration without temporal succession involves a "process".

of thinking of these matters. But I will not be able to go into all that in this essay. Assuming that the Whiteheadian conception is intelligible, let us see how it could be used to form a conception of process without temporal succession in the divine life.

The answer to that "how" question is very simple, in outline. We think of God as a single infinite actual entity, whose "extensive standpoint" is unlimited in space and time. As an actual entity, God will undergo concrescence, a development of Himself, His distinctive unity of experience, out of His prehensions of the other actual entities. And since He is a single actual entity, not a "society" of temporally successive actual entities, like you or me, the various stages of His life will not occur successively in time but will occur or "be given" in one unity of felt immediacy. A finite actual entity, though enjoying the common privilege of all actual entities—of concrescence without temporal succession—nevertheless occupies a particular finite position in the spatiotemporal continuum. But since God's concrescence is unlimited, His "position", if we may use that term, is the whole of time and space. He is subject only to the kind of process involved in concrescence, not to the temporally successive process involved in "transition" from one actual entity to its successors.

On my reading, this is just Whitehead's own conception of God. Throughout *Process and Reality* he refers to God as *an* actual entity. But then, unless Whitehead is going to "treat God as an exception to all metaphysical principles, invoked to save their collapse" (*PR*, 521), he must hold that there is no temporal succession in the divine life, just as there is none in the concrescence of any other actual entity. This is, indeed, a controversial point in Whitehead exegesis,[28] but I can see no other plausible way of reading the text. Let me mention two other points in support of my reading. (1) Whitehead repeatedly makes the point that the divine concrescence differs from the concrescence of finite actual entities in taking its start not from "physical" prehensions of other actual entities but from a "conceptual" prehension, the "unconditioned complete valuation" of all eternal objects.[29] But, by the nature of the case, there can be only one such *unconditioned* valuation. Hence God can only undergo a single concrescence. (2) The world is objectified in God's "consequent nature" without loss of immediacy.

---

[28]See, e.g., Charles Hartshorne, "Whitehead's Idea of God," in *The Philosophy of Alfred North Whitehead*, ed. P. A. Schilpp (New York: Tudor, 1941); John B. Cobb, Jr., *A Christian Natural Theology* (Philadelphia: Westminster, 1965), pp. 176–92; Lewis S. Ford, "The Non-Temporality of Whitehead's God," *International Philosophical Quarterly*, 14 (March 1974).

[29]*PR*, 134, 528.

The perfection of God's subjective aim, derived from the completeness of His primordial nature, issues into the character of His consequent nature. In it there is no loss, no obstruction. The world is felt in a unison of immediacy. The property of combining creative advance with the retention of mutual immediacy is what . . . is meant by the term 'everlasting'. (*PR*, 524–25)

But mutual immediacy is retained only within a single concrescence, not in the transition from one concrescence to another. Again, we get the conclusion that the divine life consists in a single concrescence.

When one reflects on Boethius' formula for the eternity of God, quoted with approval by Aquinas,[30] "the simultaneously whole and perfect possession of interminable life," one may well be struck by its affinity to the Whiteheadian concept of an infinite concrescence. I would say that one of Whitehead's signal achievements was to develop a conceptual scheme for handling this classical notion of divine eternity, a scheme that does the job much better than any used by the classical theologians themselves.

It must be admitted that Whitehead's view of God as a single infinite actual entity is incompatible with his principle that there is no prehension of contemporaries. Since God, on this view, is contemporary with every finite actual entity, being neither in the past nor in the future of any other actual entity, God, on the principle in question, would be able neither to prehend nor to be prehended by any other actual entity, a conclusion more radically at variance with religious experience and practice than the doctrine Whitehead was invoked to repair. In addition, such a windowless monad of a God would fail to perform His basic metaphysical functions in the Whiteheadian system. Hence God would somehow have to be made an exception to this principle, as Whitehead explicitly makes Him an exception to the principle that the concrescence of an actual entity begins from physical prehensions. In this essay I am not concerned with how, or how successfully, this modification might be carried out. It is not my job here to develop or defend Whitehead's metaphysics. I have merely sought to point out a way in which we might think of a nontemporal God as undergoing process, thereby reinforcing the point that the Hartshornean position on divine relativity, potentiality, and contingency does not necessarily carry with it the Hartshornean position on divine temporality.

Finally, the issue over temporality is intimately bound up with the issue over how to understand divine perfection. Hartshorne took this issue as the opening wedge of his battle with Thomism in *MVG*. In

---

[30]*Summa Theologiae*, Iae, Q. X, art. 1.

chapter 1 of that work Hartshorne distinguishes between *absolute* unsurpassability, impossibility of being surpassed by anyone, even oneself, and *relative* unsurpassability, impossibility of being surpassed by anyone else, but leaving open the possibility of being surpassed by oneself.[31] This distinction has a point only for a temporal being. A being that does not successively assume different states could not possibly surpass itself, i.e., come to be in a state superior to its present state. The concept of surpassing oneself has application only to a being that is in different states at different times. Not surprisingly, Hartshorne takes advantage of the possibilities opened up by a temporal conception of God, and plumps for *relative* unsurpassability. At a later stage of his thought this becomes the notion of perfection as "modal coincidence"—God, at any moment, actually is everything that is actual at that time (through his perfect "objectification" of everything in the world), and potentially is everything that is possible as of that moment.[32] God's actuality includes all actuality, and his possibilities include all possibilities. But if we are correct in holding that the Hartshornean position on relativity, contingency, and potentiality is compatible with a nontemporal conception of God, then it follows that the Hartshornean position on those Group 1 attributes is compatible with taking God to be absolutely unsurpassable, since, as we have seen, relative unsurpassability differs from the absolute variety only for a temporal being. The Thomistic, as well as the Whiteheadian, God cannot surpass Himself at a later time, for He does not move from one time to another. He simply is what He is in one eternal now (Thomas), or in one indivisible process of becoming (Whitehead).

There is, to be sure, Hartshorne's often repeated argument that since the simultaneous actualization of all possibilities is logically impossible (since some logically exclude others), the notion of a unique maximum of perfection makes no sense.[33] But this argument construes perfection in a crude, quantitative way that is, to say the least, not inevitable. Absolute unsurpassability need not be so construed that to be absolutely perfect a being would have to be both in Paris and not in Paris at a given time (since these are both possibilities), and so on. Nor have the main classical theologians done so. Sometimes they say things that are not clearly enough distinguishable from this, as when Thomas speaks of the perfections of all things as being in God,[34] but there is

---

[31]He also distinguishes between being surpassable in all, some, or no respects, but we will not need to attend to this and other distinctions that he draws in that chapter.

[32]*LP*, 34–40.

[33]*MVG*, 22, 37; *DR*, 144; *LP*, 36.

[34]*Summa Theologiae*, Iae, Q. 4, art. 2.

really no warrant for reading him as holding the absurd view that God actualizes every possibility. And Anselm's idea that "God is whatever it is better to be than not to be"[35] is poles apart from the notion of the actualization of all possibilities. If one thinks of the perfection of God along Anselmian lines, it remains to be shown that there is any logical impossibility in this being exemplified in a single state of a being.

V

I began this paper by contesting Hartshorne's claim that the classical and neoclassical conceptions of God must each be accepted or rejected as a whole, that each is so tightly unified as to make it impossible to accept or reject one component without thereby accepting or rejecting the whole package. I have opposed this claim in the most direct way possible—by doing what is claimed to be impossible. Actuality is the most compelling proof of possibility. More specifically and more soberly, I have presented strong reasons for viewing the matter in the following way. The points on which the two conceptions differ (and I have said nothing about the many points of agreement) can be divided into two groups. Group 1 contains such classical attributes as absoluteness (construed as absence of internal relatedness), total necessity, pure actuality, and simplicity—along with their neoclassical counterparts, relativity, contingency, etc. Group 2 contains such classical attributes as creation ex nihilo, omnipotence, incorporeality, nontemporality, and absolute unsurpassability, along with their neoclassical counterparts. The neoclassical position on Group 1 does not entail the neoclassical position on Group 2, though it is, of course, consistent with it. On the contrary, the neoclassical Group 1 attributes can be combined with the classical Group 2 attributes into a consistent and coherent conception that captures the experience, belief, and practice of the high theistic religions better than either of Hartshorne's total packages. (I have not argued for that latter claim in this paper.) Thus there is a rent in these supposedly seamless fabrics along the lines indicated by my division of the attributes into two groups. To be sure, this rent is not as extensive as it might conceivably be; I have not argued, nor does it seem to be the case, that one group of attributes in one conception *implies* the other group of attributes in the other conception. Indeed, I have not even suggested that the classical Group 1 attributes are consistent with the neoclassical Group 2 attributes, and it is pretty clear

---

[35]*Proslogium*, chap. 5.

that they are not. How could an absolutely simple, purely actual deity be mutable and temporal? Nevertheless the rent is sufficiently serious to be worth our notice. Because of it we are faced with a much more complex choice that Hartshorne would have us believe.[36]

[36]This paper was presented at a conference on Hartshorne's thought at the University of Chicago in November 1981. All the papers were responded to by Hartshorne. I would like to express appreciation to my teacher, Charles Hartshorne, and to other participants at the conference for many valuable criticisms.

Divine-Human Dialogue
and the Nature of God

I

Prayer comes in all shapes and sizes. Commonly recognized forms include meditation, contemplation, thanksgiving, intercession, and petition. It is petitionary and intercessory prayer that has provoked the most perplexity. If God orders all things for the best, how could this ordering be influenced by our requests? Why would God do something He wasn't going to do anyway just because some human being asked Him to? A number of thinkers have made impressive contributions to this discussion, and I do not propose to add yet one more suggestion to that list. Instead I shall shift the focus to a set of issues concerning a more general feature of prayer of which divine compliance with requests is only one form. This more general feature is *divine response* to our prayers. (This feature, in turn, is a special form of a still more general feature, divine responses to what we *do*.) *Divine response* extends beyond the granting of petitions in several directions. At the first remove there is divine refusal to grant a petition; but I am more interested in wider variations. There is an infinite variety of things that God might conceivably do in response to one or another prayer. I ask God for vengeance on my enemies and in response He inspires a redoubling of efforts to spread the gospel of love. I thank God that I am not as other men—adulterers, taxgatherers . . . , and in response He brings it about that I suffer a humbling decline in my

From *Faith and Philosophy*, 2 (January 1985), 5–21. Reprinted by permission of the Editor.

fortunes. The general category of divine responses on which I shall be concentrating is *replies*. I ask God what I should concentrate on in my work. God replies that I should concentrate on a certain book I once began to write. I protest that this seems so far removed from serving others or working for His kingdom on earth. He tells me to let Him worry about that.... Thus I will be concerned with divine-human dialogues, or at least that subset that involves a divine *reply* to a human utterance, leaving aside only those dialogues initiated by God that end with a single human response. To be sure, some divine replies are themselves the granting of a petition, e.g., where the petition takes the form of a request for guidance. This is illustrated by the first reply in the four-step dialogue just presented. But a divine reply need not be a response to a petition, as is illustrated by the second divine reply in the same dialogue.[1]

I should make it explicit that I am not restricting divine replies to cases in which the human recipient hears audible speech that he/she attributes to God, or to cases involving inner auditory imagery. But neither am I excluding such cases. I take it that God has a variety of means at His disposal for communicating with His creatures, and that He uses now one, now another as the occasion requires. In addition to externally perceived words, spoken or written by a human being or not, these include auditory imagery and thoughts that simply pop into one's mind.[2]

How important is divine-human dialogue in prayer, more specifically in the prayer life of a Christian? If the Bible is any guide, very important. A large proportion of the Scriptures consists of records of divine-human communication. Of course, a considerable proportion of that is restricted to God's giving the word to some prophet with the

[1]Note that divine answers to questions do not, in general, pose the severe problems that attach to favorable divine responses to certain sorts of petitions. If I (we) pray for peace in Central America and, in response, God brings this about, the question inevitably suggests itself as to why God should have waited for our request to bring about peace. But God could hardly have replied to my question before I asked it. It is true that, without my asking, God could have done what He did under another description, viz., "telling me that I ought to finish that book". But even under that description, it is quite understandable that God should have waited for the opportune moment to deliver this exhortation, and that this was the moment at which I asked Him what I should do, thereby rendering myself open to His exhortation.

[2]Needless to say, the human recipient will not take this last phenomenon to embody a message from God unless certain contextual indications are present. For example, the thought that I ought to finish that book may often occur to me without my taking it to be an exhortation from God. But if the thought forms itself distinctly in my mind just after I have asked God what I should concentrate on and have kept my mind blank in expectation of an answer, and, moreover, if this thought is accompanied with a strong sense of conviction, then I will take it to be God's reply to my question.

human recipient just taking it; no divine reply to a human utterance is involved. But there is plenty of back-and-forth conversation as well. Here is a famous example.

> The Lord said . . . 'The outcry of the Israelites has now reached me; yes, I have seen the brutality of the Egyptians towards them. Come now; I will send you to Pharaoh and you shall bring my people Israel out of Egypt.' 'But who am I,' Moses said to God, 'that I should go to Pharaoh, and that I should bring the Israelites out of Egypt?' God answered, 'I am with you. This shall be the proof that it is I who have sent you; when you have brought the people out of Egypt, you shall all worship God here on this mountain.'
> Then Moses said to God, 'If I go to the Israelites and tell them that the God of their forefathers has sent me to them, and they ask me his name, what shall I say?' God answered, 'I AM; that is who I am. Tell them that I AM has sent you to them.' (Exodus 3:9–14. New English Bible)

> But Moses said, 'O Lord, I have never been a man of ready speech, never in my life, not even now that thou hast spoken to me; I am slow and hesitant of speech.' The Lord said to him, 'Who is it that gives man speech? Who makes him dumb or deaf? Who makes him clearsighted or blind? Is it not I, the Lord? Go now; I will help your speech and tell you what to say.'[3] (Exodus 4:10–12)

I imagine that some sincere Christians, in the spirit of "the age of miracles is past", would feel that such conversations are reserved for the biggies of the Bible, and that they are not for the likes of us. For such souls prayer consists *solely* of our dispatching our messages out into the silent beyond. (Of course, for all or most of us that is what it frequently is.) But I suspect that this attitude is less common among Christians than it was fifty years ago. On a questionnaire I issued at the beginning of an adult education series I gave at my church, the following question appeared:

> Do you ever feel that God speaks to you? (Not necessarily in audible words. The question could be phrased: do you ever feel that God is communicating a message to you?)

---

[3]Some may deny that these exchanges are, or involve, *prayer*. One may reserve 'prayer' for divine-human communication initiated by the human participant. I don't want to get involved in controversy over the word 'prayer'. I want to discuss divine-human dialogue over its full range, when it is properly called 'prayer', and when, if ever, it is not.

The tally on that one was Yes–17, No–2. Admittedly, this is a self-selected group of people who took the trouble to attend an adult education series, and they are hardly a random sample of the churchgoers even of that particular parish, much less Christendom as a whole. Nevertheless, this result was a real eye-opener to me. In this paper I shall be assuming that divine-human dialogue is an essential component of at least the more developed Christian spiritual life, and that the conditions of the possibility of such dialogue put a significant constraint on our conception of God.

The issues I will be discussing concern what God must be like if divine-human dialogue is to be possible. They all have the form: Is it possible for God to reply to human utterances if God is ____? I will discuss three such questions, involving omnidetermination, omniscience, and timelessness.[4] Even though I am restricting explicit discussion to divine replies to human utterances in prayer, all the points I will be making apply equally to any divine responses to anything we do.

Before launching onto these specific problems I should like to set them in a more general context. Our understanding of prayer is one of the prime loci of the pervasive tension in Christian thought between "the God of the philosophers and the God of the Bible", between God as "wholly other" and God as a partner in interpersonal relationships, between God as the absolute, ultimate source of all being and God as the dominant actor on the stage of history. One thing that seems to force us into the second and away from the first pole of these dichotomies is the personal communication involved in prayer. Each of our three problems is one form this basic tension takes in application to divine-human dialogue. Each issue has the form: "Is it possible for us to engage in back-and forth dialogue with a being that is transcendent in this way? Is it conceivable that such a being should enter into genuine interpersonal communication?".

II

Let's begin with the doctrine that I have called "omnidetermination". This is the thesis that God has decided every detail of His creation, including all the putatively free choices and actions of human

[4]Many contemporary philosophers feel that there is also a serious, and perhaps insoluble, problem as to how an immaterial being could "speak," or communicate messages in any way, or, indeed, act in any way. My reasons for thinking that this difficulty can be resolved are set out in some detail in Essay 2. Essays 4 and 10 are also highly relevant to the issues of this essay.

beings. It has been widely held in the history of Christian theology, counting such distinguished adherents as Augustine, Aquinas, Luther, and Calvin. Nevertheless, it seems to me plainly incompatible with genuine divine-human dialogue, and much else in the Christian life as well. Dialogue requires two independent participants, neither of which wholly controls the responses of the other. There is no genuine communication *between* Edgar Bergen and Charlie McCarthy. Bergen, the ventriloquist, issues all the messages, some of which he issues through his dummy, McCarthy. It is just a complicated way of talking to oneself. If there is to be genuine communication, each participant must be over against another participant that is responsible for one end of the exchange. Otherwise I am as misguided in regarding it as genuine communication as I would be in eagerly looking forward to receiving a letter I wrote to myself.[5]

Note that my claim has to do not with *any* sort of determination, but rather with the effective *choice* of A's utterances by the other participant, B. I am not arguing here, though this may also be true, that any sort of causal determination of utterances, or any sort of causal determination of utterances by another person, is subversive of true communication. The claim is rather that A and B are not in genuine communication if A is exercising an ability to determine B's moves in accordance with A's intentions. It is this intentional effective control of one participant by the other that I am claiming to rule out genuine communication.

It may be felt that my ventriloquist example is unfair, in that the trouble lies in the lack of complexity of one partner, rather than in his total subservience to the other. Well, let's complicate things. I ask questions of my computer and receive answers. To get closer to divine omnidetermination, let's suppose that I built the computer and devised the program. We can make the computer as complicated as you like. Is this a genuine dialogue? Here, unlike the ventriloquist case, I do not decide each individual utterance of the computer. It often provides new information and sometimes even surprises me. But is the computer *responding* to me in the way we suppose ourselves to respond to God in prayer? I am inclined to say, No; but rather than embark on the long, and perhaps, futile attempt to establish this, I shall content myself with the following point. Any inclination to suppose there to be genuine dialogue here stems from the facts that (1) I have not individually

---

[5]Of course, we can think of circumstances in which I would not be misguided in looking forward to this. For example, I have forgotten what I wrote and am eager to have my memory refreshed. But it still fails to qualify as a case of interpersonal communication.

determined each computer response but have only deliberately instituted conditions that in turn determine those responses, and (2) that as a result I do not, in general, know in advance what those responses will be. Now condition (2) certainly does not hold of the divine-human case, under the assumption of omnidetermination. And although God certainly could determine my behavior by instituting conditions that determine it, he could equally well determine it directly, and hence even if He chooses the indirect route, given that He knows exactly what all the outcomes will be, He could hardly regard each action of mine as anything other than a carrying out of His specific intention. Whereas I cannot regard the details of each computer response as a carrying out of a specific intention of mine. Thus the features of the example that support the diagnosis of genuine communication do not hold of the divine-human case on the assumption of omnidetermination.

Finally, to come closer to home, consider a "conversation" between hypnotist and subject, in which the latter is doing nothing but carrying out posthypnotic suggestions. (It is irrelevant whether posthypnotic suggestion can in fact determine such fine details.) Here the one party, the hypnotist, really is effectively deciding just what the other says, and the other is as complicated as a human being, in fact *is* a human being. Here we have as close an analogy to divine omnidetermination as we are likely to find, and the verdict, I suppose, would be clear. This is a charade, not a genuine case of communication. The hypnotist is going to enormous trouble to institute a complicated form of talking to himself. Nothing but the complexity of the mechanisms involved distinguishes this from the ventriloquist case.

I conclude that the reality of divine-human dialogue is incompatible with divine omnidetermination. This result will be less disturbing when we realize that the proponents of omnidetermination have been mistaken in supposing it to be required, or even strongly supported, by the doctrine of divine omnipotence. It is quite conceivable that God should be omnipotent, able to do anything conceivable, including determining every detail of the creation, but voluntarily refrain from doing so. After all, almost all theologians recognize that God refrains from doing many things He can do, e.g., create some other possible world instead of this one, or annihilate His creation in 1870 A.D. Why should His omnipotence be incompatible with his voluntarily refraining from determining the putatively free choices and actions of human beings?[6]

---

[6]For an effective presentation of this possibility, see Nelson Pike, "Overpower and God's Responsibility for Sin," in *The Existence and Nature of God*, ed. A. J. Freddoso (Notre Dame, Ind.: University of Notre Dame Press, 1983).

III

Now let's consider whether divine *omniscience* is incompatible with genuine dialogue in prayer. The case for incompatibility is not nearly so strong as it was with omnidetermination, but there is a case. The knowledge of God that creates the problem is, of course, God's foreknowledge of the moves by the other party. Given that God knows in advance exactly how I will react at each point, can He be said to enter into genuine interpersonal communication with me? Doesn't that require each party to be responding to the other as the dialogue develops, so that each party is actively involved at each stage, confronted at each stage with the task of deciding how to respond to what is proffered by the other at that point? This is what it takes for genuine reciprocity, in which both parties are involved in the same generic fashion, each dependent on the other to provide, at each point, the occasion for a fresh response, newly minted on the spot. But this is what we fail to get where one party knows in advance how the other will react to any move by the former (or, indeed, given omniscience, to any given situation). The absence of living involvement on the part of the foreknower can best be seen by noting that under these conditions the all-knowing one could turn his/her part of the proceedings over to a preprogrammed robot that would operate purely mechanically (not excluding electronically). Since h/she can know in advance how the other will react to any move h/she makes, h/she is in a position to decide in advance how h/she will react to any of those reactions. There is no need to wait until the other actually makes a move to construct a response. but then no real shaping of response, in the light of the activity of the other, would take place at each stage. The foreknower could have made creative decisions in planning the whole thing, determining what his/her response would be to what h/she knew the other would be doing at each stage. But there is no such active involvement as the putative dialogue unfolds; the one party has made all his/her decisions and is now reduced to passively watching the foreseen sequence of events. It is as with omnidetermination, though for a different reason, a charade, play-acting. It is a mock dialogue, not the real thing.

Thus far I have argued only that an omniscient being *could* plan the whole exchange as far in advance as you please, thus avoiding any living involvement in the proceedings when they actually occur. But then what about the other possibility? Couldn't an omniscient being choose to forgo that privilege and, for the sake of genuine interaction, wait until the other party makes a given move to decide how h/she will react? No, that is not possible. An omniscient being will, necessarily, know in advance what h/she is going to do at any given time. Otherwise prior to that time there would be something of which h/she is ignorant, and h/she would not be omniscient. God, if omniscient, not only may but must decide in advance how He will freely act at any given moment.

At the risk of fatuity, let me note that it is no answer to the above argument to point out that one can enter into genuine communication with another person one knows so well as to be able to anticipate how the other will react. Such knowledge, as actually possessed by human beings, is highly fallible and incomplete. People often surprise even those who know them best; and such knowledge as I have of how, e.g., my wife will react extends only to certain kinds of situations. I would be rash indeed to claim to *know*, exactly and in detail, how she would react to my announcement that I had just returned from a trip around the galaxy. It is because of these limitations of our knowledge even of our closest intimates that the possibility of genuine communication is not subverted. Because of these limitations I am not able to program a robot to hold up my end, secure in the knowledge that it will all go as predicted. But divine knowledge does not suffer from those limitations. Hence the analogy fails at the crucial point. If ignorance is not bliss, it at least is, or makes possible, mutuality.

Here I must pause to consider the following objection. "Let's agree that 'living involvement' is precluded by perfect foreknowledge. And if living involvement is required for 'genuine dialogue' or 'real interpersonal communication', then that is ruled out too. But so what? Is it really so important that our contact with God be characterizable in those terms? What difference does it make *when* God decided how the conversation would go? We may naively suppose that God is shaping His responses on the spot, just as we do; but in many cases we have to revise our naive conceptions of God and His relations to His creation. Why shouldn't this be one of those cases? And what, of crucial value, would be lost in the shift? So long as God has freely decided to initiate contact and to respond to our initiations and responses in the way He has decided, what essential difference does it make when He made those decisions? Doesn't that still leave us with all we need and want in the way of sending messages to God and receiving messages from Him, and isn't that the crucial point? Have we lost anything more than a naive picture of the situation that represents God more anthropomorphically than is theologically warranted?"

It was in anticipation of this objection that I said at the beginning of this section that the case against omniscience was weaker than the case against omnidetermination. I don't see how anyone could respond to the argument against the latter by saying that omnidetermination still leaves us with everything essential. Surely it is essential to divine-human interaction that the human participant is playing some role in determining his/her side of the proceedings. But, with respect to the difficulties about omniscience, I will grant this much to the objection. We could learn to live with divine foreknowledge if we had to. The reconception of divine-human dialogue thereby enforced is not such as to rob it of its most essential value as communication. But if we can avoid this reconception, without violating any legitimate theological constraints, so much the better. I shall now proceed to argue that we can.

IV

To carry this out I must explain how our third problem, concerning *timelessness,* becomes enmeshed with the second. If the divine being is not subject to temporal succession, this will alleviate the strain that omniscience places on mutuality. The above argument depended on thinking of God as knowing *in advance* how a given human being would react in any situation, as well as knowing *in advance* what He will do at any given moment. That is, the argument depicts God as temporal, performing a given action at a time and knowing, at a time, that so-and-so. It supposes that God's actions and states can be dated, and that God moves through a succession of moments. But this is not the dominant conception of God in the Christian tradition, though the tradition has come under heavy attack on this point in this century. What if we think of God, God's knowledge, and God's activity as timeless? How will that affect the above argument?

It will subvert it entirely. If God is timeless, God does not know anything *in advance,* because God does not know anything *at any time.* God timelessly knows that I issue a certain utterance at t_1, feel queasy at t_2, and so on. *What* God knows, in these instances, is dated, but God's knowledge of them is not. God, as the infinite eternal *now,* is all at once simultaneous with every moment of time, and with everything that is happening in time.[7] Thus insofar as God's knowledge of what I do at t_1 stands in anything like a temporal relation to my doing it, it is simultaneous with my doing it, not earlier than my doing it. God knows what I do at t_1 by seeing me do it right then and there, not by virtue of being

[7]See Eleonore Stump and Norman Kretzmann, "Eternity," *Journal of Philosophy,* 78 (1981), 429–58, for a special concept of simultaneity that is designed for this application.

able to anticipate it.[8] Since God doesn't know *in advance* what I will do and what He himself will do, He is in no position to decide the whole thing in advance and let it run off mechanically according to a prearranged program. He is no more in a position to do that than to do anything else that requires occupying temporal positions and undergoing succession in His own life and activity. Since God's knowledge of anything that happens in time is simultaneous with that happening, His relations with those happenings and with the creatures involved need suffer no loss of "living or active involvement" or "decisions on the spot" by reason of His omniscience.[9]

"But," it may be said, "we have indeed jumped from the frying pan into the fire. For divine timelessness poses difficulties for divine-human dialogue far more severe than those posed by the omniscience of a temporal deity. As we have seen, genuine interpersonal interaction requires that each party engage in a continuous process of shaping and modifying its responses in the light of the developing contributions of the other. And this shaping must take place at the appropriate juncture in the proceedings. Unless I respond to your move when (just after) you make it, I am not engaged in active communication with you. But if God is timeless God doesn't do anything *at any time;* therefore He doesn't do anything when, or just after I ask Him what I should concentrate on in my work. Hence God never *responds* to anything done by a human being. And much less does He engage in a 'continuous process of shaping and modifying His responses in the light of the developing contribution of' the human side of the supposed dialogue. In short, since dialogue is essentially a temporal process, involving temporally interrelated messages and replies, a timeless being is logically

---

[8]If we accepted omnidetermination we could say, with Aquinas, that God knows what I do by virtue of knowing that He willed it. But since I don't accept divine determination of human free choices and actions, I can't accept that as an account of all divine knowledge. (See below, pp. 158–59.) I am forced to say that God's knowledge of events He does not determine must stem from God's "seeing" them happen. To be sure, since Aquinas combined this account of divine knowledge with a doctrine of divine timelessness, he no more thought of God's knowing events *in advance* than I do. God's willing my action at t_1, by virtue of knowing which God knows what I do, no more precedes my action than the knowledge does. It too is a timeless activity of God.

[9]This move is precisely parallel to the way in which the difficulties allegedly posed for human free will by omniscience are alleviated by the doctrine of divine timelessness. Here too, so long as we think of God's knowing *in advance* what I do at t_1, it would seem that this is incompatible with my having two or more genuine alternative possibilities from which to choose at t_1. But if God is timeless, He doesn't know *in advance* what I will do. He knows what I do because He "sees" me doing it. Contemporaneous knowledge of my doing what I do poses no threat to the real possibility of the alternatives between which I choose.

debarred from participation.[10] The objection to temporal omniscience was that the responses were shaped at the wrong time. The objection to timelessness is more radical; there are no responses at all."

I believe this assessment to be unwarranted, and I can indicate why by making use of the standard way of showing how a timeless deity can perform acts in time.[11] That way consists in distinguishing the aspect of the action that is internal to the agent, in this case God, and the aspect that consists in some effect produced by that agent. In the case of God that internal aspect will simply be an act of will; since God is bodiless He acts in the world by directly producing worldly effects of His volitions, not by producing those effects by movements of His body. The crucial point is that the two aspects can differ in temporal status. The worldly effect will be at a time. But it is quite compatible with this that the divine volition should be timeless, should be embraced with all other divine activity in the one eternal *now*. The action is in time by virtue of its effect, but not by virtue of the immediate activity of the agent. In speaking to Moses God wills that Moses should hear certain words in certain circumstances at a certain time. The hearing of those words by Moses is dated, but the divine volition is not. How can a timeless being act in the temporal world? By timelessly performing acts of will that have temporal effects.[12]

Now it may seem that even if this provides a wholly satisfactory answer to the question: "How can God, though timeless, have said that p to Moses at a certain moment?", as I am convinced it does, it does not suffice to answer the question: "How can a timeless God, in saying that, be *replying* to a question Moses had asked just before?". And it must be admitted that more is required for God's replying to Moses at t_1 that p than is required for God's saying at t_1 that p. Not everything that God says is a reply, much less a reply to that question. However the question before the house is not: "What are the necessary and sufficient condi-

---

[10]Cf. Nicholas Wolterstorff, "God Everlasting," in *God and the Good*, ed. C. J. Orlebeke and L. G. Smedes (Grand Rapids, Mich.: Eerdmans, 1975), p. 197: "some of God's actions must be understood as a response to the free actions of human beings. . . . And I think it follows, given that all human actions are temporal, that those actions of God which are 'response' actions are temporal as well."

[11]See, e.g., St. Thomas Aquinas, *Summa Contra Gentiles*, II, 35–36; Stump and Kretzmann, "Eternity," pp. 447–50.

[12]In (human) action theory we are familiar with the point that the date of what an agent most immediately does in an action can differ from the date of one or another effect that is a necessary condition of the performance of an action of that type. X willed to pull the trigger, and did so, at 10 P.M. on August 28, but the victim did not die until September 6. When did X kill Y? There is no single date of the action; instead we have one for the volition (and what it immediately issued in) and another for the effect ultimately aimed at. The present point differs from this only (!) by the fact that the "date" of the volition is the eternal *now*.

tions for God's saying that *p* in reply to Moses' asking what God's name
is?" The question is as to whether divine timelessness would prevent
anything God says from being a reply to something some human being
said. More specifically, we are considering the claim that it would prevent this just because a timeless God can't say anything *after* a human
utterance X and this is required for anything's being a reply to X. And
the standard treatment of the temporal acts of a timeless being does
give us all we need to take care of this.

The crucial point is simply that the standard treatment shows us the
sense in which an utterance of a timeless God can be temporally later
than a human utterance, viz., with respect to the worldly effect involved. God willed that Moses should hear "I AM; that is who I am" or
rather an equivalent sentence in the appropriate language, just after
Moses had asked his question, and in such a way that Moses would take
this to be a message from God. The effect on the receiver occurred just
after the question being answered, and it was intended by God to occur
then. Why should we suppose that any more is required in the way of
temporal placement for God to be credited with replying to Moses? If
this is sufficient to date what God did, then that dating should be
sufficient to satisfy temporal conditions for counting as an answer to
Moses. Why should we suppose that the initiatory volition of the an-
swerer must also be assigned a later date? Even with communication
between human beings the fact that A's voluntary initiation of a reply
to B's utterance always comes later than B's utterance is due to human
limitations rather than to requirements imposed by the concept of a
reply. Suppose that you emit a cry of despair and I offer consolation.
As we are actually constituted I will not initiate my attempt at consolation until some finite time (however short) after your cry. But isn't that
just due to our limitations? If I could be so closely tied to you as to
apprehend your cry while you are in the act of producing it, and if I
were able to offer my consolation (or at least do the most immediate
part of this, the volition) at that very same moment of apprehension,
would I not still be responding to your cry? We can't actually bring this
off, we can't respond that quickly, but that has no bearing on the *concept*
of a reply. I recognize that the concept prevents anything I do *before* X
from being a reply to X, but simultaneity is ruled out only by human
limitations.[13] And if a response to X that is simultaneous with X, from

[13]It is also true, no doubt, that human limitations require that you *receive* my consolation,
apprehend my response, after that to which I was responding, to avoid jamming the
communication channel. But that does not prevent my willing to issue the consolation at
the same moment as your cry. This is the same distinction between the time of volition, or
the most immediate issue thereof, and the time of certain crucial effects.

the side of the respondent, is a conceptual possibility even for a human responder, we certainly can't rule out responses to human actions by a timeless deity on the grounds that none of His volitions temporally succeed any human action.[14]

I believe that this is a sufficient answer to the objection. But we can further defend and elucidate the possibility of dialogue with a timeless deity if we explore further just how a timeless deity can reply to a human utterance. And to do that we must bring out what is required for an utterance, Y, to be a reply to a human utterance, X, over and above Y, on its effect side, being later than X.

In order for Y to be a reply to X, in the full-blooded sense in which we are interested, it must be, as we might say, issued "as a reply" to X.[15] But what does that involve? As a start, Y was done *because of* X.[16] If S was not influenced in any way to issue Y by the fact that T had issued X, then S could not be deemed to be replying to X in issuing Y. But not just any sort of influence will do. If T, by saying the code phrase 'I am hungry' releases a noxious substance in the air, and this leads S to say 'What is that awful smell?', S does not thereby reply to T. One crucial lack here is that S need not have known that T said what he did in order for S to remark on the smell; S did not utter Y "in the light of" T's having uttered X; an awareness of X played no role in leading S to utter Y. And so a second component is that S utters Y *in the light of* T's utterance of X. The fact that T has uttered X plays an essential role in S's reasons for uttering Y. But even this is not enough. Suppose that having overheard you say to Smith at a cocktail party "It's in the bag," I say to Jones that you are a conceited ass. I made my remark in the light of your having made yours; my awareness of your saying 'It's in the bag' played a major role in leading me to say what I said. Yet I wasn't replying to you. I am still not uttering Y *as a reply* to X. What is missing here is that I do not utter Y in order to communicate a message to you,

[14]Stump and Kretzmann, "Eternity," pp. 450–51, in treating this problem say that for an action to be an answer to a prayer it must be made *because of the prayer but need not be later than* the prayer. I agree that something like a 'because of' is the heart of the matter (see below, where, however, I choose a much richer term than 'because of'), but in saying flatly that being *later than* is not required Stump and Kretzmann fail to take account of the distinction between the way that requirement does hold (date of the crucial effect) and the way it does not (date of the initiatory volition).

[15]I have specified a full-blooded sense in order to exclude defective or border-line cases, e.g., those in which something I said was, in effect, a reply to your question, although I didn't intend to be replying to you.

[16]This is as far as Stump and Kretzmann carry the matter. ("Eternity," pp. 450–51.) The ensuing discussion will reveal the inadequacy of this phrase. It should be noted that 'Y occurred because of X' is not intended to entail that X causally determined Y, but only that X played some role in the replier's issuing Y.

the issuer of X, a message that is appropriate to your having uttered X. (I am assuming that I do not intend you to hear what I said to Jones.) Thus a third condition is that S utters Y *in order to communicate an X-appropriate message to T*.[17] This condition includes the other two. I couldn't utter Y with that intention without doing it in the light of X, and hence without X's playing some role in my uttering Y. But be that as it may, I shall sum up these three conditions in the phrase 'utter Y *as a reply to X*.'[18]

Thus the question I wish to consider is whether a timeless deity can say something *as a reply* to a human utterance. And I propose to approach this issue by first asking whether an *omnidetermining* deity could satisfy that condition. Could a God who decides every detail of His creation *reply* to a question from Moses? Well, in a way this is possible. God's masterplan for creation could include as components (a) Moses' asking this question, and (b) immediately afterward Moses' hearing the words 'My name is I AM' and hearing those words in such a way as to be convinced that this is a message from God. In that case, wouldn't God be sending that message to Moses as an answer to his question? Wouldn't God be saying that in the light of Moses' having asked his question, and in order to communicate to Moses a message that is appropriate to that question? And as far as the *'because of'* condition is concerned, the usual counterfactual requirements for causal influences are satisfied. If Moses had not asked that question at t_1 God would not have said that to Moses, in such a way that Moses received the message at t_2. For if God had not brought about the question at t_1 He would not have brought about the hearing of the answer at t_2.

[17]This is a cumbersome formulation, but I don't know how to say anything smoother that will cover the whole territory. Specific forms of X-appropriate utterances include giving an answer to a question, refusing to answer a question, offering consolation to an expression of anguish, sneering at someone's recital of failure, making an objection to a thesis propounded, saying something on the same subject as X, where that is in order, and so on.

Note that since "X-appropriate message" occurs in an intentional context, "in order to communicate an . . .", this condition can be satisfied without the message's being in fact appropriate to X. Suppose that you asked "Is he still feigning?", and I, supposing you to have asked "Is it still raining?", reply, "Yes, it's coming down cats and dogs". I replied to you, even though I did not in fact produce an X-appropriate message, for I did say what I said in order to communicate to you an X-appropriate message.

[18]We have been restricting ourselves to the concept of a *reply* because we are specifically concerned with *dialogue*. But the concept I have been adumbrating is a special form of a more general concept of a *response*, where a response is not necessarily a communicative utterance and not necessarily a response to a communicative utterance. Our discussion could be expanded into a general treatment of divine responses to human actions; but to do so would entail drawing boundaries around the concept involved here, the concept of free, voluntary, intentional responses, a concept which excludes, e.g., "responses" typically dealt with in "stimulus-response" theory, as well as unintentional "responses".

Nevertheless, although in a sense God's utterance could be performed *as a reply* to Moses' question, we still have to say that this fails to be a reply in the full-blooded sense that is required for "genuine dialogue". What, then, is missing? Just this. The X putatively responded to in no way "stands over against" God as something independent of His will, something introduced into the situation by the initiative of another, something to which He has to adjust His conduct, something that requires a special ad hoc "response" on His part. In "replying" to Moses' question God is merely adjusting one decision of His to another. The dynamics of the affair are wholly internal to the divine conation. He is not confronted with something to which He has to *fashion* a response. The supposed response is simply another link in the initial (and in this case final) chain of systematically interrelated decisions. Without an other that is sufficiently outside my control to make its own independent contribution to what is going on, there is nothing for me to reply to.

Thus if the *uttered as a reply* condition is to be sufficient for genuine dialogue, we must specify that the X in question is, to some degree, independent of S's will. This enriched condition constitutes an impassable roadblock for a traditionally prominent form of Christian theology, according to which God is always agent, never patient; always cause, never effect. Since such a theology must endorse omnidetermination, it cannot recognize divine *responses* to human beings, in a full-blooded sense of 'response'. We have already seen that omnidetermination is incompatible with genuine divine-human dialogue from the human side, since it rules out the human being's playing any real role in the proceedings. What we have just seen is that it is equally incompatible from the divine side. It equally prevents God from making the kind of contribution required for genuine dialogue, viz., a genuine response to the contributions of the other party.

Now let us consider the question of whether, and if so how, a timeless deity can utter Y as a reply to X, once we enrich that concept to require that X be, to some degree, independent of God's will. There is no doubt that this additional stipulation poses a problem over and above that posed by the kind of response that is compatible with omnidetermination. With the latter we simply have to think of God as performing one all-inclusive act of will. That will take care of everything: the existence of the temporal world in all its details and the appropriate interlocking of creaturely activity and divine action, with "responses" on each side to action on the other. Since all this is determined by the divine will, the one fell swoop, to adapt Quine's pun, can be a full sweep. Furthermore God's knowledge of His creation can be wholly contained in His knowledge of what He wills. There will be nothing in the former that is not in the latter. On this story there is obviously no need for temporal succession in the divine activity. One creative act of will, together with God's awareness thereof, will be sufficient. But once we allow (or rather once God allows) some creatures to determine some details of their activity, once God refrains from deciding just what actions they perform, the divine activity takes on an additional complexity. It can no longer be confined to a single creative act of will. Even apart from divine *responses* to human actions, if God is to have knowledge of the latter that knowledge will stem from something other than His knowledge of His own will. He must, so to say, "see" what Moses is doing when Moses is doing it. So our problem is this. Can we (or rather can God) cram the initial creative volition, all the awarenesses of what free creatures are doing freely, *and* the responses to these (including adjustments that are made in the overall plan) into the eternal now? Can it embrace all that without spilling over into temporality?[19] We have already noted that the divine response to a free human action (or at least the volition thereto) could be simultaneous with that action; and so they at least are fitted for cohabitation in the eternal now. Moreover if, as I am taking Stump and Kretzmann to have shown, it is possible that God should, without undergoing temporal succession, be all at once aware of everything that happens throughout time, there is no bar to the awareness of each and every free act, along with the responses thereto, occupying the one eternal now. So the question boils down to whether this totality of awarenesses of, and responses to, human free acts, can find a place in the eternal now *along with* the basic creative act of will by which God determines everything that He determines in the world.

Well, why not? If an omnidetermining divine volition can itself be timeless, I cannot see that this additional complexity poses any new bar. Why should it be any more "difficult" to combine all this in the eternal now than simply to combine all the infinite detail of God's creative activity? And in any event, this talk of how difficult it is or how God brings it off is not to be taken seriously. God is omnipotent, and we are in no position to determine "how" He does what He does. If there are

---

[19]Strictly speaking, if created agents do sometimes act in ways not fully determined by God, then more than these actions will fall outside the scope of the initial creative act of will. For these free actions of created agents will themselves affect many subsequent states of affairs in the world; hence none of those states of affairs will be fully determined by God either. Since this further complexity adds no further difficulties about timelessness, I shall, for simplicity of exposition, proceed on the simplifying fiction that it is only free creaturely actions that God fails to uniquely determine.

no logical impossibilities in the supposition, it is within the divine power. And once we fully grasp the point that a timeless deity can be all-at-once simultaneous with every temporal state of affairs, we can see that there is no logical impossibility in God's creating the world, "hearing" Moses ask a question, and answering that question, all in the same timeless *now*.[20]

Thus I conclude that a timeless omniscient God an enter into genuine dialogue with human beings in prayer. But I must also conclude that God has achieved this capacity by forgoing the complete determination of His creation.[21]

V

I had originally intended that the high point of this paper would be an argument for the possibility that God, though not essentially or necessarily temporal, had freely decided to enter into the temporal process Himself, so as to be able to interact with His creatures. This position was to be opposed both to the tradition of Augustine, Anselm, and Aquinas, for whom God is essentially and necessarily timeless, and to process theology, for whom God is essentially and necessarily tem-

[20]The strongest objections to this position I can think of are easily answered. It might be felt, for example, that if two acts of will are simultaneous one cannot be in the light of the fact that p, whereas the other is not. But there are clear counterexamples to this within human volition. I can simultaneously will to scratch my head and to reply to your question, even though the latter but not the former is done in the light of the fact that you asked your question. Various other allegations might be made as to the impossibility of simultaneous realizations of states or activities we are attributing to God, but I cannot see that any such allegations have greater force than the one just considered.

[21]Let me note that when we think of God as timeless we shortcircuit human analogues of the sort I invoked in connection with omnidetermination and omniscience. One might try to argue against the compatibility of timelessness and genuine dialogue by invoking the abnormally prescient human being I introduced in Section III. Such a person can foresee all the responses of his/her partner to anything h/she might say and, being in such a position, could turn the whole affair over to a suitably programmed robot. In that case the hyper-prescient one would lack any real living involvement in the moment-by-moment development of the conversation. Thus it would not be genuine dialogue. And, so the argument goes, don't we have to say the same of a timeless God who does not have to have to wait and see what the human partner will say at a given moment? But the analogy fails at a crucial point. Just because God is timeless, God does not known *in advance* what Moses will do at t_1. This completely subverts the supposed analogy. A timeless God neither can, nor has any occasion to, *pre*-program a robot (*in advance*) and turn the matter over to it. Cannot, because this requires a temporal position. Has no occasion, or need, to, since a timeless God *is* directly involved in the moment-by-moment development of the conversation by virtue of His simultaneity with each moment of the temporal process. This is essentially the same point we made earlier in invoking divine timelessness to resolve the difficulties (for dialogue) presented by divine omniscience.

poral. According to this intermediate position, God is essentially timeless in the sense that, apart from His free choice to the contrary, none of His actions or states would be datable nor would He live through temporal succession. But God has the capacity to freely choose to render His activity, or portions thereof, temporally ordered. And this permits Him to enter into genuine interaction, conversational and otherwise, with temporal creatures. I was going to spring this rabbit out of the hat after arguing that such genuine interaction is impossible for a timeless deity. However in the course of working out the paper I changed my mind on that crucial issue, with the result you have just witnessed. Nevertheless, I still feel that my intermediate position is rather interesting, and worthy of more than the little or no attention it has received thus far. And so I commend it to your attention. In particular I commend it to the attention of those undoubtedly numerous persons who have failed to be convinced by my argument for the compatibility of divine timelessness and genuine divine-human interaction.[22]

[22]This paper was presented at a symposium on prayer at the meeting of the Society of Christian Philosophers held at the 1983 meetings of the Eastern Division of the American Philosophical Association. Fellow symposiasts were Joshua Hoffman and Eleonore Stump. I would like to express appreciation for the comments I received at that meeting.

Divine Foreknowledge
and Alternative Conceptions
of Human Freedom

I

Nelson Pike's important 1965 paper, "Divine Omniscience and Voluntary Action,"[1] presents an interestingly novel version of the old argument from divine foreknowledge to our inability to do (choose) other than what we in fact do.

1. "God existed at T_1" entails "If Jones did X at T_2, God believed at T_1 that Jones would do X at T_2."
2. "God believes X" entails "'X' is true."
3. It is not within one's power at a given time to do something having a description that is logically contradictory.
4. It is not within one's power at a given time to do something that would bring it about that someone who held a certain belief at a time prior to the time in question did not hold that belief at the time prior to the time in question.
5. It is not within one's power at a given time to do something that would bring it about that a person who existed at an earlier time did not exist at that earlier time.
6. If God existed at T_1 and if God believed at T_1 that Jones would do X at T_2, then if it was within Jones's power at T_2 to refrain from doing

From *International Journal for Philosophy of Religion*, 18, no. 1 (1985), 19–32. Copyright © 1956 by Martinus Nijhoff Publishers. Reprinted by permission of Kluwer Academic Publishers.
[1]*Philosophical Review*, 74 (1965), 27–46.

X, then (1) it was within Jones's power at T_2 to do something that would have brought it about that God held a false belief at T_1, or (2) it was within Jones's power at T_2 to do something which would have brought it about that God did not hold the belief He held at T_1, or (3) it was within Jones's power at T_2 to do something that would have brought it about that any person who believed at T_1 that Jones would do X at T_2 (one of whom was, by hypothesis, God) held a false belief and thus was not God—that is, that God (who by hypothesis existed at T_1) did not exist at T_1.

7. Alternative 1 in the consequent of item 6 is false (from 2 and 3).
8. Alternative 2 in the consequent of item 6 is false (from 4).
9. Alternative 3 in the consequent of item 6 is false (from 5).
10. Therefore, if God existed at T_1 and if God believed at T_1 that Jones would do X at T_2, then it was not within Jones's power at T_2 to refrain from doing X (from 6 through 9).
11. Therefore, if God existed at T_1, and if Jones did X at T_2, it was not within Jones's power at T_2 to refrain from doing X (from 1 and 10).[2]

This argument has stimulated a flurry of discussion that shows no signs of abating.[3] But in this literature there is little attempt to spell out the intended sense of such crucial terms as 'power', 'ability', 'could have done otherwise', 'free', and 'voluntary'. And even where some attention is given to these terms there is no recognition that they might be used differently by different parties to the discussion. This is all the more surprising since, in another part of the forest, one finds elaborate analyses of competing senses of these terms. I refer, of course, to the extensive literature on free will. It is high time the fruits of this latter activity were brought to bear on Pike's argument, which, after all, is concerned to show that human actions are not free in some sense, that human beings lack the power, in some sense, to do other than what they do. I will be asking (1) what concepts of power, etc., Pike and other participants in the controversy mean to be using, and (2) how such concepts will have to be construed if their arguments are to be successful, or as successful as possible.

[2]Ibid., pp. 33–34.
[3]In addition to the contributions that will be discussed in this paper, see Marilyn Adams, "Is the Existence of God a Hard Fact?," *Philosophical Review*, 76 (1967), 209–16; Joshua Hoffman, "Pike on Possible Worlds, Divine Foreknowledge, and Human Freedom," *Philosophical Review*, 88 (1979), 433–42; and the latest entry, so far as I know, John Martin Fischer, "Freedom and Foreknowledge," *Philosophical Review*, 92 (1983), 67–79. At a recent Pacific Regional meeting of the Society of Christian Philosophers, Pike presented a discussion of Fischer's paper, which was responded to by Marilyn Adams and Fischer, so that the conferees were treated to hearing Adams on Pike on Fischer on Adams on Pike, and Fischer on Pike on Fischer on Adams on Pike. "Enough!", you may well cry. And yet the beat goes on.

Rather than attempt to follow all the twists and turns in the free will literature, I will focus on the crucial distinction between a "libertarian" and a "compatibilist" understanding of terms like 'within one's power'. I will not attempt a full characterization of either interpretation. Instead I will focus on one basic respect in which they differ, viz., on whether its being within one's power to do A at t requires that it be "really possible" that one do A at t. What is *really possible* at t is what is "left open" by what has happened up to t; it is that the nonoccurrence of which is not necessitated by what has happened up to t. Now there are various ways in which previous states of the world can necessitate, prevent, or leave open a state of affairs. It is the causal way that has dominated the free will discussion. A previous state of affairs, F, *causally* necessitates E at t if the necessitation is by virtue of causal laws.

> I. E is causally necessitated by a previous state of affairs, F = $_{df}$. E is entailed by the conjunction of F and some causal laws, and E is not entailed by either conjunct alone.[4]

And to say that E is *causally possible* is to say that not-E is not causally necessitated by any previous states of affairs.

> II. E is causally possible at t = $_{df}$. There is no state of affairs prior to t, F, such that not-E is entailed by the conjunction of F and some causal laws without being entailed by either conjunct alone.

Being causally ruled out by the past is not the only threat to real possibility. Contemporary thinkers who suppose that God's fore-knowledge rules out human free choice do not typically suppose that divine knowledge causes us to act as we do.[5] They think, rather, that since God is necessarily infallible the fact that God believes at t_1 that Jones will do X at t_2 *by itself* logically entails that Jones will do X at t_2, and hence is, by itself, logically incompatible with Jones's refraining from doing X at t_2. Let's say that a state of affairs is "situationally logically necessitated" when it is entailed by a previous state of affairs alone.

---

[4]This last requirement is designed to prevent causal necessitation from ranging over logical necessitation, in which a previous state of affairs alone entails E.

[5]Some classical theologians, e.g., St. Thomas Aquinas (*Summa Theologiae*, I, Q. 14, art. 8) hold that divine knowledge causes what is known. But Aquinas never had the opportunity of discussing Pike's argument.

III. E is situationally logically necessitated by a previous state of affairs, F, = $_{df}$. E is entailed by F alone.

And let's say that a state of affairs is "situationally logically possible" ('S-logically possible') when its nonoccurrence is not entailed by past facts alone.

IV. E is S-logically possible at t = $_{df}$. There is no state of affairs prior to t, F, such that not-E is entailed by F.

We may think of an event as "really possible" when it is both causally and S-logically possible.

V. E is really possible at t = $_{df}$. There is no state of affairs prior to t, F, such that either (a) not-E is entailed by the conjunction of F and some causal laws without being entailed by either conjunct alone, or (b) not-E is entailed by F alone.

This formulation can be simplified. Clearly if not-E is entailed by the conjunction of F and some causal laws, this covers both the case in which both conjuncts are needed for the entailment and the case in which not-E is entailed by F alone. Hence the following is logically equivalent to V.

VI. E is really possible at t = $_{df}$. There is no state of affairs prior to t, F, such that not-E is entailed by the conjunction of F and some causal laws.

However, IV is more perspicuous in that it brings out the way in which a really possible event escapes being ruled out by the past in both of two ways.

Since the basic claim of the libertarian is that I am not really free to do X at t if doing X is ruled out by what has already happened, she will want to use the broader notion of real possibility for a necessary condition of freedom. She will want to make it a necessary condition of being free to do E (having it within one's power to do E) that E is neither causally nor S-logically necessitated by past events.

Recently, under the influence of William of Ockham, a distinction between "hard" and "soft" facts has been injected into the discussion of these and related issues.[6] Roughly, a dated fact is a "hard" fact about the time in question if it is wholly about that time, if it is completely

---

[6]See, e.g., Marilyn Adams, "Is the Existence of God a Hard Fact?"; John Fischer, "Freedom and Foreknowledge"; Joshua Hoffman and Gary Rosenkrantz, "Hard and Soft Facts," *Philosophical Review*, 93 (1984).

over and done with when that time is over. Otherwise it is a "soft" fact about that time. Thus the fact that I was offered the job at t is a hard fact about t; it embodies only what was going on then and is fully constituted by the state of the world at t. On the other hand, the fact that I was offered the job two weeks before declining it is not a hard fact about t, even if t is when I was offered the job. That fact is not fully constituted until two weeks past t. This distinction is relevant to our account of real possibility in the following way. A soft past fact can entail the occurrence of non-E without thereby preventing E from being really possible. The fact that I was offered the job two weeks before declining it at t entails that I did not accept it at t; but this obviously fails to show that it was not really possible for me to accept the job at t. Of course my not accepting the job at t is entailed by any fact that includes my declining it as a conjunct; but that has no bearing on whether accepting it was a real possibility for me at the moment of choice. Thus III–VI must be understood as restricted to states of affairs that have completely obtained before t, i.e., to *hard* facts about times prior to t.

Some recent thinkers, again following Ockham, have sought to draw the teeth of arguments like Pike's by claiming that a divine belief at t is not a hard fact about t; and hence that the fact that 'God believes at t_1 that Jones will do X at t_2' entails 'Jones will do X at t_2' does not show that Jones's refraining from doing X is not a real possibility for Jones at t_2.[7] If that contention is accepted, Pike's argument never gets out of the starting gate, and the question of the kind of freedom it shows to be impossible does not arise. Since the issue is controversial, I feel free to preserve my problem by simply assuming, for purposes of this discussion, that a divine belief at t_1 is a hard fact about t_1. Setting aside this additional complication will enable us to focus on the differential bearing of the argument on different conceptions of freedom.

Returning to our two senses of 'within one's power', the "compatibilist" interpretation of 'within one's power' was specifically devised to ensure a compatibility of free will and determinism. It does this by adopting the following account of what it is for something to be within an agent's power.

VII. It is within S's power at t to do A = $_{df}$. If S were to will (choose, decide, . . .) at t to do A, S would do A.

---

[7]Alfred J. Freddoso, "Accidental Necessity and Logical Determinism," *Journal of Philosophy*, 80 (May 1983), 257–78; Alvin Plantinga, "On Ockham's Way Out," *Faith and Philosophy*, 2 (July 1986), 235–69.

In other words, its being within S's power to do A at *t* is simply a matter of S's being so constituted, and his situation's being such, that choosing to do A at *t* would have led to A's actually being done at *t*. As far as A is concerned, S's will would have been effective. To have been able to do other than what one actually did, in this sense, is obviously compatible with causal determinism. Even if my choice and action were causally necessitated by antecedent factors, it could still be the case that *if* I had chosen to do otherwise that choice would have been implemented. That counterfactual could be true even if it were causally impossible for me to choose or to do anything else. This is all quite analogous to the following physical analogue. Where only ball A hit ball C at *t*, it could still be true that *if* ball B had hit ball C at *t* instead, C would have moved differently from the way it in fact moved; and this can be true even if all these motions are causally determined.

Thus in the compatibilist's sense of 'A is within one's power' the causal possibility of A is not a necessary condition. And, by the same token, the S-logical possibility of A isn't either. Even if Jones's mowing his lawn logically follows from God's antecedent beliefs, that would seem to be compatible with the claim that *if* Jones *had* decided not to mow his lawn nothing would have prevented that decision from being implemented.[8] Hence we may say that neither form of real possibility is a necessary condition of A's being within one's power in a compatibilist sense of the term.

II

Turning now to the application of this distinction to the debate over foreknowledge and free will, I first want to ask what concept of 'within one's power' Pike was employing. He is not very forthcoming about this. In the original article his focal term was 'voluntary', and about this he says, "Although I do not have an analysis of what it is for an action to be *voluntary*, it seems to me that a situation in which it would be wrong to assign Jones the *ability* or *power* to do *other* than he did would be a situation in which it would also be wrong to speak of his action as voluntary."[9] This makes 'voluntary' depend on 'within one's power', but it gives no hint as to the understanding of the latter. Nor does Pike offer any further clues in his responses to critics.

Faced with this situation we should perhaps follow Wittgenstein's

---

[8]This may be contested. See the next section.
[9]"Divine Omniscience and Voluntary Action," p. 33.

dictum: "If you want to know *what* is proved, look at the proof."[10] In that spirit, let's ask: in what sense of 'within one's power' does Pike's argument show that divine foreknowledge is incompatible with its being in anyone's power to do anything other than what one does? Or, not to take sides between Pike and his critics, in what sense of 'in one's power' is Pike's argument the strongest?

There would seem to be a clear answer to this question. We have distinguished the two concepts in terms of whether its being within one's power to do A requires that one's doing A is really possible. But Pike's argument is naturally read as being designed to show that, given God's forebelief that Jones mows his lawn at t_2, it is *not* really possible that Jones refrain from mowing his lawn at t_2. Underneath all its complexities Pike's argument essentially depends on the thesis that *God's believing at t_1 that Jones will do X at t_2* entails that *Jones will do X at t_2*, and hence that Jones not doing X at t_2 is not really possible. It is because of this entailment that in order for Jones to have the power at t_2 to refrain from doing X he would have to have the power to bring it about that the entailing fact did not occur, either because God did not exist at t_1 ((3) of Pike's step 6) or did not believe at t_1 that Jones would do X at t_2 ((2) of step 6), or would have to have the power to bring it about that the entailment does not hold ((1) of step 6). But if this entailment is the heart of the matter, the argument can be construed as an attempt to show that Jones's refraining at t_2 is not really possible, from which we conclude that it is not within his power to refrain. But we get this last conclusion only on a conception of *within one's power* that, like the libertarian conception, takes real possibility as a necessary condition. On the compatibilist conception the real impossibility of Jones's refraining cuts no ice. Thus it seems that Pike's argument shows, at most, that it is not within Jones' power to refrain from mowing his lawn in a libertarian sense of that term.

This may be contested. It may be claimed that the argument shows that Jones can't refrain even in a compatibilist sense. For if a necessarily infallible deity believes in advance that Jones mows his lawn at t_2, then Jones would do that even if he did decide to refrain. A mere momentary human decision surely wouldn't override eternal divine foreknowledge in the determination of what will happen. Hence if God believes in advance that Jones will do X at t_2, then even if Jones were to decide not to do X he would still do it. And so Pike's argument shows

---

[10]Ludwig Wittgenstein, *Philosophical Grammar* (Berkeley: University of California Press, 1974), p. 369.

that it is not within Jones's power to refrain, even in a compatibilist sense.[11]

Thus we have plausible-looking arguments on both sides. This is not an unusual situation with counterfactuals, which are notoriously slippery customers. If Jones had made a decision different from the one he in fact made, what would have ensued depends on what else would have been different from the actual world. It is clear that there can't be a world different from the actual world only in that Jones decided at t_2 to refrain from doing X. For the actual decision will have resulted from certain causes and will in turn contribute to the causation of subsequent events.[12] Hence if Jones had decided at t_2 to refrain from X the causal influences on his decision-making would have been different; otherwise that decision to refrain would not have been forthcoming. And, in turn, the consequences of the decision to refrain from X will be different from the consequences of a decision to do X. The only alternative to this would be a change in causal laws that would permit this decision to refrain to be inserted into precisely the actual causal context. Hence a world in which Jones decides at t_2 to refrain from doing X will be different in *some* other respects from the actual world. And whether the counterfactual, 'If Jones had decided to refrain from X, he would have refrained from X', is true depends on just what additional differences from the actual world are being presupposed, implied, or allowed for. If we hang onto the actual causal laws and keep the causal context as similar as possible, then the decision to refrain would lead to refraining, and God's forebelief that Jones does X at t_2 would have to be different.[13] On the other hand, if we keep God's actual beliefs unaltered so far as possible then Jones will still do X at t_2, which implies that either some further causal influences on his behavior are different, or that causal laws are not as they are in the actual world. So which is it to be?

I believe that it can be shown fairly easily that as the compatibilist

---

[11]I am indebted to Pike for suggesting this line of argument, though he should not be taken as committed to it.

[12]Since the compatibilist typically assumes causal determinism, we are conducting this discussion on that assumption. If decisions, actions, and so on, are not strictly causally determined, similar points will hold, though the discussion would, perforce, be more complicated.

[13]I am assuming that the actual situation is such that there is nothing to prevent either a decision to do X or a decision to refrain from doing X from being carried out. This is a situation in which human beings often find themselves. If divine foreknowledge were to rule out the power to do other than what one in fact does, it would have to rule it out in this kind of situation.

understands his counterfactual, and as causal counterfactuals like this are commonly understood, the question of whether the proposition is true *is* the question of what would be the case if causal laws and causal factors were as much like the actual world as possible. When we wonder what Jones would have done had he decided differently, or whether that match would have lit if it had been struck, or whether Smith would have fallen from the ledge had the fireman not rescued him, we want to know what further difference this difference would have made, given our actual causal laws, and given the actual situation so far as it is logically compatible with this difference. If we are told that Jones still would have done X, despite the decision to refrain, if his behavior had been under radio control from Mars and the Martians in question had decided that Jones should do X, or if Jones's brain were organized in a quite different way, or if causal laws were quite different, that is all irrelevant to what we are asking. And it is equally clear that this is the way in which the compatibilist understands the counterfactual. For when the compatibilist maintains that, even given causal determinism, Jones *could* have refrained, in the sense that if he *had* decided to refrain he would have done so, what she is concerned to insist on is the point that the actual situation in which Jones found himself is such that a contrary decision, inserted into *that situation,* would give rise to a contrary action. Hence, as the compatibilist understands 'in one's power', divine forebelief that Jones does X at t_2 has no tendency to imply that it is not within Jones's power to refrain from doing X at t_2. The crucial counterfactual will still be true, even though in the counterfactual situation God's belief as to what Jones does at t_2, as well as God's belief as to what Jones decides at t_2, will be different.

It may be useful to look at the matter from another angle. It is often held that when we wonder whether Y would have happened if X had happened, what we want to know is whether Y happens in a situation in which X happens and which is otherwise as similar as possible to the actual situation. In a recently popular possible-worlds formulation, the question is as to whether Y is the case in all the X-worlds (worlds containing X) that are "closest" to the actual world. (For purposes of this highly compressed discussion let's understand 'closeness' as 'similarity'.) Now it may look as if there is a real contest on this point between those who think Pike's argument does apply to freedom in the compatibilist sense (extremists) and those who think that it does not (moderates). For the moderate will say that a Jones-decides-to-refrain world in which causal laws are the same and the causally relevant surroundings of Jones's decision are as much like the actual world as possible (but where God's belief about what Jones does at t_2 is different) is closer to the actual world than a Jones-decides-to-refrain world in which God's belief that Jones does X at t_2 is the same, but there are differences in causal laws or causally relevant factors. And the extremist will make the opposite judgment. This looks like a thorny issue as to which makes the *larger* difference from the actual world: (a) differences in causal laws or causal factors, or (b) differences in God's beliefs. And how do we decide a question like that?

But this appearance of a deep impasse is deceptive. There is really no contest. This can be seen once we set out the differences from the actual world that obtain in the worlds claimed by each side to be closest. The worlds favored by the extremist as closest we will call 'Set I' and the worlds favored by the moderate as closest we will call 'Set II'. Let's begin by enumerating the differences apart from God's beliefs.

Differences from the actual world[14]

Set I	Both	Set II
Some additional causally relevant features of Jones's situation, or some causal laws, to block the implementation of the decision	Jones decision to refrain at t_2, together with whatever changes in the past are required to produce this decision, and some differences that result from the decision.	Jones refrains from doing X at t_2

Intuitively it looks as if Set I worlds are further from the actual world than Set II worlds. But, says the extremist, it only looks that way until we realize that Set II, but not Set I, worlds will also differ from the actual world by the fact that God believes that Jones refrains from doing X at t_2. Hence, at the very least, it is not clear that Set II worlds are closer to the actual world. However, a moment's reflection should assure us that this observation cuts no ice. Just as we have to add to the differences specified above for Set II the additional difference that God believes that Jones refrains from doing X at t_2, so we have to add to the differences specified above for Set I the additional difference that God believes that all these differences obtain. Thus bringing in differences in God's beliefs *could not* affect a previously existing difference in closeness. If world A is closer to the actual world than world B on all counts other than God's beliefs, then it can't be further away with God's beliefs taken into account. For since the beliefs of an omniscient and infallible deity will exactly mirror what is the case, the dif-

---

[14]This is oversimplified a bit. For example, there may well be other differences in Set II that intervene between decision and execution. Moreover, each of the differences specified will ramify causally both backwards and forwards in time.

ferences introduced by God's beliefs will exactly mirror differences in other respects. And so if Set II worlds have the edge in closeness with God's beliefs left out, they will necessarily retain that edge with God's beliefs taken into account.

III

On the basis of all this I will take it that Pike's argument is designed to show that it is not within anyone's power to do otherwise in a libertarian sense of that term. In what sense of the term are his critics contesting this?

The earliest published criticism of Pike's 1965 article was John Turk Saunders' "Of God and Freedom".[15] In considering the three alternatives embedded in step 6 of Pike's argument, Saunders concedes that Jones cannot have the first power, but he finds no bar to attributing the second or third. However, he first reformulates these powers, since he takes Pike to have been construing them as powers to causally influence the past.

> . . . it is contradictory to speak of a later situation causing an earlier situation, and consequently, it is contradictory to speak of its being in Jones's power to do something at t_2 which causes God not to exist, or not to have a certain belief, at t_1. But, while such powers are contradictory, there is no good reason to think that Jones must possess such powers if he has the power to refrain from X at t_2. The power to refrain from X at t_2 is, indeed, the power so to act at t_2 that either God does not exist at t_1 or else God does not at t_1 believe that Jones will do X at t_2. But Jones's so acting at t_2 would not bring it about that God does not exist at t_1, or that God does not hold a certain belief at t_1, any more than Jones's doing X at t_2 brings it about that God believes, at t_1, that Jones will do X at t_2. Jones's power so to act at t_2 is simply his power to perform an act such that if that act were performed, then certain earlier situations would be different from what in fact they are.[16]

Backwards causation turns out to be a nonissue however, since in his reply to Saunders Pike disavows any causal interpretation of 'bring it about' and acknowledges that Saunders' formulations might well do a better job of expressing his intent.[17]

---

[15]*Philosophical Review*, 75 (1966), 219–25.
[16]Ibid., p. 220.
[17]"Of God and Freedom: A Rejoinder," *Philosophical Review*, 75 (1966), 371.

Thus, it looks as if there is a head-on confrontation between Pike and Saunders with respect to the possibility that Jones has the second and third powers mentioned in step 6. But this is so only if they are using 'within one's power' in the same sense. And this is definitely not the case, for it is clear from Saunders' article that he understands such terms in a compatibilist way.

> ... suppose that at t_1 I decide to skip at t_2 rather than run at t_2, that conditions are "normal" at t_1 and t_2 (I have not been hypnotized, drugged, threatened, manhandled, and so forth), and that I have the ability (knowhow) both to skip and to run. Suppose, too, that the world happens to be governed by empirical laws such that if ever a man in my particular circumstances were to make a decision of this kind, then he would not change his mind and do something else but would follow through upon his decision: suppose, that is, that, under the circumstances which prevail at t_1, my decision is empirically sufficient for my skipping at t_2. Clearly, it is in my power to run at t_2, since I know how to do so and the conditions for the exercise of this ability are normal. If I were to exercise this power then I would not, at t_1, have decided to skip at t_2, or else the circumstances at t_1 would have been different.[18]

> ... although it (logically) cannot be both that my decision, under the circumstances, is empirically sufficient for my doing what I decide to do and also that I change my mind and do not do it, it does not follow that it is not in my power to change my mind and run instead. It follows only that I do not change my mind and run instead: for the fact that I know how to run, together with the fact that it is my own decision, under normal conditions, which leads me to persevere in my decision and to skip rather than to run, logically guarantees that I skip of my own free will and, accordingly, that it is in my power to change my mind and run. To maintain the contrary would be to suppose that some sort of indeterminism is essential to human freedom, on grounds that if ever, under normal conditions, my own decision is empirically sufficient for my doing what I do, then my own decision compels me to do what I do.[19]

Saunders plainly does not take the real possibility of S's doing A at t to be a necessary condition of its being within S's power to do A at t. He insists that even if antecedent events are causally sufficient for my doing B at t it could still be within my power to do A at t instead, and, indeed, that this will be within my power, provided I know how to do A, conditions are normal, and nothing is preventing whatever choice I

---

[18]"Of God and Freedom," p. 221.
[19]Ibid., p. 222.

make between A and B from issuing in action. This is obviously compatibilism; we even have the standard compatibilist line that to require indeterminism for freedom is to confuse causation with compulsion.

Thus Saunders and Pike are arguing past each other. The conclusion of Pike's argument is to be construed, as we have seen, as the claim that it is not within Jones's power at t_2 to refrain from doing X in a libertarian sense of 'within one's power'. Whereas Saunders holds that it is often within our power to do other than what we actually do in a compatibilist sense of 'within one's power'. They are simply not making incompatible claims.

IV

The other exchange I wish to examine is that between Pike and Alvin Plantinga. In *God, Freedom, and Evil*[20] Plantinga contends, like Saunders, that the powers Jones must have in order to be able to refrain are not, when properly understood, impossible at all. From now on let's concentrate on Pike's (2), the power, as Pike originally put it, to bring it about that God did not hold the belief He held at t_1.[21] In working toward his own version of this power Plantinga does not, like Saunders, first set aside a backwards causation interpretation. Instead he first considers the following version.

> It was within Jones' power, at T_2, to do something such that if he had done it, then at T_1 God would have held a certain belief and also *not* held that belief.[22]

Quite sensibly rejecting the supposition that Jones has any such power as this, Plantinga proposes instead the following as quite sufficient for Jones's having the power at t_2 to refrain from doing X.

> It was within Jones' power at T_2 to do something such that if he had done it, then God would not have held a belief that in fact he did hold.[23]

Let's call the power so specified, 'P'. The attribution of P, Plantinga

[20]Grand Rapids, Mich.: Eerdmans, 1974.
[21]I do so partly for the sake of greater focus in the discussion, and partly because more recent controversy over Pike's argument has centered around this part of the problem.
[22]*God, Freedom, and Evil*, p. 71.
[23]Ibid.

says, would be "perfectly innocent". Note that this is substantially equivalent to Saunders' formulation.

We have seen that Saunders is a card-carrying compatibilist. This enables us to understand how he can regard P as "innocent". For, as we have seen, even if a necessarily infallible God believed at t_1 that Jones would do X at t_2, it could still be true that Jones could have refrained from doing X at t_2, in the sense that *if* he had decided to refrain nothing would have prevented the implementation of that decision. Hence in *that* sense he could, given God's antecedent infallible belief that he would do X, have the power so to act that one of God's antecedent beliefs would have been other than it was in fact. But how can Plantinga regard the attribution as innocent? It can't be for the same reason. Plantinga has made it abundantly clear that he takes what I have been calling the "real possibility" of S's doing A to be a necessary condition of its being within S's power to do A, and the real possibility of both doing A and refraining from doing A to be a necessary condition of S's freely doing A, or freely refraining from doing A.

> If a person is free with respect to a given action, then he is free to perform that action and free to refrain from performing it; no antecedent conditions and/or causal laws determine that he will perform the action, or that he won't. It is within his power, at the time in question, to take or perform the action and within his power to refrain from it.[24]

But if Jones's having a power to do A at t_2 requires that "no antecedent conditions and/or causal laws" determine that Jones does not do A at t_2, how can Jones have power P? For clearly *God believes that p at t_1* entails *Jones does not do something at t_2 such that if he had done it God would not have believed that p at t_1*. And so if divine beliefs are "antecedent conditions" in the relevant sense, i.e., hard facts about the time at which a given such belief is held,[25] then Plantinga's condition for something's being within a person's power is not met by Jones and power P. Hence Plantinga, and anyone else who takes real possibility as a necessary condition for something's being within one's power, cannot regard the attribution of P to Jones as "innocent", at least not without denying that divine beliefs are "hard facts".

To support this verdict I will look at the way Plantinga defends his "innocence" claim. As a preliminary, let's specify the proposition Plantinga numbers (51).

---

[24]Ibid., p. 29.
[25]Plantinga does not question the "hardness" of divine beliefs in *God, Freedom, and Evil*.

(51) God existed at T_1, and God believed at T_1 that Jones would do X at T_2, and it was within Jones' power to refrain from doing X at T_2.[26]

Now the defense:

For suppose again that (51) is true, and consider a world W in which Jones refrains from doing X. If God is essentially omniscient, then in this world W He is omniscient and hence does not believe at T_1 that Jones will do X at T_2. So what follows from (51) is the harmless assertion that it was within Jones' power to do something such that if he had done it, then God would not have held a belief that in fact (in the actual world) He did hold.[27]

We can see that there is something wrong with a libertarian's taking this line when we reflect that just the same case could be made for holding that its being within Jones's power to refrain from doing X at t_2 is compatible with *Jones's doing X at t_2* being causally determined. Here is that parallel case. Instead of (51) we will have its analogue for causal determinism.

(51A) Causal factors obtained prior to t_2 that determined Jones to do X at t_2, and it was within Jones's power to refrain from doing X at t_2.

Suppose that (51A) is true, and consider a world W in which Jones refrains from doing X. If causal determinism holds in this world W then either causal laws in W are different from what they are in the actual world or some of the causal factors that affect what Jones does at t_2 are different from what we have in the actual world. So what follows from (51A) is the harmless assertion that it was within Jones's power to do something such that if he had done it, then (assuming causal determinism still holds) either causal laws or causal factors would have been different from what they are in the actual world.

This is at least as strong as the case for the compatibility of divine foreknowledge of Jones's doing X, and Jones's power to refrain. If Jones can have it within his power to do something such that if he had done it then what God believed prior to that time would have been somewhat different, then surely Jones can have it within his power to do something such that if he had done it causal factors or causal laws

[26]Ibid., p. 69.
[27]Ibid., p. 71.

would have been somewhat different.[28] Thus if Plantinga were in a position to argue as he does for the compatibility of *Jones's being able to do otherwise* with divine foreknowledge, he would equally be in a position to argue for the compatibility of *Jones's being able to do otherwise* with causal determinism. And that is just to say, once more, that Plantinga's argument goes through only on a compatibilist conception of 'within one's power'. It is not surprising, then, that in "On Ockham's Way Out" Plantinga finds a different way to oppose Pike's argument—by arguing that the beliefs of a necessarily infallible being at *t* are not hard facts about *t*.

V

The moral of all this is a simple but important one. If we are to consider attempts to show that it is within no one's power to do other than what one does, we had better attend to the variant possibilities for understanding 'within one's power', and we had better make explicit how it is being understood in a particular context. Else we run the risk of arguing to no purpose.[29]

[28]There are two significant differences between the two cases. First, Plantinga takes it that God necessarily exists; the nonexistence of God in W does not constitute a possible difference between W and the actual world. Hence the nonexistence of God is not one of the ways in which W could accommodate Jones's refraining from X at t_2. Whereas since causal determinism fails to hold in every possible world, its absence in W is one of the ways in which W could accommodate Jones's refraining from X at t_2. Second, even if determinism holds in W, the causal laws that hold there might be different in such a way as to permit Jones's refraining from X in the face of the same causal factors. But the theological analogue to the specific content of causal laws, viz., the infallibility of God, is taken to be necessary and so not to vary across possible worlds. Note that these two differences do nothing to shake the point that if Jones has the power to refrain from what is entailed by past facts he also has the power to refrain from what is causally necessitated by past facts. On the contrary, the two differences mean that there is even more room for variations across possible worlds in what *causally* determines what actually happens than there is with respect to what *theologically* determines what actually happens.

[29]I have greatly profited from discussing the issues of this paper with Jonathan Bennett, Nelson Pike, Alvin Plantinga, and Peter van Inwagen.

Does God Have Beliefs?

Beliefs are freely attributed to God nowadays in Anglo-American philosophical theology.[1] This practice undoubtedly reflects the twentieth-century popularity of the view that knowledge consists of true justified belief (perhaps with some additional component). After all, no one supposes that God has beliefs in addition to, or instead of, knowledge. The connection is frequently made explicit.[2] If knowledge is true justified belief, then whatever God knows He believes. It would seem that much recent talk of divine beliefs stems from Nelson Pike's widely discussed article, "Divine Omniscience and Voluntary Action".[3] In this essay Pike develops a version of the classic argument for the incompatibility of divine foreknowledge and free will in terms of divine forebelief. He introduces this shift by premising that 'A knows X' entails 'A believes X'.[4] As a result of all this, philosophers have increasingly been using the concept of belief in defining 'omniscience'.

> . . . a being B is omniscient if and only if *for every true proposition p, B knows p; and for every false proposition q, B does not believe q.*[5]

From *Religious Studies*, 22 (1987), 287–306. Reprinted by permission of Cambridge University Press.

[1]See, e.g., R. G. Swinburne, *The Coherence of Theism* (Oxford: Clarendon Press, 1977); Anthony Kenny, *The God of the Philosophers* (Oxford: Clarendon Press, 1979); Alvin Plantinga, *God, Freedom, and Evil* (Grand Rapids, Mich.: Eerdmans, 1974).

[2]Stephen T. Davis, *Logic and the Nature of God* (Grand Rapids, Mich.: Eerdmans, 1983), p. 26; Swinburne, p. 169.

[3]*Philosophical Review*, 74 (January 1965), 27–46. All of the books I have cited contain discussions of Pike's article.

[4]Ibid., p. 28.

[5]Davis, p. 26. See also Plantinga, p. 68.

Indeed, in a later essay Pike goes so far as to define omniscience solely in terms of belief.

> A being counts as omniscient just in case (1) that being believes all true propositions; and (2) that being believes no propositions that are false.[6]

Pike neglects to tell us what has happened to the other components of knowledge.

In this essay I shall present reasons for taking this practice of attributing beliefs to God to be misguided. Since, as just noted, no one thinks of God as having beliefs over and above His knowledge, the issue as to whether God has beliefs boils down to the question of whether beliefs are constituents of divine knowledge. I shall argue that they are not, whichever position we take on a fundamental issue concerning divine knowledge. That issue concerns whether divine knowledge is properly represented as "propositional" in the sense that it is made up of cases of *knowledge that p,* where what replaces '*p*' in each case is some declarative sentence that expresses a proposition. God is often spoken of as knowing *that so-and-so,* as knowing that the Israelites are worshiping idols, as knowing that Adam will sin, and so on. Unless such talk is accompanied by a codicil to the effect that it does not accurately represent the way it truly is with divine knowledge, it represents God's knowledge as "propositional" in character. Some thinkers, by contrast, have maintained that God's knowledge is not broken up into proposition-sized bits in this way, but rather constitutes a seamless whole, an undifferentiated intuition of all there is. In this essay I will not try to decide between these positions. Instead I will argue that on neither position is God properly thought of as having beliefs. I offer the reader a choice as to whether divine knowledge is propositional. Whichever way she will have it, divine beliefs must go.

I

First consider the position that God's knowledge is not propositional. St. Thomas Aquinas provides a paradigmatic exposition of this view. According to Aquinas, God is pure act and absolutely simple. Hence there is no real distinction in God between his knowledge and its object. Thus what God knows is simply His knowledge, which itself is

---

6"Divine Foreknowledge, Human Freedom and Possible Worlds," *Philosophical Review,* 86 (April 1977), 209.

not really distinct from Himself.[7] This is not incompatible with God's knowing everything. Since the divine essence contains the likenesses of all things, God, in knowing Himself perfectly, thereby knows everything.[8] Now since God is absolutely simple His knowledge cannot involve any diversity. Of course what God knows in creation is diverse, but this diversity is not paralleled in His knowledge of it. Therefore "God does not understand by composing and dividing".[9] His knowledge does not involve the complexity involved in propositional structure any more than it involves any other kind of complexity. God does not mentally distinguish subject and predicate and then unite them by a copula. He does not analyze reality into various separate facts, each of which is itself internally complex, and then organize them into a system.

> . . . He knows each thing by simple intelligence, by understanding the essence of each thing; as if we, by the very fact that we understand what man is, were to understand all that can be predicated of man. This, however, does not happen in the case of our intellect, which proceeds from one thing to another, since the intelligible species represents one thing in such a way as not to represent another. Hence, when we understand what man is, we do not forthwith understand other things which belong to him, but we understand them one by one, according to a certain succession. On this account, the things we understand as separated we must reduce to one by way of composition or division, by forming an enunciation [proposition]. Now the species of the divine intellect, which is God's essence, suffices to manifest all things. Hence, by understanding His essence, God knows the essences of all things, and also whatever can be added to them.[10]

But although God's knowledge, in itself, consists wholly of His simple intuition of His own essence, nevertheless He does not thereby miss anything, including whatever can be "enunciated", i.e., formulated in propositions.

> Now just as He knows material things immaterially, and composite things simply, so likewise He knows what can be enunciated, not after its manner, as if in His intellect there were composition or division of enuncia-

---

[7]*Summa Contra Gentiles*, I, 48. *Summa Theologiae*, Ia, Q. 14, art. 2.

[8]*Summa Contra Gentiles*, I, 51–53. *Summa Theologiae*, Ia, Q. 14, arts. 5, 6.

[9]*Summa Contra Gentiles*, I, 58.

[10]*Summa Theologiae*, Ia, Q. 14, art. 14, trans. Laurence Shapcote, O.P., ed., Anton C. Pegis. *The Basic Writings of Saint Thomas Aquinas*, vol. 1 (New York: Random House, 1945), p. 158.

tions, but He knows each thing by simple intelligence, by understanding the essence of each thing. . . .[11]

So although it is not strictly accurate to say that God knows *that Detroit won the 1984 World Series,* that does not imply that God is missing something cognitively, that God fails to make effective noetic contact with some aspect of reality, perhaps through lack of interest in baseball. He is in no state that embodies the complexity of the proposition that Detroit won the 1984 World Series. Nevertheless whatever is knowable in this fact, along with all else, is somehow contained in His simple intuition of His own essence.

No doubt, we are quite unable to envisage just *how* the full extent of reality can be known by, or in, God's intuition of His essence. And it is not just that we cannot work through all the details; it is not that we get stuck only on particularly tough cases like counterfactuals or modal facts. We cannot even make a start at seeing how it is brought off. We do not have any real understanding of how so simple a state of affairs as that *this rose is red* could be known by a subject without that subject's cognitive state somehow reflecting the complexity of that fact. Hence when we have occasion to speak of God's knowledge we are forced to represent it on the model of human knowledge, and speak of God as knowing, e.g., *that the Israelites were being held in slavery in Egypt,* even if we hold that this is not how God's knowledge is in itself. Aquinas would not dispute this. He would be quick to acknowledge, indeed to insist, that we have no real *understanding* of what God is like, or of what it would be like to be God. We can know *that* the divine knowledge is in accordance with the above characterization. But we cannot grasp the way in which a knowledge of that sort could embrace all things. Aquinas would take this not as a defect of his account but as a recommendation. Why should we expect to attain any concrete understanding of the way God's knowledge works?

Without in any way wishing to deny our severe limitations in this regard, I suggest that we might make progress in getting some sense of what nonpropositional divine knowledge might be like, by switching from the Thomistic view that God knows the world through knowing His own essence to the idea that God directly intuits the world. In that case we might think of divine knowledge as like our initial visual perception of a scene, where we have not yet begun the job of extracting separately statable facts, rather than like our propositional perceptual knowledge of the fact that the table is darker than the chair. To be

[11]Ibid.

sure, it is controversial whether adult human percipients enjoy any perceptual awareness of the physical environment that is wholly free from propositional structuring. It has been widely maintained that I cannot see anything without taking it *as* something, e.g., as a house with trees in the background, even if I do not consciously put this to myself in so many words. But even if this is so, we can still distinguish, within a particular complex of perceptual experience, an aspect of sheer givenness or sheer awareness of something, from the judgmental activity of taking this given as such and such. It might further be speculated that in early stages of individual psychological development, and in relatively unorganized psychological conditions, as when just waking up, we have the bare awareness element without the propositional structuring. Considerations like this may give us some sense of what a purely nonpropositional knowledge would be like.

To be sure, this model suffers from the disability that it is a poorer, not a richer cognitive state than the propositional knowledge into which it develops. Whereas God's simple awareness of His essence is supposed to be richer in cognitive value than any possible propositional knowledge. This suggests that we might turn to F. H. Bradley's portrayal of the human cognitive condition. In a highly truncated version it goes something like this. At the base of our cognition is a condition of pure immediacy, a state of pure "feeling" in which there is no distinction of any kind between subject and object, or between different objects of knowledge. This condition scores high on unity and felt oneness with the object, but it scores very low on every other relevant dimension, including comprehensiveness, articulation, and understanding. In our drive to achieve these goals we shatter this primeval unity and build up ever more complex systems of propositional knowledge. But no matter how elaborate these become, and no matter how much we achieve in the way of logically articulated systems of explanation, we can never, by this route, reinstate that original condition of felt unity and immediacy; as a result, discursive thought will never be wholly satisfactory. All the relevant desiderata can be combined only by a "higher immediacy" that includes all the richness and articulation of the discursive stage in a unity that is as tight and satisfying as the initial stage. This is the ideal, the ultimate goal of thought, one which Bradley thought of as actually realized, not in any human being or other finite subject, but in the Absolute.[12] Strangely enough, this bit of British Hegelianism serves rather well as a model for the Thomistic conception of divine knowledge and of the way in which it compares with human

[12]*Appearance and Reality*, 2d ed. (Oxford: Clarendon Press, 1987), chaps. XIV, XV, XIX, XXI.

knowledge. Bradley too would recognize that we are incapable of forming any concrete idea of what this higher immediacy is like. We can
draw up its specifications only in the most general and abstract of
terms. We can say what it must contain, but we cannot see how.

My task in this essay is not to recommend the Thomistic conception
of divine knowledge, but only to lay it on the table and consider what
implications it has for the question of whether God has beliefs. Nevertheless, I will just briefly consider how it might be supported. For
Aquinas it is an immediate consequence of the doctrine of divine simplicity. Since propositional structure involves complexity, it cannot be
involved in the way God knows.[13] But the Thomistic doctrine of simplicity is a lot to swallow. Is there any more modest way of supporting
the nonpropositional view? Here is such a way. It seems plausible to
suppose that the propositional character of human knowledge stems
from our limitations. Why is our knowledge parceled out in separate
facts? For two reasons. First, we cannot grasp any concrete whole in its
full concreteness; at most we cognize certain abstract features thereof,
which we proceed to formulate in distinct propositions. Second, we
need to isolate separate propositions in order to relate them logically,
so as to be able to extend our knowledge inferentially. Both these
reasons are lacking in the divine case. God can surely grasp any concrete whole fully, not just partial aspects thereof. And God has no need
to extend His knowledge, inferentially or otherwise, since it is necessarily complete anyway. Hence there would be no point in God's carv-
ing up His intuition of reality into separate propositions. We have to
represent divine knowledge as the knowledge of this or that particular
fact; but this is only one of the ways in which we are forced to think of
God's nature and doings in terms of our own imperfect approxima-
tions thereto.

Now we can turn to the implications of the nonpropositional view for
the issue of divine beliefs. The matter can be dealt with summarily.
Whatever else a belief may be, it is obviously a *propositional* attitude, a
psychological state that involves the structural complexity of some
proposition. We have no inkling of how some psychological state could
be a belief without being a belief that *p,* where '*p*' stands for a sentence
that expresses a proposition. Hence a being whose knowledge involves
no propositional structure or complexity has no beliefs as part of its
knowledge. On any nonpropositional conception of divine knowledge
there can be no case for supposing that God's knowledge involves
beliefs.

---

[13]*Summa Contra Gentiles,* I, 58; *Summa Theologiae,* Ia, Q. 14, art. 14.

II

Now let us consider the more commonsensical view that God's knowledge is propositional, that it is correctly represented as made up of components, each of which is a knowledge that *p*, and consider whether this knowledge involves beliefs. If divine propositional knowledge conforms to any kind of "true belief + . . ." conception of knowledge—true *justified* belief, true *reliably formed* belief (perhaps with extra conditions to deal with Gettier problems)—then in knowing that *p* He will ipso facto believe that *p*. But that is just the question. Is His knowledge correctly thought of as true belief + . . . ? I shall argue that it is not.

First I want to foreswear a cheap way of winning a victory: by taking belief to be exclusive of knowledge, by conceptual necessity. It is sometimes supposed that part of what one is saying in saying 'S believes that *p*' is that S does not know that *p*. This is suggested by dialogues like the following:

A (calling from the second floor). What's that noise in the kitchen?

B (from the kitchen). I believe that the faucet is leaking.

A. You *believe* it's leaking? Can't you see whether it is or not?

A seems to be taking B's statement that she believes that *p* to imply that she does not know that *p*. And there is no doubt but that 'believe' is often used contrastively with 'know'. Clearly, if 'does not know that *p*' is part of the meaning of 'believes that *p*', then God has no beliefs; for God will never be in the position of having a belief that does not count as knowledge.[14]

However, it is not necessary to admit that 'does not know' is part of what is meant by 'believes'. We can explain dialogues like the above by a Gricean "conversational rule", according to which one is not to make a weaker statement than one is in a position to make, where the context would make the stronger statement relevant. Where knowledge is relevant and I say 'I believe that *p*' I thereby suggest that I do not know that *p*, not because 'not knowing' is part of what is meant by 'believing', but because if I do know I am violating the conversational rule in merely saying that I believe. But whether or not that is the correct explanation, and whether or not there is a familiar sense of 'believe' in which belief semantically excludes knowledge, it remains true that philosophers

---

[14]Note that this is an argument against construing *any* knowledge, not just God's knowledge as true belief +. . . . However, though it is an argument against that construal of human *knowledge*, it is not an argument against the existence of human beliefs; for we, unlike God, can and do believe something without knowing it.

typically mean to be using 'believe' in a more neutral sense in which a belief may or may not count as knowledge. Without attempting anything like an analysis of such a sense, we may characterize it as follows. To believe that p, in this wide neutral sense, is to "accept" the proposition that p, where the acceptance need not be a full-dress, conscious proceeding. Such acceptance is typically manifested in, e.g., being disposed to assert that p when the occasion arises and being disposed to act as if it is true that p. I shall take it that there is such a neutral sense, and that those who speak of God's beliefs are employing that sense. Hence I am blocked from taking this shortcut to my conclusion.

The next shortest argument for my conclusion runs as follows. Even if we understand 'believe' in such a way that a belief may count as knowledge, still the point of attributing beliefs to a subject is that some of the propositional "acceptances" or "assents" of the subject *may* not qualify as knowledge. The concept of belief has a place in our conceptual scheme just because human beings sometimes take it that p without really knowing that p, either because it is false that p or because other conditions of knowledge are not satisfied. A human being, S, can be, and often is, in a state that is like knowledge in that S has a positive attitude toward a proposition, p (has a sense of conviction with respect to p, is disposed to assert that p, is disposed to act as if p is true), but nevertheless fails to know that p. Thus we need a term for this imperfect approximation to knowledge, and 'believe' fits the bill. Now consider a subject that never "accepts" a proposition without knowing it to be true; 'believe' would have no application to such a subject, since the whole point of attributing the term would have evaporated. This is still more the case if there is no *possibility* of this subject's failing to know what it accepts. But God, Who is necessarily omniscient, is precisely such a subject. To accept a proposition without knowing it to be true, would be a cognitive imperfection and so not attributable to God. Therefore the distinction between belief and knowledge has no relevance to God, and it cannot be correct to think of God as believing that Jones will mow his lawn three weeks later.

But this line of argument may well be contested. Although we do not have the same reasons for using 'believe' with respect to God that we have with respect to human beings, that does not show that God does not have beliefs. After all, the conditions under which there is a point in saying that p often diverge from the conditions under which it is true that p. There may well be no point in my going around saying to people 'I exist', but it is true nonetheless. Where it is perfectly obvious to all concerned that I see you there is no point in my saying 'I see you', but still it is true that I see you. Here is a closer analogue. The point of distinguishing one's purposes or intentions from what one actually does is that (1) sometimes one fails to achieve the purposes for which one does what one does, and (2) sometimes one fails to act on one's intentions through sloth, fear, or weakness of will. Now God never fails to accomplish what he sets out to do, nor does He ever swerve from the carrying out of His intentions. Does it follow that He has no purposes, that He never does A in order to carry out His purpose to achieve E? Hardly. Even if God is not subject to gaps between purpose and fulfillment, it can still be true that, e.g., God brought about the downfall of Jerusalem in order to carry out His purpose of punishing the Judaeans for their sins.

Thus, even if the divine case does not exhibit the same kind of contrast between belief and knowledge that we have in the human case, it does not follow that God does not have beliefs as components of His knowledge. We must dig deeper.

We might conduct a frontal assault on the application of the "true belief + . . ." conception of knowledge to God by considering what must be added to true belief to make knowledge and then arguing that this cannot be attributed to God. To carry this out we would have to survey all the plausible candidates for these extra conditions, and show the inapplicability to God in each case. Consider, for example, the idea that one thing that must be added to true belief to make knowledge is *justification* of the belief in a deontological sense of 'justification'. In this sense to say that one is justified in believing that p is to say that one has not violated any of one's intellectual obligations in believing that p. One is in no way subject to blame for having that belief; one is within one's rights in so believing.[15] We might then seek to show that the concept of intellectual obligations does not apply to God. Such an argument might appeal, e.g., to the principle that a being is subject to obligations only if principles of obligations can play a governing or directive role with respect to that being.[16] And this is possible only if that being has, or might have, some tendency to act in violation of those principles. But God, being necessarily perfectly good, could have no tendency to act in violation of principles of obligation. Hence God cannot be thought of as subject to obligations.

However, I do not regard this as a promising way to establish that God's knowledge is not true belief +. . . . First, and most important, it would require us to survey all sufficiently plausible candidates for such

---

[15]See my "Concepts of Epistemic Justification," *The Monist,* 67 (1 January 1985), 57–89, and various references given there for an account of this and other concepts of justification.

[16]See Essay 12.

conditions; and it is not at all clear just what and how many items should be put on such a list. Second, it may not be possible to show, for each such plausible candidate, that it could not be attributed to God. Hence I will employ a more positive approach. I will contend that there is another construal of divine knowledge that is superior to any true belief + . . . construal.

My candidate for this superior construal is the traditionally important "intuitive" conception of knowledge, as I shall call it. This is the view that knowledge of a fact is simply the immediate awareness of that fact. In H. H. Price's felicitous formulation, knowledge "is simply the situation in which some entity or some fact is directly present to consciousness".[17] Despite the curious conviction of many contemporary Anglo-American epistemologists that the true-justified-belief conception of knowledge is "the traditional conception", the intuitive conception has been much more prominent historically. It was certainly the dominant conception in the seventeenth and eighteenth centuries, appearing in such guises as Descartes' conception of clear and distinct perception and Locke's definition of knowledge as the perception of the agreement and disagreement of ideas.[18] On this view, knowledge is quite a different psychological state from belief. Obviously I can believe that p without its being the case that p. But I cannot be in the state of knowledge that p, so construed, without its being the case that p; for that state just consists of the presence of that fact to my consciousness; without that fact there could be no such state. Knowledge is not a state that could be just what it is intrinsically without the actual existence of the object; it has no intrinsic character over and above the presence of that object to consciousness. Thus knowledge, on this construal, is infallible in a strong sense; its inherent nature guarantees the reality of the object. Whereas a belief that p is, by its very nature, a state that can be just what it is whether or not there is any such fact that p.[19] Intuitive theorists differ as to whether I can also believe (judge) that p at the same moment that I know that p; but they are united in affirming that

[17]"Some Considerations about Belief," *Proceedings of the Aristotelian Society*, 35 (1934–35), 229. Price's formulation is designed to handle knowledge of particulars as well as knowledge of facts, but we shall be concerned only with the latter.

[18]For the latter, see *Essay Concerning Human Understanding*, bk. IV, chap. 1, section 2.

[19]We have to make an exception to this generalization for beliefs with certain special contents. For example, my belief that I believe something could not be the state it is (a belief of mine) unless its propositional object were true. (I owe this point to Robert Audi.) But this is because of the special character of that propositional object. It is still the case that, unlike knowledge on the intuitive conception, there is nothing about belief as such that prevents a belief from being the psychological state it is even if its propositional object is false.

knowledge is a different kind of psychological state from belief (judgment); it is not a belief that meets certain further conditions.[20]

Many philosophers, especially since Hegel, have argued that there can be no immediate awareness of facts that is free of any belief or judgmental element. They have typically held that the supposition of such an awareness is confused, incoherent, or worse.[21] The usual line of argument goes something like this. The alleged immediate awareness of the fact that X is P will be, or at least involve, being aware of X *as* P. But I can be aware of X as having any property, P, only by applying the concept of P to X, only by *taking* X to be P. It is not as if the *fact that* X is P is just sitting out there awaiting my notice, the way in which X may be. To achieve any sort of cognition *that* something is of a certain sort, I must utilize my concept of that sort; I must utilize my capacity to class things as being of that sort. But to apply the concept of P to X, to take X to be P, is just to form the judgment or belief that X is P.[22] Hence the immediate awareness of a fact turns out to contain a belief or judgment as an essential component. It *is* just a belief of a special sort, one that structures or organizes awareness in a certain way. Hence the idea that knowledge of *p* can be immediate awareness of *p*, rather than a true belief that *p* that satisfies certain further conditions, is vitiated from the start. Its favored candidate inevitably carries along with it that which it was designed to supplant.

Various questions might be raised about these claims, even as applied to the human condition; but on the whole I find the argument sound in that application, and so I shall refrain from quibbles. Instead I shall contend that even if belief-free immediate awareness of a fact is not a possibility for us, it does not follow that God is similarly limited. To make this point I need not challenge the application to God of the thesis that to be aware of the fact that X is P one must possess and deploy the concept of P, must be utilizing one's capacity to recognize something as being P. No doubt, what it is for God to possess and to

---

[20]See Price, p. 229. In Descartes' *Méditation IV* it is the faculty of the understanding that achieves knowledge; the will is then faced with the task of forming judgments or beliefs in accordance with that. See also Locke, bk. iv, chaps. 5 and 14. In chapter 14 Locke clearly affirms that one judges that *p* only where one does not know that *p*; but in chapter 5 he seems to hold that one may also judge that *p* where one does know that *p*, though the knowledge is still distinct from the judgment.

[21]See, e.g., F. H. Bradley, *The Principles of Logic* (London: Oxford University Press, 1922), bk. ii, pt. i, chap. vi; Brand Blanshard, *The Nature of Thought* (London: George Allen & Unwin, 1939) chaps. i, ii, xxv; Wilfrid Sellars, "Empiricism and the Philosophy of Mind," in *Science, Perception, and Reality* (London: Routledge & Kegan Paul, 1963), pp. 127–96; Michael Williams, *Groundless Belief* (New Haven: Yale University Press, 1977), chap. 2; Laurence Bonjour, "Can Empirical Knowledge Have a Foundation?," *American Philosophical Quarterly*, 15 (January 1978), 1–13.

[22]For purposes of this discussion I will not distinguish between judgment and belief.

utilize such a capacity is radically different from what all that comes to in the case of a human being, but that is not our present concern. My contention will be that what the argument infers from this for the human case fails to follow for the divine case. Even if it is true for us that to apply the concept of P to X is, or necessarily involves, *believing* that X is P, in a sense of 'belief' in which a belief is the sort of thing that may or may not be true, no such conclusion can be drawn for the divine case. Since God is necessarily infallible, even if, in being aware of the fact that X is P, God is applying a concept of P to X, it does not follow that God is thereby *judging* or *believing* that *p*, where that claim commits us to holding that God possesses a belief that is intrinsically capable of being false. God's necessary infallibility protects us from the requirement of any such admission. Hence we are not constrained to concede that God's immediate awareness of the fact that *p* can constitute knowledge that *p* only by way of involving a belief that *p*. We are, so far as the above line of argument is concerned, free to hold that God's immediate awareness of *p* is itself His knowledge that *p*, without any belief being involved.

With this defense of the legitimacy of an intuitive conception of knowledge, at least in application to God, let us move on to the question of whether God's knowledge is best construed as intuitive. In the human case, even if the intuitive conception does have a possible application, contrary to the above argument, there are conclusive reasons for denying that it gives us an adequate account of human knowledge; but none of these reasons applies to the divine case. For one thing, the intuitive conception is too episodic for our condition. It limits knowledge that *p* to those moments at which I am directly aware of the fact that *p;* but that is intolerably restrictive. I am capable, at best, of having one or two facts present to my consciousness at a time. But surely there are many things that I know right now. And equally surely there are many things that I know continuously over a long period of time. I have known that $2 + 2 = 4$ for many years now, and not just at odd moments during those years; but at most I am only infrequently aware of that fact. Hence the intuitive conception fails to bring out the way in which I know what I know when my conscious attention is not on it. A suitably dispositionalized concept of belief is just what is needed to bring out this largely "latent" character of human knowledge. If my knowledge is a true belief that meets further conditions, I can be said to have this knowledge at times when it is not occupying my attention. However, God is not limited in this way. He could be directly aware of all facts at every moment, or aware of all facts timelessly if that is the mode of His existence.

The second reason for denying that the intuitive conception captures the character of human knowledge is this. If I know anywhere near as much as I ordinarily suppose myself to know, then I know much more than can ever be directly present to my consciousness. How can I know anything about history or the contemporary character of distant lands on this conception of knowledge? How can facts concerning the micro-structure of matter be directly present to my consciousness? But again these considerations have no relevance to the divine situation. Nothing could prevent God from being directly aware of facts of every sort.

This may suffice to show that God's knowledge could be of the intu-itive rather than of the *true belief* + variety; but we have not yet argued that it is better construed as intuitive. I shall now proceed to do so. The basic point is that the intuitive conception represents the fullest and most perfect realization of the cognitive ideal. We reject the intuitive account for human knowledge, not because we suppose ourselves to have something better, but because it represents too high an aspiration for our condition. If we could be continuously directly aware of every fact of which we have knowledge, that would be splendid; but we must settle for something more modest. Immediate awareness of facts is the highest form of knowledge just because it is a direct and foolproof way of mirroring the reality to be known. There is no potentially distorting medium in the way, no possibly unreliable witnesses, no fallible signs or indications. The fact known is "bodily" present in the knowledge. The state of knowledge is constituted by the presence of the fact known.[A] This is the ideal way of "registering" a fact and assimilating it into the subject's system of cognition and action guidance. Hence this is the best way to think of God's knowledge. Since God is absolutely perfect, cog-nitively as well as otherwise, His knowledge will be of this most perfect form. It would be fatuously unjustified at best, and blasphemous at worst, to attribute to Him some second-rate mode of knowledge, one that is of value only for limited creatures that can do no better.

III

I take the argument of Section II to be conclusive. God can have beliefs only as components of knowledge. But God knows what He knows in a way that does not involve any beliefs. Hence God has no beliefs. Nevertheless it may be illuminating to approach the issue from a different perspective. Without considering whether beliefs figure in knowledge, we can consider various fundamental features of beliefs and ask what bearing each of these has on the question of whether beliefs are attributable to God. In raising these questions I will be relying on the conclusions of Section II.

What fundamental features beliefs have depends, of course, on what sorts of entities beliefs are. Following H. H. Price's admirable book-length treatment,[23] we can distinguish between "occurrent" and "dispositional" accounts of the nature of belief. ". . . in the traditional Occurrence Analysis of belief, attention is concentrated on a special sort of mental occurrence or mental act, which may be called assenting".[24] This is to be construed as the taking up of a certain attitude to a proposition. Whatever is to be further said about this mental act, the basic point to be made in the present connection is simply a different application of a point made in Section II, to the effect that higher forms of cognition in God exclude lower forms. In its present guise the point is that if God is immediately aware of all facts, there is no point to His *assenting* to propositions. Such activity has a point only when one does not already have effective access to the facts. If one's best shot at reality is to pick out those propositions that, so far as one can tell, have the best chance of being true and assenting to them, well and good. But if one already has the facts themselves, what is the point of *assenting* to propositions? It would be a meaningless charade.

On the dispositional analysis, a belief is essentially a complex disposition. A full-blown version of this, as in Robert Audi's "The Concept of Believing",[25] will cite dispositions to a variety of manifestations—cognitive and affective as well as behavioral; but for this abbreviated discussion we can restrict ourselves to dispositions to actions. Let us think of a belief that *p* as, at least in part, a complex of dispositions to act, in appropriate situations, in ways that are appropriate to its being the case that *p*, given the subject's aims, desires, standards, and so on. Thus to believe that my Aunt Jennifer is coming for a visit tomorrow is, *inter alia*, to be disposed to get the guest room ready. Now we might argue against the attribution of dispositions of any sort to God on the grounds that God, as pure act, excludes all potentiality and hence all dispositions. It could never be true that God is disposed to do something that He is not already doing. Again, it could be argued that God can have no dispositions because His mode of existence is timeless rather than temporal; and a disposition can be attributed to a being only if it is possible for that being to be doing something at some future time that it is not doing now, viz., the action to which it is disposed. A

[23]*Belief* (London: George Allen & Unwin, 1969).
[24]Ibid., p. 204.
[25]*The Personalist*, 53, no. 1 (1972), 43–62.

disposition that could not exist unactualized is hardly worthy of the name. But I need not go into all that for present purposes. Let us agree that God does have various dispositions to action. He is disposed, let us say, to forgive any sinful human being who turns to Him with true repentance.

So if God has action dispositions of the sort that are ingredient in belief, why should we not attribute beliefs to Him? (We may assume for purposes of this discussion that the other sorts of dispositions that are constitutive of belief can also be attributed to God.) Let us consider a disposition that might be thought to constitute a good part of a belief. Take the disposition to send plagues on Egypt if the Pharaoh does not release the Israelites. This disposition might be thought to be partly constitutive of the belief that the Israelites are being forcibly detained in Egypt. If we are prepared to hold that God had that disposition prior to the Exodus, why should we abstain from crediting Him with the corresponding belief? The answer is, of course, that since God has unlimited intuitive knowledge, that suffices for the action guidance function and serves to ground such behavioral dispositions as He possesses. It is because God *knew* that Israel was enslaved in Egypt that he was disposed to inflict plagues on the Egyptians if that were necessary to get the Israelites released. Having perfect knowledge He has no need of mere beliefs to guide His behavior. His dispositions to act in one way rather than another stem from His knowledge of the situation. Again the better drives out the worse. (Here theology displays its superiority to economics.) The action guidance aspect of cognition does not distinguish between belief and knowledge; they share in it equally. Hence it can serve as no basis for the attribution of belief rather than, or in addition to, knowledge.

Finally let us consider the plausible view that a belief involves some inner mental representation of what is believed. If this inner representation aspect is essential to belief, it provides yet another reason why beliefs are not to be attributed to God. A creature in our condition needs inner representations in order to be able to think about absent states of affairs, since the facts are rarely if ever directly present to our consciousness. But since God enjoys the highest form of knowledge He is never in that position, and so He has no need for inner representations that He can "carry around with Him" for use when the facts are absent. The facts are never absent from His awareness; thus it would be fatuous to attribute to Him any such mental map. When we have arrived at our destination we can fold the map away.[26]

[26]This paper has greatly benefited from comments by Robert Audi, William Hasker, Norman Kretzmann, Alvin Plantinga, Alfred Stenner, Eleonore Stump, and Charles Taliaferro.

Notes

A. William Hasker, in a critical discussion of this essay ("Yes, God Has Beliefs!", forthcoming in *Religious Studies*), questions whether a direct awareness of a fact deserves to be called "propositional" knowledge, since there is nothing with a propositional structure serving as a representation of the fact. The answer is that the fact itself has a propositional structure. Facts, in fact, just are what true propositions correspond to, and that correspondence involves an isomorphism of structure.

PART III

GOD AND
THE WORLD

God's Action
in the World

1. The Problem

In this essay I seek an understanding of the notion of God's acting in the world, where this is to be understood as going beyond God's creation and preservation of the world, and as involving God's intentionally producing various particular effects in the world. The general notion covers a wide variety of putative cases. On the one hand, there is a variety of ways in which God is thought to deal "directly" with human beings: communicating messages to them, judging them, forgiving them, sustaining them, enlightening or guiding them. Then there are more public displays, the Cecil B. De Mille spectaculars, such as parting the waters of the Sea of Reeds, sending the plagues on Egypt, and raising the dead to life. In my discussion I will be taking this whole spectrum into account, though at times I will narrow the focus.

It goes without saying that this problem will assume different forms, depending on how we view God and how we view the world. Let me explain the setting within which I am raising the question. God is the ultimate source of being for everything other than himself: everything other than God exists only because of the divine creative activity. It is not simply that God initially brings each creature into existence; God's creative or sustaining activity is continually required to keep the creature in being. God's existence, on the other hand, depends on nothing

From *Evolution and Creation*, ed. Ernan McMullin (Notre Dame, Ind.: University of Notre Dame Press, 1986), pp. 197–220. Reprinted by permission of University of Notre Dame Press.

outside Himself. God exists necessarily; He exists in every possible world. God is unlimited in every perfection: knowledge, power, goodness, and so on. As such He is immaterial, not limited by the conditions of corporeality. I also think of God as not Himself being in, or moving through, time, but the details of my discussion will not reflect that conviction. I shall take it that talk of God as a temporal agent, at least my talk of God as a temporal agent, can always be translated into talk of God as a timeless agent that produces temporal effects. In most of these respects I am siding with classical theism against the process theology of Whitehead, Hartshorne, and their followers.

Moreover, I think of God as literally a personal agent. By a "personal agent" I mean a being that acts in the light of knowledge to achieve purposes, a being whose actions express attitudes and are guided by standards and principles, a being that enters into communication and other forms of personal relations with other personal agents. In saying that God *literally* acts in the light of knowledge and purposes, I do not mean to imply that knowledge, intention, and other psychological states and processes are realized in God in the same way they are realized in human beings. What it is for God to intend something may be, and undoubtedly is, radically different from what it is for a human being to intend something. But this is quite compatible with the basic sense of terms like 'know' and 'intend' holding constant across the divine-human gap.[1] For example, despite the radical differences in divine and human nature, the existence of an intention (together with the power to carry it out) can have the same sorts of implications in both cases. Thus, from "God intends to establish his kingdom on earth", together with "God is omnipotent", we can infer that God's kingdom will be established on earth. In taking God to be literally a personal agent my view is distinguished from pan-symbolists like Paul Tillich and John Macquarrie. If I were to agree with Tillich that divine will and intellect are "symbols for dynamics in all its ramifications and form as the meaningful structure of being-itself",[2] and that providence is the "divine condition which is present in every group of finite conditions and in the totality of finite conditions, . . . the quality of inner directedness in every situation"[3] I would not draw such implications from attributions of intentions to God.

I will not say much about the world. I use the term to designate the

---

[1]For an elaboration of this idea see Essays 3 and 4.
[2]Paul Tillich, *Systematic Theology* (London: Nisbet, 1953), vol. 1, p. 274.
[3]Ibid., p. 296.

whole of creation, the totality of everything that exists other than God. In this essay I will be focusing on the physical universe, including human beings, leaving to one side whatever else there may be to creation. No doubt, the details of an account of God's action in the world will differ somewhat from one cosmology to another, but I doubt that any of the issues I will be discussing are affected by detailed differences between cosmologies. In the course of the discussion I will consider both sides of one issue about the creation, whether everything that happens is determined to happen in just that way by natural causes.

2. Determinism and Divine Agency

The most basic issue that arises when, against this background, we try to understand the action of God in the world is this. Must we think of *everything* that happens in the world, including those happenings that are due to natural causes, as actions of God, as something that God does? Or is it only some, perhaps very small, subclass of happenings that deserves that appellation? We are pulled both ways here. On the one hand, as we shall see in a moment, there is a considerable case to be made for the thesis that everything that happens in the world (with the possible exception of free voluntary acts of created agents) is God's doing. But, on the other hand, it seems that when we take some particular occurrence to be an action of God, we mean to be contrasting it with more humdrum happenings that are purely the work of created agents. When the waters of the Sea of Reeds part to let the Israelites through, but close when the Egyptians seek to follow, that is seen as an act of God. But the normal rippling of the water before and after this event is not thought of as God's doing, at least not in the same way. We single out an act of God against a massive background of the purely worldly. In the remainder of this section I will look at the case for holding that everything, or almost everything, is done by God. The rest of the paper will be devoted to exploring the idea that happenings of some relatively small subset are actions of God in some special sense.

There is a widespread view in Christian theology that I will call "omnidetermination". This is the thesis that God wills, intentionally brings about, every detail of creation. It can boast such distinguished adherents as Augustine, Aquinas, Calvin, and Luther. For example, Aquinas argues that all things are subject to the divine government, including contingent events and things that happen by chance.[4] To say

---

[4]Aquinas, *Summa Theologiae (ST)*, Ia, Q. 103, art. 5. Aquinas, *Summa Contra Gentiles (SCG)*, III, 64.

that something happens by chance is simply to say that it is not determined by some particular kind of natural causes; to say that something happens contingently is to say that its proximate causes are not sufficient to determine it uniquely.[5] But nothing falls outside the order instituted by the divine will. God, as first cause and first mover, is responsible for all existence and all activity. And since God's causation is by His will, guided by His intellect, every activity in the world was willed by God and so carries out a divine intention. This even includes human volition, which, Aquinas insists, is free, but free in the sense that no created being outside the agent causes the agent to will one alternative rather than another, and contingent in that its proximate cause, the created will in question, is not determined by its nature to will in just one way.[6] Since God wills every created happening, God is the agent of every happening. "God works in every agent."[7]

Thus Aquinas seeks to establish omnidetermination, and hence universal divine agency, from very general considerations concerning the nature of God and the relations He must have to *any* created world. I do not find the arguments convincing, but to explain why, I would have to go deeply into Thomistic theology and philosophy, something I have no time for in this essay. I shall simply assume that the fundamental nature of God, as briefly adumbrated at the beginning of this section, leaves open the extent to which God determines every detail of His creation. God could determine everything; He has the power to do so. But He also has a choice as to whether to be omnidetermining. His nature does not constrain Him either way. It is quite conceivable that He proceeds as Augustine, Aquinas, and others suppose, but it is also quite conceivable that God has deliberately refrained from deciding certain details, for example, the free voluntary choices of human beings.

Proceeding in that spirit, I shall explore the prospects for universal divine agency on one or another assumption about the universe. And first I shall indicate how universal divine agency follows from a certain possible feature of the universe, namely, *causal determinism.* Determinism is the thesis that everything that happens in the universe is uniquely determined to happen in just that way by natural causes. Thinking of the universe in this way, let us consider a particular naturally determined event. A cow eats some grass and is thereby sustained. We would say, of course, that the cow is nourished by the grass and that

---

[5]*ST*, Ia, Q. 103, art. 7. *SCG*, III, 72, 74.
[6]*ST*, Ia, Q. 105, art. 4. *SCG*, III, 89, 90.
[7]*ST*, Ia, Q. 105, art. 5. *SCG*, III, 67, 70.

the grass does the nourishing. Does that rule out God's doing the nourishing? By no means. After all, God instituted and maintains the natural order by which this nourishing takes place. God created the entities involved and established the laws by which their behavior is governed. Since He did this knowingly and since He acts purposefully, we must suppose that He set all this up in order, inter alia, that this cow should be nourished by this grass at this time.[8] Thus we must hold that God used the grass to nourish the cow and hence that God is the ultimate doer of the deed, just as when I use a hammer to drive in a nail, it is I who drove in the nail, even though I used a hammer to do so. In the latter case I intentionally bring about certain dispositions of the hammer vis-à-vis the nail in order to get the nail imbedded in the wood. In the former case God, via creating and sustaining the natural order, intentionally brings about a certain disposition of the grass vis-à-vis the cow in order to get the cow nourished. Thus in both cases the agent who intentionally brings about the immediate cause of E in order to produce E is rightly said to have produced E. Indeed, God has, if anything, a better right to be regarded as the nourisher of the cow than I have to be regarded as the driver of the nail, for He is more fully responsible than I for the intended effect. I merely make use of an instrument I find ready to hand, whereas God is responsible for the existence of His instrument. Even if I forged the hammer, I merely transformed preexisting materials. I did not bring them into existence out of nothing.

Indeed, we do not even need the doctrine of continuous divine preservation to arrive at the conclusion that God brings about every effect. Suppose that God simply brings created substances into existence, ordains deterministic laws that govern their behavior, and then leaves them alone. It is still the case that God intentionally set up the natural order as He did, knowing how it would work out at every time and place. We can hardly deny that He did this in order to accomplish His

[8]Of course it may be that God didn't really care whether *this* cow ate *this* grass at *this* time. Perhaps he cared about cows being nourished but wasn't specifically concerned about precisely how it is carried out in each instance. In that case the particular details of this ingestion constitute a foreseen but unintended result of the natural order. If this is the right way to look at it we will have to modify the strong statement in the text; but there will still be plenty of aspects of the world that do constitute a carrying out of divine purposes.

The view in the text will have to be more drastically modified if, as Peter van Inwagen suggests in his "The Place of Chance in a World Sustained by God" (in *Divine and Human Action,* ed. Thomas V. Morris [Ithaca: Cornell University Press, 1988]), God leaves some of the basic structure of the world to chance, e.g., just how many basic particles there are. But even on this view there will still be many aspects of nature that constitute the carrying out of divine purposes.

purpose, and hence that in exercising His creative activity, He was intentionally bringing about what ensues in the world. We have as much reason, on this hypothesis, to say that God nourished the cow as we have for saying that the person who booby-trapped a car killed the driver. In both cases some arrangements were made in order to lead to a result, and after a passage of time they did lead to that result, even though the agent did not actively intervene after the initial arrangements were made. If God continuously sustains everything in being, this gives His agency, so to say, more immediacy, but it is not required for the pervasive reality of divine agency.

Note that the doctrine of divine agency in the world, as I have been presenting it, is not simply the doctrine of creation and preservation expressed differently. The thesis that God is the intentional agent of all worldly happenings follows from the doctrine of divine creation (and preservation) *provided* that it is conjoined with (a) the thesis of determinism and (b) the assumption that it is God's purpose to bring about all that He does bring about.

To be sure, since God's claim to have nourished the cow rests on the fact that God intentionally and knowingly brought about a state of affairs that led to that nourishment, we cannot limit the instrument God used for this action to the grass ingested. For God no more directly brought about the ingestion than he did the resultant bovine metabolism. That herbaceous ingestion was itself brought about by the use of a previous state of affairs, and that, in turn, all the way back to the Big Bang, or back indefinitely if the universe is temporally infinite. But it is hardly a matter for surprise that God should use instruments on a cosmic scale.

It is sometimes thought that universal divine agency is incompatible with the reality of created agency, so that if we hold that God nourished the cow, we must deny that the grass did. To dispel this impression we only need note that the action involves different roles for different agents and that the filling of one role by no means implies that the others are empty. Whenever an agent uses an instrument to do something, both the (ultimate) agent and the instrument are doing something, and if they were not both doing their job, the effect would not be forthcoming, at least not in that way. The hammer will not pick itself up and drive in the nail, but neither can I drive the nail by my bare hands. Just so, the grass will not nourish the cow unless God endows it with its properties and sustains it in being. To be sure, God could perfectly well bring it about that the cow is sustained without using grass or any other created agency. However, if God chooses to nourish the cow by the ingestion of grass, the grass must do its thing metabolically if God is to do it that way. Similarly, suppose that I could drive the nail with my bare hands if I so choose. Even so, when I choose to use the hammer, the hammer has an essential role to play; if the hammer did not knock the nail in (propelled and guided by me), then I would not drive the nail in that way, by using a hammer. Thus we must reject the theological version of the National Rifle Association principle: "Diseases don't kill people; God kills people." We can recognize that both God and the disease kills, both God and the grass nourishes, each in its distinctive way.[9]

Thus far I have been proceeding on the assumption of determinism. Here the case for universal divine agency, on the assumptions of classical theism, is quite straightforward. But many thinkers today hold that the results of quantum mechanics show that no physical events are strictly causally determined, though for macroscopic events the chances of things having come out differently are negligible. It would be interesting to explore the bearing of a quantum mechanical point of view on the case for universal divine agency. Could we think of God as having nourished the cow if he used means that are only very, very, very likely to bring it about? I would think so. But here I want to concentrate on another kind of possible exception to causal determinism, human voluntary actions. If they are causally determined, the above account of bovine nourishment applies equally to them. We would all be divine instruments in the same straightforward sense as the grass. But what if, as libertarians think, human voluntary actions are not causally determined? On that assumption can God be said to perform those actions? Aquinas, as we have seen, insists that God intentionally brings about every event, whether uniquely determined by natural causes or not. But having set aside that position, we want to know what follows concerning divine agency of human voluntary actions, from the tenets of classical theism as set out in Section 1, plus a libertarian account of human voluntary action.

There is no doubt but that the situation is significantly different from what it is on the thesis of complete determinism. Here we cannot say that God instituted the natural order knowing that it would lead to my freely choosing to become a professional philosopher. Hence we lack that reason for holding that God is the agent of that choice. Even if God foreknows all free human actions, it does not follow that He intentionally brought them about in order to achieve his purpose. It is true that God cannot escape all responsibility for a given naturally undetermined event, for example, that choice of mine. For, being omnipotent,

---

[9]Cf. Aquinas, *SCG*, III, 69, 70.

He could have made it impossible, either by creating a wholly deterministic universe that excluded it, by refraining from allowing some of
the conditions of its possibility (for example, not endowing me with the
capacity to make such a choice), or by interfering before I could bring it
off. Thus God bears the kind of responsibility for naturally undetermined events that I bear for something I could have prevented but did
not, for example, my small child's beating his fists on the wall in rage.
But the fact that I could have prevented that action does not imply that
I did it, that *I* beat my son's fists against the wall; the same point holds
for God and human free action.

This last result underlines the point that the doctrines of divine
omnipotence and continuous divine conservation do not by themselves
imply that everything that happens in the world is done by God. For
free autonomous created agents, as much as other creatures, exist and
exercise their powers only because God continuously sustains them in
existence. And the divine omnipotence extends to them as much as to
other creatures; God could have refrained from creating them as autonomous agents, and He can interfere with their activities at any time.
But despite all that, the above considerations show that God is not
properly regarded as the agent of their actions.

I cannot discuss the status of human voluntary actions in this essay,
but I want to consider the bearing of the libertarian position on the
extent of divine agency. I have already noted that causally undetermined human actions or volitions cannot be regarded as divine actions
in a full sense. But, in addition, the libertarian position greatly compli-
cates the case for divine agency of causally determined happenings.
Recall that the case for universal divine agency, given universal determinism, rested on the thesis that every worldly happening issued from
the order God instituted in order to produce those happenings. But in
allowing some created agents a say in what they do, God is also giving
them a share in causally determining other sorts of events. Human
voluntary actions themselves have effects as much as any other worldly
happenings. At least on or near the surface of the earth very little
happens that is totally causally independent of past human activity.
That leaves the rest of the universe; yet apart from the prospects for
human exploration outside our solar system, if there are free created
agents elsewhere in the universe, a like situation obtains there. To be
sure, there are gross features of the environment that are, thus far,
independent of human manipulation. We have not yet altered the cycle
of the seasons or the location of the seas. But even here the precise
details of the weather or of the sea level are affected by our doings. So
there are a vast number of causally determined happenings whose

causal determinants did not stem solely from God's choice. In fact, the above-mentioned bovine nourishment is undoubtedly one of them. Assuming that this is a domesticated cow, she would not have been in just that place, in a position to eat just that grass, apart from the voluntary activity of husbandmen. So what is the case for divine agency of those causally determined happenings that are influenced by free human choices?

Let us remind ourselves that we have a problem here because the earlier case for universal divine agency depended on the assumption that God *chose all* worldly happenings by creating the constituents of the world and ordaining laws governing their interaction. But since that cow would not be eating that grass if some human had not made certain choices that God did not determine, even indirectly, the previous argument does not apply. So what is God's role in a happening that partly depends on free human choices? It is still true that God partly determines the event; human choices make a partial contribution at most. If God had not endowed cows and grass and numerous other things with the powers they have, no cow would be eating any grass anywhere. But the crucial difficulty here comes not from the extent of divine causal involvement in the outcome, but rather from divine intentions. Can we think of God's having intended just this outcome, considering the role of human free choice in producing it? We cannot, as before, hold that God knew that this result would be forthcoming just by instituting the natural order. Of course, it is conceivable that God acts directly to shape the situations that are influenced by human voluntary activity. But at this point we are confining ourselves to happenings that are determined by natural causes.

Let us make a fresh start. It seems clear that God can intentionally produce an effect that is completely determined by created causes only by way of His institution of the causal order. Is there any way in which God could do that if other, independent sources of determination are involved? (Even if those sources owe their independent voice to God's permission, they still make their contribution in ways not specifically chosen by God.) This could happen if God could foresee those independent contributions *and on the basis of that* adjust the details of the natural order so that the outcomes of those creaturely choices would always be in line with His intentions: not necessarily in line with what He would have chosen had He been calling all the shots (His antecedent will), but at least in accordance with His intentions, given that free created agents will act as they will (His consequent will). But if God is to adjust the natural order in light of this knowledge, it cannot be direct intuitive knowledge of the actual occurrence of the free actions, whether this is a contemporaneous awareness of them in the divine eternal now (on the assumption that God is timeless) or a special cognitive power of directly intuiting what will happen in the future (if God is temporal). For the direct intuition of the actual occurrence of the free choice is logically posterior to that choice; it presupposes the constitution of that choice. But that means that it also presupposes the constitution of the causal order that produced the situation in which the choice was made. Human free choices, even if not uniquely determined by their natural environment, are surely heavily influenced by that environment. If my natural environment were different from what it is in certain respects, I would not even have the same alternatives from which to choose. In an appropriately different environment I would not have the opportunity to choose whether to be a professional philosopher. Moreover, given those alternatives, various features of my situation determine what influences me one way or the other. Hence if God's only "foreknowledge" of human free choices is an intuitive awareness of the actual choices, this "comes too late" to permit Him to adjust the natural order so as to carry out His intentions in the light of those choices. He would already be stuck with one natural order rather than another.

Thus it seems that if God is to produce intentionally the sustenance of the cow, via the institution of the natural order, He will have to know how free created agents *would* act in various possible situations, as well as knowing how they will act in actual situations. That is, He will have to have "middle knowledge."[10] (God's "middle knowledge" is his conditional knowledge of future contingent events. The controversial doctrine of *scientia media* was devised originally by Molina in an attempt to secure both God's foreknowledge and the reality of human freedom, the latter of which he thought to be undermined by the standard Thomistic accounts.) I myself am dubious about the possibility of such knowledge, not because I think God might be limited in his cognitive powers, but because I doubt that there are any true-or-false propositions, any facts of the matter to be known, about how free agents would act in this or that situation. There may well be truths to the effect that the probability of a given free agent doing A in situation S is so-and-so. But I doubt that there are any truths as to precisely what a free agent would do in a given situation. How could there be such truths if the

---

[10]This term was introduced by the sixteenth-century Jesuit theologian Luis de Molina. For a discussion of this type of knowledge, together with historical references, see R. M. Adams, "Middle Knowledge and the Problem of Evil," *American Philosophical Quarterly*, 14 (April 1977), 109–17.

agent does indeed have a free choice in such a situation? How could there be such a truth if the agent were not somehow determined to do A in that kind of situation? But be that as it may, it would seem that only if God has middle knowledge could He adjust the laws of nature in the light of human free choices. God needs that knowledge of how the agent would act in various situations if He is to have a realm of possibilities within which the free choice and the laws of nature can be mutually adjusted so as to produce consequences in line with His intentions.

But even in the absence of middle knowledge, and given libertarian assumptions about human voluntary action, it can still be true that God intentionally brings about various not completely specific features of causally determined states of affairs influenced by human voluntary action. God can limit the scope of human free choice, so as to prevent it from threatening various features of His world He wishes to preserve. And He can see to it that His world contains enough counterinfluences to prevent the most disastrous possible consequences of human sin. But on those assumptions God would not unqualifiedly be the agent of all naturally determined happenings.

Let me summarize the results of this section. Given an unrestricted thesis of determinism, there is a straightforward derivation of universal divine agency of worldly happenings from the classical theism we are presupposing. If there are naturally undetermined happenings, whether human voluntary actions or otherwise, this line of argument does not apply to them, and God is not their agent unless He directly produces them. Furthermore, it is only on the assumption that God has "middle knowledge" that He could be the agent of naturally determined happenings that are causally influenced by naturally undetermined happenings. Finally, even where God is not, in the full sense, the agent of certain happenings, He could still see to it that they do not deviate too widely from His intentions.

3. Is Direct Divine Intervention Possible?

Now for the opposite pull, the conviction that some happenings are acts of God in a way in which most happenings are not. Believers sometimes single out particularly noteworthy happenings as acts of God in a special sense. For example, when a boy is the only survivor of a highway collision and then in later life discovers a cure for some dread disease, one may be inclined to regard his survival of the wreck as an act of God in a way in which the collision itself and the dispersion of the wreckage are not. But if all naturally determined happenings are acts of God in a quite straightforward and full-blooded sense, what is this special sense in which only a small subclass deserves that appellation?

To be sure, in the previous section I expressed doubt about the doctrine of middle knowledge that is required if God is to be the agent of all naturally determined happenings, assuming human free will in the libertarian sense. Of course, even if we reject middle knowledge, God will be the agent of many naturally determined happenings that we do not pick out as "acts of God" in a special way, and we will still be faced with the question of the basis on which those special items are picked out. But to simplify the discussion I shall henceforward stifle my doubts about middle knowledge and take God to be the agent of all naturally determined events, even those influenced by free human acts.

There is a well-known traditional answer to the question of what makes special divine acts special, and I am sure you have been impatiently wondering why I had not mentioned it earlier. Only some events are acts of God in the strongest sense, because only in these cases is God *directly* bringing about some effect in the world rather than using natural causes to do so. God normally works through the natural order He has created, but from time to time He bypasses this and brings about some state of affairs just by willing it. These cases are marked out by the fact that things happen otherwise than they would if produced in the usual way by natural causes: a man walks on water, water suddenly becomes wine, the sun remains fixed in the heavens, a blind man regains his sight at the touch of a hand, and so on. It is because we realize that something is happening contrary to the usual course of nature that we are impelled to credit the effect to the direct action of the Creator. This, in brief, is the traditional view of "miracles". And there is no doubt that this view embodies a sense of "(direct) act of God" different from that in which Section 2 shows all naturally determined events to be "acts of God".

This traditional view has encountered some stormy seas in the last two hundred years or so. First there was the Humean argument that we can never have sufficient reason for supposing that an act of God in this sense (indeed, anything outside the usual course of nature) has occurred. Naturalists have condemned the belief in miracles as contrary to determinism. And underneath these theoretical arguments is the fact that belief in special divine interventions runs counter to the deeply rooted modern faith that for any occurrence, no matter how bizarre, it is in principle possible to find a scientific explanation. In these latter days many theologians have gone over to the opposition and decried the belief in miracles as "unacceptable to the contemporary mind".

> The traditional conception of miracle is irreconcilable with our modern understanding of both science and history. Science proceeds on the assumption that whatever events occur in the world can be accounted for in terms of other events that also belong within the world; and if on some occasions we are unable to give a complete account of some happening— and presumably all our accounts fall short of completeness—the scientific conviction is that further research will bring to light further factors in the situation, but factors that will turn out to be just as immanent and this-worldly as those already known.[11]

Indeed, some of their statements branding the belief as "unintelligible" or "meaningless" go beyond anything to be found in the pages of atheists, who typically are willing to concede that the belief in miracles gets so far as to be false.

> I want to emphasize that the problem we are considering does not arise in the first instance out of difficulties connected with conceiving a transcendent agent; it is rather the difficulty—even impossibility—of conceiving the finite event *itself* which is here supposed to be God's act. . . . An "event" without finite antecedents is no event at all and cannot be clearly conceived; "experience" with tears and breaks destroying its continuity and unity could not even be experienced . . . it is impossible to conceive such an act either as a natural event or as a historical event, as occurring either within nature or history; in short it is impossible to conceive it as any kind of event (in the finite order) at all. Our experience is of a unified and orderly world; in such a world acts of God (in the traditional sense) are not merely improbable or difficult to believe: they are literally inconceivable. It is not a question of whether talk about such acts is true or false; it is, in the literal sense, meaningless; one cannot make the concept hang together consistently.[12]

> Miracles cannot be interpreted in terms of supranatural interference in natural processes. If such an interpretation were true, the manifestation of the ground of being would destroy the structure of being; God would be split within himself.[13]

[11]John Macquarrie, *Principles of Christian Theology*, 2d edition (New York: Scribner's, 1977), p. 248.

[12]Gordon Kaufman, "On the Meaning of 'Act of God'," in *God the Problem* (Cambridge: Harvard University Press, 1972), pp. 134–35.

[13]Tillich, *Systematic Theology*, p. 129. One cannot help noting that in this passage Tillich, to use his own terminology, seems to be absolutizing the natural order of causality and making an "idol" of it.

I am afraid I do not find any of this very impressive as an argument for denying that divine interventions do, or can, occur. Let it be granted that the belief in such interventions runs counter to various features of the contemporary mind-set. But unless we have reason to think that our age is distinguished from all others in being free of intellectual fads and fancies, of attachments to assumptions, paradigms, and models that far outstrip the available evidence, of believing things because one finds one's associates believing them, and so on, this is hardly of any probative value. I fear that theologians who appeal in this way to the contemporary climate of thought are doing nothing more intellectually respectable than considering what it takes to sell the product, or rather, what would inhibit the sale of the product.

> It is this traditional account of the distinctiveness of miracle that makes the concept very difficult for modern minds, and might even suggest to the theologian that "miracle" is a discredited and outmoded word that ought to be banished from his vocabulary. The way of understanding miracle that appeals to breaks in the natural order and to supernatural interventions belongs to the mythological outlook and cannot commend itself in a post-mythological climate of thought.[14]

And even in this they are misguided. A little market research would surely reveal that the most flourishing business is done by fundamentalist sects for whom direct divine interventions are a matter of course and who have scant respect for "the modern understanding of science and history" and the "post-mythological climate of thought".[15]

The more respectable arguments for the impossibility of miracles invoke the doctrine of determinism, directed not against causally undetermined happenings, but against happenings that are determined by supernatural rather than natural causes. But I think it is fair to say that this doctrine is accepted on faith by its devotees. It is true that with the progress of science we have greatly advanced in our knowledge of

---

[14]Macquarrie, *Principles of Christian Theology,* pp. 247–48.

[15]Revisionist theologians also object on theological grounds to supposing that God sometimes directly intervenes in nature. They take such behavior to be "unworthy" of God, since it presupposes a lack of power or foresight, a defect of will or intellect. They assume that only if God were unable to set up the natural order in such a way as to achieve all His purposes by its normal working would He seek to carry out any intentions by direct intervention. But why should we assume that God would prefer to attain His goals only by working through the natural order if He could? What basis do we have for that assumption? Even if we can see why God should choose to work sometimes through the natural order, we certainly cannot see why he should choose to work exclusively in this way. It is presumptuous for any human being to claim that degree of insight into the divine preference order.

the natural conditions on which one or another outcome depends, but we are almost as far as we were a thousand years ago from being able to show in a particular instance that the outcome was causally determined in the last detail. For example, by now we pretty much know the conditions of the putrefaction of meats. But that by no means implies that we have established such laws of putrefaction as will enable us to show in a given case that the precise pattern and mode of putrefaction, down to the molecular details, could not have been other than it was. I do not say that the progress of science, or, indeed, our prescientific knowledge of natural regularities, carries no presumption of determinism. By a not unreasonable extrapolation from what we know, we can suppose that every detail of every event is determined to be just what it is by natural causes. But all our evidence is equally compatible with the view that causal determination is sometimes, or always, only approximate. The antecedent causal factors determine the gross outline of the result, but that only sets limits to the freedom or spontaneity of the agents' responses. The evidence we have, or any evidence we can foresee obtaining in the future, does not put us in a position to claim to know that determinism is true or to brand as irrational one who rejects it.[16]

At this point I would like to say something about the common view that a miracle (direct action of God in the world) would be a "violation of a law of nature". It is worth considering whether this is so, because it is often used against the believer in miracles. If the argument were explicitly set out, it would run something like this. "A law of nature tells us what *must* happen under certain circumstances. But in an alleged miracle what, according to the law, *must* happen does not. The man standing upright on the lake does not sink. But clearly what must happen must happen. Therefore. . . ."[17]

To be sure, even if a direct action of God would be a violation of a law of nature, I do not agree that this would render such actions impossible. The alleged impossibility of a freely falling body's reversing course and moving upward is, at most, an impossibility *within the natural order,* not an unqualified impossibility. The omnipotent author and

[16]For a more elaborate version of this line of thought, see Peter van Inwagen, *An Essay on Free Will* (New York: Oxford University Press, 1983), pp. 198–201. The argument of this paragraph has been quite independent of considerations from quantum mechanics. If that were brought into the picture, the prospects for establishing determinism would be even dimmer.

[17]It is worth noting that this argument can be mounted only on a fairly strong interpretation of natural laws, according to which they have modal force. Laws as mere records of observed regularities or mere extrapolations of observed regularities, or mere universally true conditionals, will not do the trick.

sustainer of that order is not bound by it; He retains His freedom to act outside its constraints as well as within. But as I see it, we do not need to invoke this consideration, because there is no need to regard God's direct action on the world as a violation of a law of nature in the first place. Whether it is depends on the form that laws of nature take. We can envisage laws of which any direct action of God would be a violation. Such laws would specify unqualified sufficient conditions. Thus a law of hydrostatics might specify as a sufficient condition for a body sinking in still water (of sufficient depth) that the body be of a density greater than the water. If a man walks on still water, that would be a violation of *that* law. But, and this is the crucial point, we are never justified in accepting such laws. The most we are ever justified in accepting in the way of nomologically sufficient conditions is a law that specifies what will (must) ensue in the absence of any relevant factors other than those specified in the law. In other terms, the laws we have adequate reason to accept lay down sufficient conditions only within a "closed system", a system closed to any influences other than those specified in the law. We are confined to laws that carry riders like this simply because none of the laws we are capable of working with take account of all possible influences; even if a formulation took account of all influences with which we are acquainted, we cannot be assured that there are no hitherto unknown influences lurking on the horizon. A man standing upright on the surface of a lake will sink—unless he is being supported by a device dangling from a helicopter, or unless he is being drawn by a motor boat, or unless a sufficiently strong magnetic attraction is keeping him afloat, or. . . . When a galvanometer in working order is attached to an electrically charged body, the needle will move unless someone holds it still, or unless a strong gust of wind prevents the movement, or. . . . Since the laws we work with make (implicit or explicit) provision for interference by outside forces unanticipated by the law, it can hardly be claimed that the law will be violated if a divine outside force intervenes. No doubt that is not the sort of outside force scientists normally envisage, but that is neither here nor there. If we were to make the rider read "in the absence of outside forces of the sort we are prepared to recognize as such", our confidence in all our law formulations would be greatly weakened, for we have no significant basis for supposing that science has identified or can identify all the factors that can influence the outcomes it studies. Once we appreciate this point, we can see that "outside the ordinary course of nature" does not imply "a violation of a law of nature".[18]

[18]This way of thinking about the matter was suggested to me by C. S. Lewis' treatment in chapter VIII of *Miracles* (New York: Macmillan, 1947), "Miracles and the Laws of Nature." I have, however, presented my own formulation of the point.

It will undoubtedly be replied that my argument depends on certain limitations of the present state of science, and that when we develop a unified science we will be in a position to exhaustively enumerate and interrelate all the factors that can influence a given sort of result. This will enable us to state unqualifiedly sufficient conditions, and the "in the absence of outside forces" rider can be omitted. Even now, though we are not in a position to *assert* laws of this form, we have good reason to suppose that there are such laws in force. My response would be to deny that we have sufficient reason to suppose that there are such laws. I recognize this to be an intelligible supposition, but we lack adequate reason to suppose it to be true. The course of science strongly suggests to me that nomological dependence is a "local" affair and it will be tight only to the extent that a system is closed to alien influences. I take the dream of a unified science in which all possible influences are systematically integrated to be just that, a dream.

4. Is Direct Divine Intervention Required?

There is much more to be said about the possibility of direct divine action on the world, but we must push on. Thus far I have been attacking the claim that direct divine action in the world is impossible and the claim that we can confidently rule out its actuality. But though I consider it a live possibility that God sometimes directly produces effects in the world, I am not at all inclined to restrict myself to this way of marking out those occurrences that are acts of God in some specially significant way. I also take it as a live possibility that God always acts through the natural order, and so I want to consider how to mark out the "special" acts of God on that assumption. There are several reasons for not restricting ourselves to the "direct intervention" account, even if we are not prepared to rule out its possibility.

First, even though divine intervention is possible, it is by no means clear that it ever does happen. I do not go along with Hume's argument in his famous essay on miracles that it is in principle impossible to be justified in believing that something has happened outside the usual course of nature, but I do recognize that we are rarely, if ever, in a position to justify conclusively such a claim. No matter how unusual or outlandish the occurrence, we cannot rule out the possibility that it was brought about by natural causes in a way that we do not currently understand. It is a truism that with respect to some occurrences attributed at one time to supernatural intervention we are, at a later time, in a position to give a scientific explanation, or at least to see the gross outlines of such an explanation. Mental illness and recovery therefrom is a signal case in point. We can be justified in dismissing the possibility of a naturalistic explanation only if we have (a) a complete description of the particular case and (b) a complete inventory of natural causes of that sort of occurrence. Armed with that, we might be able to show that there were no available natural causes that could have produced that result. But when are we in a position to do that? If we insist that what makes something a "special" act of God is that it is a direct act of God on the world, we cannot be assured that there are any "special" acts of God.

Second, not all the occurrences we feel inclined to treat as special acts of God even appear to be independent of natural causes. The contrary impression is fostered by preoccupation with the standard biblical "superspectacular" miracles: the parting of the waters of the Sea of Reeds, walking on water, changing water into wine, and so on. These do *appear* to stem from special divine intervention, whatever our final judgment. But other cases do not immediately strike us that way. Think of all the cases in which one takes oneself to have been guided or strengthened by God. When I take God to have guided me in making a decision, or to have enabled me to meet a crisis without collapsing, the phenomenology of the situation may present nothing outlandish. On the surface nothing untoward happens. In the guidance case I weigh the alternatives, think about them, pray about the problem, try to imagine alternative outcomes, and so on. In the strengthening case I simply meet the crisis, doing what seems called for at each point, perhaps frequently calling on God for help. Or consider a case in which I take God to have spoken to me. This *may* involve an apparent miracle—the clouds open and a booming voice seems to emerge from the empyrean vault. But more commonly we get something like the following: I ask God in prayer what I should concentrate on in my work, after which the thought forms in my mind that I should give priority to administration rather than scholarship, accompanied by a strong conviction that this is God's message for me. Again, on the surface nothing happens in a way that seems outside the order of natural causality. In all these cases we have events of quite ordinary sorts, occurring in contexts in which they frequently occur. Or again, consider events taken to be "providential", like the boy's emerging unhurt from the accident in which all others perished. This may be mildly unusual, but it is by no means unprecedented. It is easy to think of natural factors that would produce such a result—place and angle of impact, positioning of passengers, what each encounters in being propelled from his/her position. In all these cases one may believe that God is working outside the ordinary course of nature to strengthen one, to preserve the person from harm, or whatever, but one is not forced into this belief by an apparent absence of the right kind of natural causes. For all we can tell by an examination of the situation itself, these thoughts, capacities, or whatever were just as much produced by natural causes as other effects of those sorts.

Third, even where we believe that God is acting outside the natural order, that belief is by no means always crucial to our taking the occurrence to be an act of God in a specially significant way. Sometimes it *is* crucial. Here we must draw some distinctions within this vaguely demarcated class of "special" acts of God. The distinctions have to do with the special role or function we take the act in question to have, what sort of thing we take God to be up to in performing it, or, more generally, what we take to be so special about it. One historically important kind of specialness that does depend on divine intervention is the way in which an act of God is supposed to authenticate some person's claim to authority, to be delivering a divine message, or to be acting under divine instructions. Thus, according to Exodus 4, when God gave Moses his commission in the wilderness, He empowered Moses to validate his claims by performing certain miracles, for example, turning a staff into a snake and then back into a staff and turning water from the Nile into blood. God confirmed Elijah's claims to authority by sending fire from heaven to consume the offering made on Mt. Carmel. Jesus' status was confirmed, for many, by the wonders he performed. When this is taken to be the special significance of an act of God, it is essential that the act be thought of as direct. The reasoning presumably runs like this. Moses did something that he could not do by his own natural powers; indeed, it was something that no creature could bring off by its natural powers. This could only happen if the creator and controller of the natural order set aside the usual rules in this particular instance and endowed Moses with special supernatural powers.[19] But He would not have done this had He not wished thereby to endorse Moses' claims. Therefore. . . .

If an occurrence is to elicit this reasoning, it must not only *be* outside the course of nature but must seem to be so. In fact, the latter is

[19]It does not matter whether we think of God as endowing Moses with supernatural powers or think of God as turning the staff into a serpent himself. In either case God has acted outside the natural order—either to bring about an event in the universe directly or to endow some creature with supernatural powers. In either case the direct action of God, in connection with the claims made by the human being, is taken to validate those claims. Some miracles are more naturally viewed in one of these ways, and some in the other. It is more natural to think of *Moses* as turning the staff into a serpent (having been granted the special power to do so by God), whereas it is more natural to think of God sending down the fire on the sacrifice, after Elijah calls on Him to do so.

presumably sufficient in itself. If and only if the occurrence runs counter to what is generally believed to be the natural outcome of the antecedent situation will it be taken as an authentication of prophetic claims. Furthermore, it must be a publicly observed occurrence if it is to be effective. In this connection we should note that the effectiveness of this procedure depends on a certain cast of mind in the audience; in particular, it presupposes that the audience will be disposed to take direct divine intervention as the correct explanation of anything that strongly runs counter to what is confidently believed to be the course of nature. Hence it will fall flat with a contemporary scientistic audience that is predisposed to take such surprising occurrences as an indication that our scientific theories need to be revised. If *they* were to witness fire falling from heaven at Elijah's request on Mt. Carmel, their reaction would be, not "God has confirmed Elijah's authority", but rather "Back to the drawing board".

However, many occurrences are taken to be special acts of God in a way that does not require the assumption of direct divine intervention. For one thing, there are God's "personal dealings" with creatures of which we spoke earlier—God's strengthening, guiding, enlightening, empowering, and speaking to the person. Again, there are all the cases that fall under the rubric of "providential care", personal and corporate. This includes, on the personal level, recovery from illness, survival of accidents, and the building of a career in ways not anticipated in advance. On the corporate level we have the rise and fall of nations, the preservation of a people from destruction, and the growth of the Church. In all these cases what is taken to be "specially significant" is the nature of the outcome, not merely as happening somehow or other but *as a carrying out of God's purposes.* We may believe in some or all such cases that God has brought about the outcome apart from natural causes, but that belief is not essential for our singling out these occurrences in the way we do. What we take to be special about them is simply that God has acted in such a way as to effect *this result,* that *this* is something that God *intended* to bring about. How God chose to do this is not the heart of the matter; it will be special in the relevant way whatever that choice. In these cases we are centrally interested in the character of the result whereas in the "authentication" cases the result could be, and often was, quite indifferent in itself, its significance residing in its being a sign of divine favor.

Many people think, and I myself at one time thought, that the belief that God enters into active interaction with His creatures, a belief crucial to the Judeo-Christian tradition, requires us to suppose that God directly intervenes in the world, acting outside the course of nature.

But the considerations of this essay clearly indicate otherwise. Just by virtue of creating and sustaining the natural order God is in as active contact with his creatures as one could wish. Merely by the use of natural causes God carries out His purposes and intentions with respect to creatures, and this surely counts as genuine action toward them. If God speaks to me, or guides me, or enlightens me by the use of natural causes, He is as surely in active contact with me as if He had produced the relevant effects by a direct fiat. Indeed, as I suggested above, we do not even need the doctrine of continuous divine preservation in order to achieve that result; although if God is actively sustaining everything in being at every moment, this does, so to speak, give God's instrumental actions more immediacy. But even without that, God is still intentionally doing everything done by the natural order he creates. After all, when one human being directly interacts with another, by speaking to or embracing the other, the agent is making use of aspects of the natural order, exploiting physical and psychological regularities; we do not know how to do it otherwise. And surely this does not imply that we are not in active contact with each other in such transactions. However necessary direct intervention may be for the authentication of messengers, it is not required for genuine divine-human interaction.

5. Special Acts of God without Direct Intervention

Because of all these considerations I am motivated to find some other way to bring out what makes some acts of God "specially significant", some way that does not require us to view them as outside the course of nature. Before launching into this, let me underscore something that has been at least implicit in my discussion. I am very much opposed to trying to limit God either to working within the course of nature or to direct intervention. In my view both the traditional "supernaturalists" and the scientific "revisionists" are wrong in seeking to restrict God to one modus operandi. I am not charging them with deliberately trying to dictate God's procedure. No doubt each side sees itself as delineating the only possible alternative. But as I have been arguing, both sides are wrong in denying the possibility of the other side's suggestion. Since I take it that in speaking to me God could be working either through the course of nature or outside it, I am content to leave it up to God which way He prefers. And I will not insist on determining which way He has chosen before listening to His word. End of sermon.

In seeking a way of construing events within the natural order as "special" acts of God I am entering onto well-trodden ground. The "revisionist" theologians who reject the view that God sometimes acts outside the natural order have been much concerned to explain why some naturally determined events, rather than others, are taken as "miracles", "acts of God", or "revelations of God". I find in their discussions two suggestions, one of which I shall reject as inadequate, but the other of which I find more promising.[20]

The most obvious suggestion to be found in the writings of, for example, Paul Tillich and John Macquarrie on this subject is that what distinguishes the "special" acts of God is something about the way in which they are experienced and responded to. According to Tillich, "A genuine miracle is first of all an event which is astonishing, unusual, shaking, without contradicting the rational structure of reality. In the second place, it is an event which points to the mystery of being, expressing its relation to us in a definite way. In the third place, it is an occurrence which is received as a sign-event in an ecstatic experience."[21] Here I want to concentrate on the third condition, that the occurrence is received "in an ecstatic experience". I am not sure exactly what Tillich means by this, but it is clear that in such an experience one has the sense of being "grasped" by something fundamental in reality and for human life. Tillich often speaks of being grasped by "the power of being", the "ground of being", the "mystery of being".[22] He calls on Rudolph Otto's analysis of numinous experience in terms of the *mysterium tremendum et fascinans* to flesh out his account.[23] Furthermore, the occurrence calls out, or tends to call out, what Tillich calls "ultimate concern", a reaction that involves such components as an absolute commitment, an absolute trust in a promise of salvation, and total devotion and worship.[24] In this experience it seems that the ultimate is present and manifesting itself to one. It is a searing and transforming experience that can reshape one's entire life, providing a focus and organization for one's existence.

Now I do not wish to deny that what are taken to be specially significant acts of God can be, and sometimes are, received and reacted to in this way. Nor do I wish to minimize the importance of such experiences

[20]These two suggestions are intimately blended in the writings of theologians such as those I will be citing, Paul Tillich and John Macquarrie. If I were trying to represent the views of these people, I would present the matter differently. My purpose here is to distinguish two ways in which one might try to answer our question and to evaluate each.

[21]Tillich, *Systematic Theology*, p. 130.

[22]See, e.g., ibid., pp. 24, 124, 126.

[23]Ibid., pp. 239–40.

[24]Paul Tillich, *Dynamics of Faith* (New York: Harper, 1957), chap. 1.

for the individual and for the shaping of religious communities and religious traditions. However, an appeal to these experiences does not suffice to give a general account of what differentiates these "special" acts of God from other events, and this for two reasons. First, we do not always react in so extravagant a fashion to what we take to be a specially significant act of God. I would agree that if a person were completely indifferent and blasé in the face of such an occurrence, that would be a good, and perhaps conclusive, reason for denying that he took it to be an act of God. But it seems clear that I *can* take God to have sustained me or guided me without being shaken to the roots of my being by the experience. Quite devout people see many or most occurrences as constituting God's dealings with us; yet many of them never have a Damascus-road experience. So we *can* take something as a "special" act of God without receiving it in the ecstatic fashion Tillich specifies. The second point is that when the ecstatic experience does occur, it can, and often does, *result* from our supposing the occurrences to be an act of God rather than *constituting* that supposition. When I become aware of the boy's "miraculous" survival of the accident, I take this to be a case of God's providential care, and this may then lead me to have the experience of being grasped by the "power of being", of being in the presence of God. Since in these cases my taking the occurrence as an act of God causes the experiential reaction, the former can hardly be constituted by it.

Note also that Tillich's account is restricted to events that are "astonishing" and "unusual". This leaves aside all the "ordinary, on the surface" occurrences we were discussing earlier as special acts of God.

But, as intimated above, the ecstatic experience is not Tillich's whole story. Even in the passage just quoted he also speaks of "an event which points to the mystery of being, expressing its relation to us in a definite way". Rather than take the time to unpack this rather cryptic formula, I shall turn to John Macquarrie, whose development of this line of thought is more lucid: "What is distinctive about miracle is God's presence and self-manifestation in the event."[25] In speaking of the crossing of the Sea of Reeds Macquarrie writes: ". . . this significance is really God's grace and judgment".[26] Again: "the miracle focuses the presence and action that underlies the whole and makes sense of the whole".[27]

From this point I would like to take the ball and run with it myself. Since Tillich and Macquarrie think of God as Being-Itself in a way that

---

[25]Macquarrie, *Principles of Christian Theology*, p. 250.
[26]Ibid., p. 251.
[27]Ibid., p. 253.

seems to them to preclude thinking of God as literally an agent who carries out intentions and acts to achieve His purpose, they do not attempt to develop the concept of an act of God with which I am working. Nevertheless, the above quotations from Macquarrie suggest to me something that I can work out as follows. In taking my coming to a decision or my forming a certain thought as an act of God (of guidance or communication) I suppose this event to be a "self-manifestation" of God's purposes (or a fragment thereof). Even if I take everything that happens in the world as an act of God, still I specially regard these events as acts of God, not because they *are* acts of God in any stronger, different, or more basic sense than myriads of other happenings I just let float by, but because in these cases I have some idea as to what God is up to. I discern, or think I discern, a bit of the divine purpose. These events "focus" for me "the presence and action that underlies the whole and makes sense of the whole". Why do I take only some of the ideas that float through my mind to be cases of God communicating with me, even though I regard all my nonvoluntary ideation as acts of God? Because in those special cases I have some idea as to what God is trying to accomplish: for example, I take it that God is forming in my mind the idea of concentrating on administration, along with a strong sense of conviction, because that is what he wants me to do. Why do I regard the escape of the boy from the wreck as a special act of God? Because I think I can see why God saved the boy, but I do not think I can see why God arranged other details of the accident as He did. Even if everything that happens is carrying out the divine purpose, it is only seldom that we have, or think we have, some insight into what that is. It is these cases that we take, in a preeminent sense, to be acts of God. Thus when I speak of "special" acts of God, the specialness attaches to our taking rather than to the action itself. This may seem to lay us open to our own criticism of the first suggestion from Tillich as being too subjective. But the criticism of that suggestion was not that it made the discrimination rest on *some* reaction of the subject, but rather that it made the discrimination rest on experiential and emotional reactions of the subject. Our account is rather in terms of how the subject is thinking about the matter, what the subject believes about it.

Note too, in case this needs emphasizing, that it is only the demarcation of "special" acts of God that is made to rest on human reactions. Members of this class share with innumerable other happenings the objective feature of being acts of God, a feature that attaches to them however we think, feel, or experience.

But if we believe that all or most naturally determined events *are* acts of God, do we not think that we see what God's intention is for any such event, however insignificant and nonspecial it appears, namely, that this event occurs? If I believe that each movement of each leaf in the wind is done by God, do I not thereby also believe that each of those movements carried out God's intention that it occur? This must be admitted. How then can I maintain that it is only where I take something to be a "specially significant" act of God that I take myself to discern a bit of the divine purpose? I think the answer must be that in those special cases we think we discern a *bit more* of the divine purpose. We think that we see at least a little way into the further purpose for which that event occurred. This is clearly the case with respect to the "superspectacular" miracles, where those who regard them as acts of God see them as instrumental in the furtherance of national destiny, the work of the Church, or the validation of prophets. Again, when we single out a pattern of events as an instance of providential care (the building of a career in science or the ministry in the face of hardship, failures, and obstacles), we think we see, to some extent, how this furthers God's purpose for mankind. Finally, the same point holds for God's "individual dealings with us". When I take a piece of ideation to be a message from God, I think I know, at least in part, what God meant to be communicating, and hence I think I know for what immediate purpose God brought it about that those ideas formed themselves in my mind at that time. Again, when I suppose God to have guided me in making a decision to go into teaching rather than the law, I believe that I have some inkling of the purpose for which God guided my deliberations in a certain way, namely, to lead me to make that decision and thereby to make such contributions as I can to my fellow human beings in that mode of activity.

I do not suppose that this is the whole story of what is involved in "special" acts of God. Indeed, I do not suppose that there is a sharp line between the special ones and the ones we acknowledge in a blanket fashion. If it is a matter of degree how special we take a certain act of God to be, our interest or involvement in the alleged divine purpose may well play a large role in determining the degree of "specialness" for us. And there may be other complexities as well. But I believe that the main lineaments of the situation are as I have depicted them.

6. Conclusion

Thus we can think of God's action in the world as pervasive, if not all-pervasive, whether or not anything ever happens outside the ordinary course of nature. And whether or not this is the case, we can understand why it is that we pick out some small subclass of happenings to be taken as divine action in a special way.[28]

[28]This paper was presented at a conference "Evolution and Creation", held by the Center for the Philosophy of Religion at the University of Notre Dame in March 1983. The paper has profited greatly from comments by Robert Audi, Richard Creel, Alfred Freddoso, James Keller, Alvin Plantinga, and Peter van Inwagen.

The Indwelling
of the Holy Spirit

I

This essay deals with certain aspects of the work of the Holy Spirit in the world. Christian theology assigns the Holy Spirit a wide variety of functions; He would seem to be quite busy. The Holy Spirit inspires, guides and enlightens a person, and, according to some versions, even takes over the normal psychological functions in prophecy, in the composition of the books of the Bible, in preaching the word of God, in speaking with tongues, and other "charismatic" phenomena. Over and above these more dramatic manifestations, the Spirit acts as an internal witness to the faith, producing a sense of conviction in the mind of the believer. The Spirit is active in the Church, the Christian community, knitting its members together in fellowship, guiding its decisions and activities, preserving its integrity. In this essay we will be concerned with another crucial function of the Holy Spirit, viz., the transformation of the believer into a "saint", into the sort of person God designed him/her to be. In other terms, it is the function of initiating, sustaining, fostering, and developing the Christian life of the believer, or, as we might well say, the "spiritual" life, thinking of that term as encompassing all the ways in which the work of the Holy Spirit is manifested in the life of the believer.[1] My topic thus falls within the

From *Philosophy and the Christian Faith,* ed. Thomas V. Morris (Notre Dame, Ind.: University of Notre Dame Press, 1988), pp. 121–50. Reprinted by permission of University of Notre Dame Press.

[1]At one time I thought that in order to understand the concept of the Holy Spirit one would first have to understand what it is for a human being to engage in spiritual

territory labeled "Regeneration" and "Sanctification" by much Protestant theology, and within certain parts of the territory labeled "Grace" in Catholic theology, particularly "Sanctifying Grace".

In focusing on the work of the Spirit in the individual I do not mean to be denigrating the importance of the corporate in the Christian life. I am alive to the point that the New Testament and the ensuing Christian tradition present the Christian life as a full participation in the community of believers and make no provision for the salvation of the solitary individual, isolated from her fellow Christians.[2] Indeed, the transformation of the individual with which I am concerned is a transformation into one who has both the capacity and the will to participate fully in the life of the Church. One cannot advance in love, patience, kindness, faithfulness, and other "fruits of the Spirit", without exhibiting these characteristics in one's interactions with others in the community. These are not aspects of "the feelings, acts, and experiences of individual men in their solitude, so far as they apprehend themselves to stand in relation to whatever they may consider the divine", to quote William James's profoundly misguided characterization of religion.[3] They are inclinations to social behavior. But having said all this we must also recognize that at least an essential part of the work of the Holy Spirit in building up the Christian community is the regeneration and sanctification of its members. Neither the New Testament nor

---

activities, to be spiritual, or to lead a spiritual life. This is, indeed, in accordance with the general rule for theological language: concepts of divine attributes or aspects are formed by derivation from concepts of human matters. However, I am now convinced that in this case the derivation is in the opposite direction. I can't see anything that marks off what in Christianity is called the "spiritual life" or "spirituality" except for their explanation by the influence of the Holy Spirit. A human being is a *spiritual* person, manifests true *spirituality,* provides *spiritual leadership,* etc., to the extent that she exhibits such characteristics as love, peace, serenity, joy, and absence of self-centeredness, self-seeking, and dependence on recognition from others. I can't see what differentiates this list of attributes from other commonly prized features of which we are capable, such as intelligence, resourcefulness, and prudence, except that the former are deemed to be especially prized by God, given special divine priority in His rescue operation for sinful human beings, and so are thought to be what the Holy Spirit is specially concerned to foster in us. Apart from this theological dimension, spirituality simply becomes a catalogue of those attainments of which human beings are capable by virtue of their mental capacities. For a couple of examples of what spirituality becomes when shorn of its theological dimension, see George Santayana, *The Realm of Spirit,* and Julian Huxley, *Religion without Revelation.*

[2]This is not to say what constitutes isolation or participation. I do not intend these remarks to constitute a condemnation of monasticism. There are many ways in which the religious, even the cloistered religious, can be in vital contact with the community of believers.

[3]*The Varieties of Religious Experience* (New York: Modern Library, 1902), pp. 31–32.

Christian experience through the ages represents the Spirit as working on what we might call a purely corporate level, in such a way as to bypass the inner psychological development of each individual. The sanctification of the individual is as fundamental for the building up of the Church as is the latter for the former. It is crucial to recognize both directions of dependence. On the one hand, the transformation of the individual is intimately dependent on the community, for without the Christian community we would not have the tradition that informs our Christian life, nor would we have the role models that play so central a part in spiritual growth. But, on the other hand, unless some members had made significant advances in the development of Christian character, there would be no communal spiritual life into which new members could be drawn and in the context of which each individual can receive resources to be used in further development.[4]

It will also be noted that I have chosen to concentrate on what might be called the "moral" aspects of the work of the Holy Spirit within the individual, the ways in which the Spirit modifies the character of the person, her values, tendencies, attitudes, priorities, and so on, rather than, e.g., the work of the Holy Spirit in "inspiring" the person to various sorts of exceptional activities, such as prophecy and speaking in tongues. Again I do not mean to imply that the latter are without value or that they are not genuine manifestations of the Spirit. I wish only to suggest that these phenomena are not the heart of the matter; they are not what the divine plan of salvation is all about. We were not created in order to speak with tongues or exhibit various forms of "enthusiasm". If these activities do have a place in the divine scheme, and I am prepared to recognize that they do, it is by way of assuring the individual and those around him of the presence of the Spirit and/or by way of communicating certain messages to concerned parties. But it still remains that, by well nigh common consent, God's basic intention for us is that we should become like unto Him, in so far as in us lies, and should thereby be in a position to enter into a community of love with Him and with our fellow creatures. And the work of regeneration and sanctification is directly addressed to the carrying out of this intention.

Although I am discussing these matters in terms of the work of the

[4]I also believe, though this is not directly relevant to this essay, that the individual's awareness of the regenerating and sanctifying work of the Holy Spirit constitutes a crucial part of his basis or ground for Christian belief. See my "Christian Experience and Christian Belief," in *Faith and Rationality,* ed. Alvin Plantinga and Nicholas Wolterstorff (Notre Dame, Ind.: University of Notre Dame Press, 1983), even though the discussion there is not explicitly in terms of the work of the Holy Spirit.

Holy Spirit, I am not concerned here with problems concerning the Trinity or concerning the nature and status of the third Person in particular. I am concerned with God's work in regeneration and sanctification, work that is traditionally assigned to the third Person of the Trinity, and I am following that language. Moreover, as we shall see, the term 'spirit' is quite appropriate for certain aspects of the phenomenology of these proceedings. Nevertheless, I want to avoid getting into controversies over which Person of the Trinity is doing a particular job at a particular time. I will adhere to the widely accepted theological principle that all Persons of the Trinity are involved in the external operations (external to the Godhead) of any Person. From this perspective the work of regeneration and sanctification is primarily attributed to the Holy Spirit because these operations are centered around the development of love in the individual, and within the Godhead the role of the Holy Spirit concerns the love borne each other by the Persons of the Trinity. By adhering to the principle just mentioned we can handle the fact that in the Pauline epistles and the Johannine writings there is quite a bit of oscillation between speaking of the Spirit and speaking of Christ as working within one. A famous passage from the Epistle to the Romans clearly illustrates this. "But that is not how you live. You are on the spiritual level, if only God's Spirit dwells within you; and if a man does not possess the Spirit of Christ, he is no Christian. But if Christ is dwelling within you, then although the body is a dead thing because you sinned, yet the spirit is life itself because you have been justified. Moreover, if the Spirit of him who raised Jesus from the dead dwells within you, then the God who raised Christ Jesus from the dead will also give new life to your mortal bodies through his indwelling Spirit" (8:9–11).[5] Here the indwelling divine presence that gives the new life is indifferently referred to as "God's Spirit", "the Spirit of Christ", and "Christ". I can see no way of reading the passage as specifying three distinct divine agents. If St. Paul does not find it necessary to distinguish between the Holy Spirit at work in one and Christ at work in one, I don't see why it should be incumbent on me to do so, even though he and I are separated by the Council of Nicea. In pursuance of this policy I shall feel free to use Biblical and other material put in terms of the indwelling of Christ, as well as material phrased in terms of the indwelling of the Spirit.

---

[5]All Biblical quotations are from *The New English Bible* (New York: Oxford University Press, 1976).

II

If this suffices for a demarcation of my subject matter I can proceed to formulate my problem. Simply stated, it is this: how are we to think of this stretch of the activity of the Holy Spirit? Just what role does the Spirit play in bringing about these changes within the person? Just how is it brought off? These questions need further specification. They are not to be construed as a request for a delineation of the divine mechanisms or the divine flow chart. Even if there are such things, we could not expect to grasp them. Moreover, we should be alive to the possibility that God works differently with different people in different situations. It may be unreasonable to expect a simple account that applies univocally to every case. What I am specifically interested in exploring are two issues. First, to what extent is the transformation wholly God's work and to what extent is a human response, human effort, human voluntary choice, assent, or cooperation involved? And second, how intimately is God involved with the individual in this process? How internal is He to these proceedings?

The first question is one that inevitably forces itself on us as soon as we reflect on the matter, for it is of the highest practical as well as theoretical importance. It obviously makes a great deal of difference to how I should proceed whether the course of sanctification is to any extent dependent on my actions, choices, or efforts; whether it is in any way "up to me" in what direction it goes, how fast it goes, or whether it goes at all. If, on the other hand, God is simply transforming me by His own immutable decrees according to some schedule of His own, that is quite a different ball game. And one or another position on this issue will have various theological and philosophical consequences that will tell for or against it and that will have an important bearing on one's conception of the divine-human relationship.

I won't say much about the second question now. It will become clear at a later stage of the discussion just what external-internal contrasts are relevant here and what is involved in choosing between them.

Now for a few preliminary points about the first question. Certain extreme views concerning regeneration and sanctification will be dismissed without a hearing. First, I shall rule out of court any view according to which God is not active at all in the process, except for the sustenance that He is always exercising with respect to the entire creation. On such a more-Pelagian-than-Pelagius position we are left on our own with just such natural capacities as we were initially endowed with by our Creator. God is not active in any special way. I take it that any such view goes radically against the mind of the Church, as embodied in scripture, tradition, and normal Christian experience. The idea that God *acts* in order to redeem sinful humanity and bring those that respond to His redemptive action into a loving relationship with Himself is so central to Christianity that its excision would leave nothing worthy of the name. Our problem is not *whether* God is active in personal transformation but *how* we should think of this activity. Second, at the other extreme we have the view that God alone is active in this matter, that God simply "takes over", replaces the human agent. God (the Spirit) lives one's life for one; the human person is simply the "location" or "receptacle" in which this particular bit of divine life takes place. There are famous scriptural passages that suggest this construal, most notably St. Paul's famous cry: "I have been crucified with Christ: the life I now live is not my life, but the life which Christ lives in me" (Galatians 2:20; in the better known Revised Standard Version, ". . . it is no longer I who live, but Christ who lives in me"). However, there are abundant reasons for taking this as a bit of hyperbole. Paul certainly does not lose his sense of continuing personal identity; he gives every indication of being aware that it is he, the same human being who once persecuted Christians, who is writing to the Galatians and pursuing his missionary journeys. Furthermore, if it really were Christ, or the Spirit, who is the agent from now on, why should it be, as it is according to universal Christian witness, including Paul's, that even after God has begun to work within them there is still a long job of combating and rooting out sinful tendencies? If it is God, not I, who is the agent from now on, whence these sinful tendencies? Finally, it is our faith that God has created us for loving communion with Him and with each other. If each of us were replaced by God as soon as he were firmly set on this path, the goal could not be reached; there would be no human agents left to enter into the desired communion. Thus any viable answer to our question must recognize both a divine and a human agent, both divine activity and human response.

Let me also point out that our problem does not pose the crucial issues for human free will that are notoriously posed by the Pelagian controversy. The latter, or at least an important segment thereof, has to do with putatively free human voluntary acts. For example, it has to do with the decisive act of repentance, of turning one's back on sin, asking for divine forgiveness and divine assistance, and resolving to do one's best to amend one's life and to follow the commandments of God. The question was as to whether it is ever up to a human agent to make such a move, or whether any such move will be made only as the outcome of the irresistible grace of God. (On the latter alternative, God may be working through the will of the human person, though this will can no longer be considered free, in that instance, in a libertarian sense. It was not, in the strongest sense, "up to the human person" whether that move was made.) The latter position on this issue really does deny that such acts of repentance are free in a libertarian sense. Likewise the position that fallen human beings cannot do anything good except when moved by divine grace implies that none of us has any real choice between good and evil. But the central problem of this essay does not concern putatively free voluntary acts; it has to do with personality or character changes, with changes in what we might call "motivational structure". That is, it has to do with changes in one's tendencies, desires, values, attitudes, emotional proclivities, and the like. It has to do with such changes as the weakening of a desire for illicit sexual intercourse, the strengthening of a desire for the awareness of God, the weakening of a tendency to be preoccupied with one's status or reputation, and the strengthening of one's interest in the condition of others. The issue is as to just what role the activity of the Holy Spirit has in such changes as these. To see that the integrity of human free will is not at issue here, consider the most extreme attribution of divine responsibility for these changes, short of the "takeover" position we have already ruled out. Say that all such changes result from God's simply effecting them directly by an exercise of His omnipotence, without in any way going through natural psychological or social processes, and without in any way evoking a response from the creature in order to carry this out. God just decides that one of my tendencies shall be weakened and another strengthened, and Presto, it is done. Even on this view I could still have as much free choice, of a morally significant sort between good and evil, as the most dedicated libertarian would affirm. That is, this would still be a possibility unless it is further stipulated, as many Christian thinkers would wish to do,[6] that these new tendencies (or new strengths of tendencies) to holiness are irresistible, that they strictly determine my volitions. But that would be an additional thesis, one that does not follow from the attribution of changes in motivational structure to direct divine volition. If we allow that my altered desires, tendencies, and attitudes influence my volitions without strictly determining them, just as with my previous tendencies, then no negative consequences with respect to human free will ensue.

---

[6]"We must know that the only thing we possess of ourselves is evil. Good, on the contrary, comes from us but also from Almighty God who, by interior inspirations so forestalls us as to make us will, and then comes to our assistance so that we may not will in vain, but may be able to carry out what we will" (St. Gregory). "All good thoughts and all good works, all the efforts and all the virtues whereby since the dawn of faith we have made our way to God, have truly God as their author" (Pope Zosimus).

After all, even the most convinced libertarian recognizes that human motivational structure results, for the most part, from factors other than the individual's own free voluntary acts and, indeed, from factors that were, to a large extent, not under any sort of voluntary control. When we first arrive at the point at which there is some possibility of taking oneself in hand and trying to do something about one's own habits, likes, interests, and desires, one already has a character that arose without one's deliberate intervention or encouragement. And even after deliberate intervention becomes a possibility, this is only one factor in personality changes, and by no means the most important. If there is any hope for libertarianism, it will have to be compatible with the fact that one's desires and tendencies are largely determined by factors over which one exercises no effective control. This being the case, why should we suppose that the effecting of personality changes by direct divine volition should be subversive of human free will?

After introducing our topic as having to do with both regeneration and sanctification, I have been discussing them together without differentiation, sometimes using 'sanctification' as a catchall label. But the two phenomena are typically treated in quite different terms, both in systematic theology and in reports of Christian experience. Regeneration, being born again, is often represented as an instantaneous transition that is vividly conscious and that involves acts of repentance and faith, while sanctification is a long, gradual process, much of which takes place below the level of consciousness. Regeneration is the decisive turning away from sin and toward God that initiates the process of which sanctification is the continuation. If these phenomena occupy such different positions in the scheme of salvation, it might well be that our central questions would be answered differently for the two.

In the interests of concision, however, I am going to continue to discuss them together. I am encouraged in this policy by the fact that by no means all sectors of Christendom carve up our general territory in the same fashion. The picture I have just presented is typical of Protestantism, more specifically of evangelical Protestantism. In traditional Roman Catholic theology there is much less emphasis on a conscious deliberate act of repentance and faith as a prerequisite for God's work of sanctification. "Divine grace" is portrayed as working largely through the sacraments of the Church. Insofar as there is a particular moment of initiation of the process it comes in baptism, often infant baptism when the individual is incapable of a conscious, deliberate repentance and acceptance of Christ as savior. And apart from theological differences, Christian experience indicates that the classic evangelical scenario is not always followed. As William James insisted, there are both "once born" and "twice born" believers. In many cases, even in evangelical circles, a person would be hard pressed to specify some particular moment at which the decisive conversion and rebirth took place.

In any event, I shall be focusing on common ground within mainstream Christianity. It is recognized on all hands that God is at work within the believer to transform her into the kind of person God wants her to be, the kind of person capable of entering into an eternal loving communion with God. I shall henceforth use the term 'sanctification' for this process of transformation as a whole, including any conscious, deliberate initiation there may be. Although I shall not assume that a rebirth of the classic evangelical sort is required in every case, I shall feel free to draw on descriptions of regeneration in seeking to understand the work of the Holy Spirit. For where these dramatic turnings do occur, the divine activity is more out in the open than in the lengthy gradual process of transformation that ensues.

In this connection I should make a general statement about the place of conscious manifestations in sanctification. We are often warned both by theologians and by spiritual writers not to identify grace or the work of the Spirit with feelings, emotional reactions, or "consolations". One shouldn't expect the process of sanctification to be a perpetual "high", an uninterrupted train of ecstasies and exaltations. Most of it is a matter of digging out some deeply entrenched roots, and planting and nurturing new shoots; and that is certainly not all fun. God may well be hard at work within us when we aren't feeling "spiritual", and feelings can, notoriously, be deceptive when they are present. But these sage counsels need to be balanced by the equally important point that spiritual transformation does manifest itself from time to time in a, perhaps obscure, awareness of what is going on; and this awareness is often affectively toned with feelings of joy, love, exaltation, etc. I shall also assume that by attention to these conscious manifestations we can get some clue to what is going on, though I would warn against expecting too much from this source.

III

Let's turn to the first of our two main questions, the one concerning the respective role of God and the believer in sanctification. The simplest answer to this question is that the psychological changes are wrought directly by the will of God. God simply wills that at a certain moment my concern for the condition of others will increase and my concern for my own comfort, repose, and recognition will decrease; and it thereby happens, just as whatever God wills to happen thereby happens without any need for a further intermediary. Such a view can marshal considerable support. Many Biblical passages are naturally read in these terms. The Psalmist sings: "Create a pure heart in me, O God, and give me a new steadfast spirit" (51:10). Ezekiel represents God as saying: "I will give them a different heart and put a new spirit into them; I will take the heart of stone out of their bodies and give them a heart of flesh. Then they will conform to my statutes and keep my laws" (11:19–20, see also 36:26–27). In the Epistle to the Philippians, St. Paul writes: "You must work out your own salvation in fear and trembling; for it is God who works in you, inspiring both the will and the deed, for his own chosen purpose" (2:13; see also 1:6). The Pauline love of paradox is such that this passage can be used to illustrate everything from the ultra-Pelagian view that it is all our doing to the ultra-Augustinian view that God has simply taken over and displaced the human agent. But, among other things, it expresses the conviction that God is at work in us, altering our action tendencies. Some of the prayers in the Pauline epistles seem to be informed by this conception of the matter. "May God himself, the God of peace, make you holy in every part, and keep you sound in spirit, soul, and body, without fault when our Lord Jesus Christ comes" (I Thessalonians, 5:23). ". . . may the Lord make your love mount and overflow towards one another and towards all, as our love does towards you" (I Thessalonians, 3:12). Though these utterances can be construed in other ways, we can see how they would encourage theologians to make statements like the following: ". . . the power which regenerates is the power of God . . . there is a direct operation of this power upon the sinner's heart which changes its moral character."[7] "In the primary change of disposition, which is the most essential feature of regeneration, the Spirit of God acts directly upon the spirit of man."[8] "But man cannot himself extricate himself from this revolt. For everything that he undertakes is infected with it. Only the Creator can overcome the revolt. He does it in the fact of reconciliation in Christ, when he cancels the revolt through His assurance which is accepted in faith. The self is restored to soundness through justification by faith."[9] "To say that God gives us grace is to say that the author of our existence realizes in

[7]A. H. Strong, *Systematic Theology* (Philadelphia: Griffith & Rowland, 1909), pp. 818–19.

[8]Ibid., p. 820.

[9]Emil Brunner, *The Christian Doctrine of the Church, Faith, and The Consummation*, trans. D. Cairns and T. H. L. Parker (Philadelphia: Westminster, 1962), p. 272.

us a quality or property grafted upon our natural being. . . ."[10] ". . . sanctifying grace: that is, of a divine sanctity which only God can give us and which cannot come from our works, but by which we are renewed and therefore capable of performing works that are really holy."[11] The same picture of God directly producing new dispositions and tendencies in us is embodied in the traditional Catholic view that by grace we are "infused" with the theological virtues of faith, hope, and love, and endowed with such "gifts of the Spirit" as wisdom, fortitude, and piety.[12] Let us dub this model of the working of the Holy Spirit in sanctification the "fiat" model.

On the fiat model the inner workings of the Holy spirit constitute the same sort of divine activity as creation. It is just as if God had originally created me with these tendencies, the difference lying only in the context within which the divine activity takes place. Thus the present view ties in well with all those New Testament passages that represent the initiation of the moral changes in question as a "new creation" or a "new birth." The former phraseology is more typical of Paul (See, e.g., 2 Corinthians 5:17; Ephesians, 2:10, 4:24; Colossians, 3:10), whereas the latter is more typical of John (e.g., John, 3:3–8). Since neither in being born nor in being created can I play any active part, the bearing on our question is the same.

Furthermore, this construal is richly illustrated in the reports of dramatic conversions and regenerations which abound in Christian literature. A common scenario has the individual in the grip of sinful tendencies, apparently helpless to do anything about it, until at a crisis point he turns to God, throws himself on the divine mercy, and receives as a gift from God the transformation he was unable to effect on his

[10]Jean Daujat, *The Theology of Grace,* vol 23 of the *Twentieth-Century Encyclopedia of Catholicism,* ed. Henri Daniel-Rops (New York: Hawthorn, 1959), p. 63.

[11]Ibid., p. 68.

[12]Consider also such traditional prayers as the following. "Almighty and everlasting God, who hatest nothing that thou hast made and dost forgive the sins of all those who are penitent: Create and make in us new and contrite hearts, that we, worthily lamenting our sins and acknowledging our wretchedness, may obtain of thee, the God of all mercy, perfect remission and forgiveness; . . ." Collect for Ash Wednesday. "Lord of all power and might, who art the author and giver of all good things: Graft in our hearts the love of thy Name, increase in us true religion, nourish us with all goodness, and bring forth in us the fruit of good works . . ." Collect for the 17th Sunday after Pentecost. "Almighty and everlasting God, . . . make us to love that which thou dost command . . ." Collect for the 25th Sunday after Pentecost. "O God, from whom all holy desires, all good counsels, and all just works do proceed: Give unto thy servants that peace which the world cannot give, that our hearts may be set to obey thy commandments . . ." Evening Prayer. These prayers and all others quoted in this essay are taken from *The Book of Common Prayer, According to the Use of the Episcopal Church* (New York: The Church Hymnal Corporation, 1977).

own. To the person it seems a bolt from the blue; it seems that God alone by His almighty power has effected a fundamental change in his personality.

Now there is no doubt that God could do things this way, and perhaps He does, at least sometimes. But there are reasons for doubting that this is His normal modus operandi. First there are general considerations concerning God's conception of human beings, His relations thereto, and His intentions for us. It is a major theme of the Christian tradition that God created us for loving communion with Himself, for the richest and fullest possible personal interaction with Him. God envisages us and created us as *persons*, beings capable of such distinctively personal activities as the formation of purposes and attempts to realize them, the acquisition and use of knowledge, the entering into social relationships, and the creation of beauty. Moreover, He has created us as persons who have a share in the determination of their own destiny by the exercise of free choice between alternatives. If we enjoy this status in creation, we could expect God to relate Himself to us in a distinctively interpersonal fashion. To be sure, our creation is not, and cannot be, an interpersonal relationship, for prior to being created no person exists on the human side to stand in relation. Again there is presumably nothing distinctively interpersonal about God's sustaining our existence at each moment. But against the background of creation and preservation, the Bible, and the Christian tradition generally, represent God as entering into distinctively interpersonal relations with human beings: making covenants, laying down requirements and prohibitions, making promises, providing guidance and support, punishing and rewarding, exhorting, condemning, communicating messages, consoling, encouraging, and so on. And there are abundant indications that the game has not changed in this regard in the New Covenant. St. Paul tells us: "The Spirit you have received is not a spirit of slavery leading you back into a life of fear, but a Spirit that makes us sons, enabling us to cry 'Abba! Father!'. In that cry the Spirit of God joins with our spirit in testifying that we are God's children; and if children, then heirs" (Romans 8:15–16).

The immediate point of all this is that on the fiat model the inner working of the Holy Spirit is not distinctively interpersonal in character. We have already noted that the present view represents the divine activity in sanctification as being of the same sort as in creation, and hence as lacking any distinctively interpersonal character. But if God is primarily concerned to enter into interpersonal relations with us, why should He relate Himself to us here in such an impersonal manner, treating us as sticks and stones, or at least acting in a way that is indistinguishable from one that is equally appropriate to sticks and stones. If one human being succeeds in altering the desires or attitudes of another without the other's consent, perhaps by some form of conditioning, wouldn't that constitute a violation of the other's personal integrity? Why, then, should we suppose that God acts in a way in which it would be fundamentally wrong for us to act? Would it not be more appropriate to our God-given nature and to God's intentions for us for God to go about our transformation in a way that is distinctively appropriate to persons, a way that would involve calling us to repentance, chastising us for our failures, encouraging us and assisting us to get started and to persevere, making new resources available to us, enlivening and energizing us, assuring us of His love, His providence, and His constant presence with us, leaving it up to us whether the desired response is forthcoming?

Indeed, the New Testament often speaks of the work of the Holy Spirit in these terms. One thinks particularly of the characterization of the Holy Spirit in the farewell discourses of the Fourth Gospel, in which the Spirit is characterized as an "Advocate", who will "bear witness" to Christ (15:27), will "teach you everything, and will call to mind all that I have told you" (14:26). Moreover, remembering that we are not restricting ourselves to what is specifically assigned to the Holy spirit, we can note other references in these discourses to a distinctively personal activity of God within the believer. ". . . because I live, you too will live; then you will know that I am in my Father, and you in me and I in you. The man who has received my commands and obeys them— he it is who loves me; and he who loves me will be loved by my Father; and I will love him and disclose myself to him" (14: 19–21). "Anyone who loves me will heed what I say; then my Father will love him, and we will come to him and make our dwelling with him . . ." (14:23). In these discourses the Holy Spirit is represented as one who will engage in such distinctively interpersonal activities as teaching, witnessing, loving, and uniting others into fellowship.

Let's be more explicit as to how God's role in regeneration and sanctification could be depicted on an interpersonal transaction model (hereinafter termed the "interpersonal model"). There are many possibilities. First and most obviously, God can *call* the individual to repentance, to obedience, to a life of love lived "in the Spirit". There are calls for deliberate, voluntary responses from the individual. And apart from voluntary responses, these communications can, suddenly or gradually, have effects on the individual's likes, desires, and attitudes through various conditioning mechanisms and other psychological processes that do not involve consciously directed effort. But the communication of divine messages, recognized by the individual as such, is only the most obvious possibility. God could affect the ideational processes of the individual in more subtle fashion. He could bring it about that facets of the person's present life appear to him in an unfavorable light and that the life of agape appears to him highly attractive, without this being consciously taken by the individual as a communication from God. Again, God could present Himself to the individual as a role model, giving the person more of a sense of things divine, thereby increasing the desire for holiness and communion with God. God could make His love and providence for the individual more obvious, more salient in the person's mind, thereby evoking responses of gratitude and yearning for closer communion. Finally, God could make new resources available to the individual, new resources of strength of will, of energy for perseverance in the face of discouragement, of inner strength that enables one to avoid dependence on the approval of one's associates. In these and other ways God would be seeking to *influence* the individual in the direction of holiness without stepping in and directly producing such a character structure by fiat. By proceeding in this more indirect fashion God would be relating Himself to the human person as a person, influencing the human being as one person influences another (albeit making use of some of His extraordinary powers in doing so), seeking to evoke responses, voluntary and otherwise from the other person, somewhat as each of us seeks to evoke responses from others. The only item on the above list that may seem not to fit this description is the "secret" manipulation of the subject's ideational processes. This is indeed something that human influencers are incapable of. But we do seek to alter the ideation of others by such means as are available to us, when we try to influence their motivations. Thus carrying out such alterations does not violate the distinctively interpersonal character of the transaction; it is just that the divine person has infinitely greater resources for the task.

For a live example of this way of approaching the matter, consider the excellent study by G. W. H. Lampe, *God as Spirit*.[13] One strand in this very rich book is an attack on "impersonal" ways of thinking of the action of the Holy Spirit. In opposition to that, Lampe suggests that in speaking of the Holy Spirit "we are speaking of God disclosed and experienced as Spirit, that is, in his personal outreach" (11). In accordance with this orientation, Lampe repeatedly emphasizes that the Holy Spirit works within us by entering into distinctively interpersonal interactions with us. That work is "a developing interaction, according

[13]Oxford: Clarendon Press, 1977.

to man's capacity, of the Spirit of God with the spirit of man" (20). ". . . transcendent God creates man from within, as the immanent personal indwelling Spirit who inspires and guides and evokes that response of faith and love which is the human side of the relationship of sonship."[14] God's "creativity involves the personal interaction of divine Spirit with human spirits, by which persons who have the capacity to accept or to reject divine love are formed into the divine likeness" (21). The Holy Spirit should be thought of as "forming the human personality from within by communion with it" (22). The concept of Spirit provides material "for the construction of a theological framework in which to interpret our experience of God acting upon, and interacting with, thinking, feeling, and willing human persons" (35).[15] "The concept of Spirit" is "more suitable as a way of thinking about personal God drawing created persons into communion with Himself" (41–42).

But can this interpersonal model of sanctification accommodate the facts? I don't think it runs into insuperable difficulties with Biblical texts. The ones I quoted above as encouraging the idea of direct divine alteration of character are typical in that they affirm that God does this but are less than wholly explicit as to how God does it. As for experiential reports, first note that the phenomenology of sanctification, properly so called, tends rather to support the interpersonal model. The gradual process of mastering sinful tendencies and strengthening holy desires is typically punctuated by frequent prayers to God and the reception of messages therefrom—guidance, encouragement, exhortation, assurance, and so on. But what about regeneration? A very common picture here is that of a new character structure just appearing out of the blue, without the usual psychosocial prerequisites. Can we suppose that this process has been carried on by a distinctively interpersonal divine-human transaction? Well, although these accounts certainly do not suggest an interpersonal model, they can be squared with it, provided we recognize that much of the action is carried on below the level of consciousness. After all, in these typical accounts of rebirth a great deal of conscious divine-human communication goes on before the crucial moment. It is clear from these accounts that God is exercising, or seeking to exercise, personal influence on the sinner for some

---

[14]To understand some of these passages one must realize that Lampe considers creation and sanctification to be different stages of a single process, both involving an activity of God as a person. We are not concerned here with that aspect of his view.

[15]The reference in this quotation to God's "acting upon" as well as "interacting with" us is only one of many indications that Lampe has not broken completely with the fiat model. Nevertheless, the main thrust of his thought is clearly in the direction of the interpersonal model.

considerable period of time prior to the decisive shift. It is just that the individual is not aware of a series of individually small effects of this influence, effects that are accumulating during the process. But it should be no news at this time of day that motivational shifts, even large ones, can occur below the conscious level. Hence, if there were sufficient reason to adopt the interpersonal model, the phenomenology of regeneration could be made to fit it.

Now that we have given the interpersonal model a bit of a run, it is time for a counterattack from the fiat model. "All this talk of respecting the integrity of the human person is quite inappropriate in the light of the actual divine-human relationship. My opponent is thinking of a relationship between *adult* human beings. True enough, if I were capable of directly modifying my wife's attitudes, whether by hypnotism, brain-washing, or whatever, and I were to use this power to bring those attitudes more into line with my wishes, I would be violating her personal integrity in doing so. I would be exercising control over her that one human being has no right exercising over another. But our status vis-à-vis God is quite different from the status of one adult human being vis-à-vis another. We should take more seriously the idea that even after having been 'born again' we are only 'babes in Christ'; we have only begun the new life. Therefore the rules governing the interactions of adult human beings are quite unsuitable for divine-human interaction. Let's think for a moment of the parent-infant relationship. The conscientious parent does everything she can, within limits set by other constraints, to mold the motivational structure of the child in what she deems a desirable direction, *without obtaining the infant's consent for these proceedings.* Of course, the human parent is not capable of instituting and extinguishing desires, scruples, and attitudes in the infant by fiat. But what if she were? Would she use this power to instill a good character in her child? I think she would. Would she be condemned for doing so? On what grounds? She certainly isn't condemned for using every mode of influence at her command to see to it that the child develops as good a character as possible. On the grounds that these changes have been brought about without the child's consent? But an infant is in no position to give consent; the infant has not developed to the point of being able to make a judgment on the matter. If the parent could accomplish her purposes by fiat she would merely have a more effective way of bringing about what she is already seeking to accomplish by the means at her command. Then why suppose that God would refrain from directly altering the character of the believer? Of course the adult believer is not incapable of making a judgment about such things, as the child is. Nevertheless, it could be argued that the 'babe in Christ' is in no position to make sound judgments as to what is best for him, what kind of person it would be best for him to be, or what kind of life he should be leading. And even if he is in a position to make sound general pronouncements on these matters he is incapable of working out the details. It is only *after* the right sort of character has developed that he is in a position to judge. The opposing view is one more manifestation of the basic sin of pride, the tendency to deny our proper relationship of subservience to God and to demand our rights before God."[16]

I will rule that this controversy between the fiat and interpersonal models is a standoff. However, there are what I take to be weightier objections to the fiat model. The basic point is this. If God is to transform me into a saint by a fiat why should He do such an incomplete job of it, at least one that is far from complete at any given moment (up to now!), and why should the transformation be strung out over such an extended period? If the process depends on the creature's responses to divine influences we can understand both of these features; but on the fiat theory they seem to be inexplicable. Of course, God *could* have reasons we cannot understand for issuing His fiats in this kind of pattern; after all, we often fail to understand why God does things as He does. But insofar as we are in a position to form a judgment on the matter, the present consideration does provide a strong reason against the fiat theory and in support of some view according to which human responses play a significant role in the process.

IV

Now I want to call attention to an inadequacy in both the fiat and the interpersonal models. Noting this will bring us to the second main issue of the paper, the externality or internality of the work of the Holy Spirit in sanctification.

The inadequacy is simply that both models represent God as relatively external to the believer. To be sure there is a way in which God is

---

[16]A more complete treatment would give consideration to a mediating position according to which the divine fiat would be confined to removing our inability to respond in the right way to divine initiatives. On this view God does not produce or install particular motivational tendencies in us by fiat. Those will develop, if they do, by response to divine influence, as on the interpersonal model. But it is not all interpersonal interaction. God does produce a crucial change in us by an act of will, viz., the removal of blocks that had hitherto made it impossible for us to make the appropriate responses. This does not determine those response, but it makes them possible.

always internal to everything in His creation. God is omnipresent. In whatever sense He can be said to be located at all He is, at every moment, located everywhere. Whatever this comes to, and there are different views on that, God's activity of sustaining a tree, e.g., in existence, and everything else He does vis-à-vis that tree, is done *within* the tree. God is always where He works. Our two models do not, of course, deny that God is internal to the person in this way in His sanctifying activity. Nevertheless, the New Testament and much other Christian literature represent God as internal to the believer in a special way in His work of regeneration and sanctification. This internality is represented as requiring the satisfaction of certain special conditions, whereas God's omnipresence obtains whatever conditions the believer does or does not satisfy. Thus in the farewell discourses of the Fourth Gospel Jesus says: "If you love me you will obey my commands; and I will ask the Father, and he will give you another to be your Advocate, who will be with you for ever—the Spirit of truth . . . he dwells with you and is in you" (14:15–17). "Anyone who loves me will heed what I say; then my Father will love him, and we will come to him and make our dwelling with him . . ." (14:23). Again, in the great figure of the vine and the branches, the integral connection of the branch to the vine is presented as optional. "No branch can bear fruit by itself, but only if it remains united with the vine; no more can you bear fruit, unless you remain united with me. I am the vine, and you the branches. He who dwells in me, as I dwell in him, bears much fruit; for apart from me you can do nothing. He who does not dwell in me is thrown away like a withered branch" (15:4–6). Finally, Christ, and the Church, *prays* for mutual indwelling, and one does not request something that will necessarily be the case. "But it is not for these alone that I pray, but for those also who through their words put their faith in me; may they all be one: as thou, Father, are in me, and I in thee, so also may they be in us, that the world may believe that thou didst send me" (John: 17:20–21). And from the Anglican Eucharistic prayer: ". . . humbly beseeching thee that we, and all others who shall be partakers of this Holy Communion, may worthily receive the most precious Body and Blood of thy Son Jesus Christ, be filled with thy grace and heavenly benediction, and made one body with him, that he may dwell in us, and we in him." But no extensive documentation is needed to make the point. It is fundamental to the whole Christian scheme of salvation that in order for the Holy Spirit to be within me in the way that is distinctive of the Christian life I must satisfy conditions over and above being a creature of God; I must "repent and believe the Gospel", or I must be baptised, or I must do whatever is necessary to be drawn into the Christian community. This indwelling is only a new-birthright, not a creatureright.

And now the point is that the fiat and interpersonal models do not embody this special mode of internality. Of course I can't demonstrate this without making explicit just what sort of internality this is; and that is a goal of the ensuing discussion (or of the larger discussion of which this essay is a fragment). Nevertheless, prior to such specification, I can at least indicate why it seems to me that the models are deficient in this respect.

First, the fiat model, as we have already shown, represents God as acting on the believer in the same fashion He acts on all the rest of His creation. The particular effects He brings about in sanctification differ from any that He could bring about in a stone or a tree, but the manner of going about it is the same. God simply wills that a certain change shall be brought about, and thereby it is. The model does not deny that God is present to the believer in some more intimate fashion, but no such fashion is built into the account.

As for the interpersonal model, it does not represent God as more internal to the believer than one human person is internal to another when they are related as intimately as possible. At least it does not represent God as any more internal to the believer than that in its distinctive account of the work of sanctification.[17] The distinctive thrust of the interpersonal model lies in its construal of the sanctifying work of the Holy Spirit on the analogy of the moral influence one human being can exert on another, by speech, by provision of a role model, and by emotional bonds. But all this leaves the parties involved external to each other in a fundamental way; they are separate, distinct persons, each with his/her own autonomy and integrity. Of course, human relationships can be more or less intimate; and at their most intimate they are even spoken of, figuratively, in the language of mutual indwelling. "I just feel that you are a part of me." "I carry some of you around with me wherever I go." *Unless* the talk of the indwelling of the Holy Spirit can be interpreted in just such a figurative manner the interpersonal model does not embody the appropriate sort of internality. Let's now turn to the crucial question of whether the indwelling of the Holy Spirit is thought of in the New Testament, in the Church, and in the articulation of Christian experience generally, as something

---

[17]This last qualification is needed because the model will recognize divine omnipresence, and that constitutes a mode of internality that is not exemplified in human intercourse. But we have seen that this internality is not what is distinctive of the indwelling of the Holy Spirit.

different from any purely human intimacy that is only figuratively a case of indwelling.

I will not aspire to coercive proof in this matter; I will merely consider what sort of language has been deemed most appropriate by those who have most to report of these matters. Here I am struck by the way in which the work of the Spirit is so often spoken of in terms of the believer being *filled, permeated, pervaded,* by the Spirit, by love, joy, peace, power, confidence, serenity, energy, and other gifts of the Spirit, and of the Spirit being *poured out* into us. (For Biblical references, see, e.g., Romans 5:5; 1 Corinthians 12:13; Ephesians 5:18, 3:19; Luke 1:67, 4:1; Acts 2:1–21, 10:45. See also such prayers as "O God, who has prepared for those who love thee such good things as pass man's understanding: Pour into our hearts such love toward thee, that we, loving thee in all things and above all things, may obtain thy promises, which exceed all that we can desire . . ." Collect for the 6th Sunday of Easter.) The experience of the Spirit seems to lend itself to an articulation in terms of something like a *force,* a *gaseous substance,* or, to go back to the etymology of *pneuma* and *spiritus,* a *breath,* a movement of the air. One is impelled to report the proceeding in terms of one's being *pervaded* by something that provides one with new resources, new directions, new tendencies, a "new spirit". This language is, of course, eminently suited to the articulation of "charismatic phenomena"—prophecy, speaking with tongues, and the like—where one seems to have been seized by a power, indeed by an agent, from without, so that what one is speaking and doing is not really being done by oneself; one is simply a means used by the agent that has taken possession of one to do *its* work. Now whatever is to be said about these phenomena, we have already rejected this "takeover" model as adequate for the process of sanctification. But, and this is the important point, it is not only in cases of "possession" that one speaks of being filled or permeated by the Holy Spirit. This is richly illustrated by the Biblical passages just cited.

These ways of talking about the work of the Spirit seem to present it as quite another matter than intercourse with another person that is separate from the believer in the way in which two human beings are separate from each other, however intimate their relationship. The root metaphor is much more materialistic than that. Being filled with the Spirit is like being plugged into a source of electricity, being permeated by fog, being filled with a liquid, or, closer to the etymology, being inflated by air. Of course these material analogies are grossly inadequate. The Holy Spirit *is* personal; the believer is in a personal relationship with the Spirit, and the goal of sanctification is a distinctively personal goal, both as being a goal that involves a state of a person and as being the kind of goal a person would have. Nevertheless, the wide consensus on the appropriateness of this language of filling and permeating indicates that the indwelling of the Holy Spirit is of a fundamentally different character from the relationship of two human persons, however intimate, different by reason of being much more an internal matter. Or so I shall suppose. I shall endeavor to cast some light on just what different and more internal sort of interpersonal relationship it is.

The answer is to be found, I believe, in the idea that by the indwelling of the Holy Spirit we "come to share in the very being of God" (2 Peter 1:4; see also 1 Corinthians 1:9), we partake of, or participate in, the divine nature. This concept has been made central in the Roman Catholic doctrine of "sanctifying grace". Thus Aquinas speaks of "the light of grace" as "a participation in the divine nature" (*Summa Theologiae*, Iae 2a, Q. 100, art. 4.).[18] As an initial fix on this idea let's think of our being "drawn into" the divine life and living it, to the extent our limited nature permits. We realize in our life and, to some extent, in our consciousness, the very life of God Himself. Once we have made this idea central, much of the Biblical and other material with which we have been dealing falls into a new sort of pattern. The "new birth" can be understood as the initiation *in us* of the divine life, this life being *grafted* onto us, so that *we* are living this life; a rebirth indeed! All the talk in John (gospel and epistles) about our becoming "sons of God" is given a new depth. We become sons of God not just quasi-legally, by proclamation or decree, but also in a more intrinsic sense; just as a biological son shares a nature with the parents, so we, to some extent, come to share a nature with God. When Jesus says in the "high priestly prayer", "as thou, Father, art in me, and I in thee, so also may they be in us. . . . The glory which thou gavest me I have given to them, that they may be one, as we are one; I in them and thou in me, may they be perfectly one" (John 17:21–23), he can be understood fairly literally as asking God to bring it about that believers may share, in the measure of which they are capable, in the same divine life that is His by nature. "God became man in order that man might become God" (St. Augustine); "Adoptive sonship is really a shared likeness of the eternal sonship of the Word" (St. Thomas Aquinas: *ST*, IIIa, Q. 3, art. 8). The Eucharistic reception of the consecrated bread and wine can be seen, according to one's sacramental theology, as an actual reinforcement of,

---

[18]See also such a traditional prayer as "O God, who didst wonderfully create, and yet more wonderfully restore, the dignity of human nature: Grant that we may share the divine life of him who humbled himself to share our humanity, thy Son Jesus Christ . . ." Collect for the Second Sunday after Christmas.

or addition to, the divine life in which one is partaking, or as a symbol of that participation. An understanding of sanctification in these terms we shall dub the "sharing model".

But perhaps this is just to explain the partially unknown by the totally unknown. What sense can we make of a creature's *sharing* in the divine life? The rest of this essay will be devoted to this issue (and much more would be required to deal with it properly), together with the attempt to understand sanctification in these terms. Here are a couple of preliminary points, to smooth the way somewhat. First, let's set aside any mystical idea of a wholesale *identification* of the human person with God. The terms 'share in', 'partake in', and 'participate in' are to be distinguished from 'is' or 'is identical with'. Otherwise all the objections to the "takeover model" come back in spades. If I were God, I would not have the sinful tendencies I do, I would not have to struggle for an increase of sanctity, and so on. A human being shares in the divine life in a way that is possible for a finite being of that sort, one that is, moreover, disfigured by sin. Just what way that is we must consider. Second, the sharing must be compatible with a protracted process of growth in holiness. So the divine life one receives at the outset is not, in every respect, all that the individual is capable of. There may be some sense in which the participation is complete from the first, but that sense will have to be such as to allow for subsequent growth in the individual's moral character.

Now I would like to consider a certain Roman Catholic interpretation of our participation in the divine nature. For this purpose I shall use the excellent presentation in *The Theology of Grace* by Jean Daujat. Quotations in this paragraph will be from this work. Since the life of God consists in a perfect knowledge of Himself and a perfect love of Himself for His own sake, our participation in the divine life will consist of our attaining a knowledge of God as He is in Himself and a love of God for His own sake (rather than for what He can do for us). Needless to say, neither the knowledge nor the love, especially the former, can be exactly like the divine exemplars thereof; but, so far as our finitude will allow, we are enabled by sanctifying grace to enjoy the kind of knowledge and love of God enjoyed by God Himself. Grace enables us to do in these regards what we are incapable of by our own nature. ". . . grace gives to our human intellect as an object of knowledge what is the proper object of the divine intelligence, that is, God himself in all his reality and all his divine perfection; and grace gives to our human wills as an object of love what is the proper object of the divine will, that is, God himself, loved for his own sake in his infinite divine goodness. Thus it is that grace deifies us, makes us share in what constitutes the very nature of God, and thereby establishes us, through the complete intimacy of knowledge and love, in a fellowship of love with God, whom we know and love in himself and for himself, as children know and love their father" (73). Since "it is impossible for man to be God substantially, . . . it is not by our substance but by knowledge and love that the divine nature is imparted to us. Our union with God by grace is not substantial unity, but only in the order of knowledge and love" (74). It is only as an *object* of knowledge and love that God is present within us by sanctifying grace. ". . . knowledge and love mean the presence of the object known and loved in the subject knowing and loving, which possesses within itself the known and loved object by knowing and loving it. Thus, then, does grace give us what does not belong to our nature, and what our nature cannot procure by itself— the possession of God present within us as the object of knowledge and love" (73).[19]

My objection to this account is that it leaves God too external and so fails to account for the distinctive sort of internality we are seeking to understand. God is present within us *only* as something known and loved. It is stipulated that the knowledge and love is of a sort of which we are not naturally capable; but the way in which the object of this higher knowledge and love is present in the subject is the familiar Aristotelian-Thomist way in which *any* object of an intentional attitude is present within the subject. On this account, God is not present to me in any different, any more intimate way than that in which my wife is present to me as an object of knowledge and love. My "sharing" and "participation" in the divine life amounts to no more than my having, in infinitely lesser measure, a knowledge and love of God *of the same sort* as that possessed by God Himself. What is shared are attributes, features, aspects. On this account I don't share in the divine life in any way other than that in which I share in your life when you and I know and love something (perhaps you) in the same way. And because the "sharing in the divine life" is of this relatively innocuous sort, the account provides us no new resources for understanding the divine role in sanctification. How does "sanctifying grace" as so understood *sanctify?* It will be by some combination of our first two models. First God, by fiat, will bestow on the individual the capacity and, presumably, the tendency, to know and love Him in this higher way. Then, by virtue of this knowledge and love, the individual is in a closer interpersonal relation with God and so in a better position to receive influences from Him by way of messages, example, loving encouragement, and so on. No new illumination of the work of sanctification is forthcoming.

By contrast, I should like to suggest a stronger, more literal construal

---

[19]See also St. Thomas Aquinas, *ST*, Ia, Q. 43, art. 3.

of the sharing notion. To my mind, all the talk of being filled, permeated, pervaded by the Spirit, of the Spirit's being poured out into our hearts, strongly suggests that there is a literal merging or mutual interpenetration of the life of the individual and the divine life, a breaking down of the barriers that normally separate one life from another. You and I might be in close personal communion, we might have mutual liking, respect, regard, affection for each other, we might share many interests, attitudes, and reactions. But still our two lives are effectively insulated from each other, with perhaps minor exceptions to be noted below, by physical and psychological barriers. Mine is lived within my skin and yours within yours. When we have similar attitudes, still I have my attitude and you have yours; when we react alike to something, still each of us must react to it on his/her own. If we can now imagine some breakdown of those barriers, perhaps by a neural wiring hookup, so that your reactions, feelings, thoughts, and attitudes, or some of them, are as immediately available to me as my own, and so that they influence my further thinking and feeling and behavior in just the same way that my own do, there would have occurred a partial merging of our hitherto insulated lives. Some of your life would have become as intimately involved with my life as one part of my life is with another. When you are moved by a scene I will *thereby* be moved with your feelings; when you find a remark distasteful I will *thereby* find it distasteful. This is not to say that you will have taken over and eliminated me. Some of your life has been caught up in mine and vice versa, but caught up alongside what would have been there anyway. The details of this could be spelled out in various ways. The merging might be wholly egalitarian, with alien attitudes, thoughts, and reactions on exactly the same footing as the natives. This might lead to considerable incompatibility and tension. Another version would preserve a privileged status for the old settlers, relegating the new immigrants to a servile position. More soberly, your thoughts and reactions might influence the further course of events in me by virtue of being immediately accessible to me, but without being strictly speaking mine until I have taken them up in a certain way. And many other arrangements would be conceivable. However, my aim at present is not to make an exhaustive catalog of modes of life-sharing, but only to suggest that the concept of life-sharing between two persons is one that can be spelled out to some extent.

Another illustration of life-sharing is found in the breakdown of barriers between one psychological subsystem and another within a single human being. It is a truism of psychotherapy that people often wall off a certain sphere of thought, affect, or conation from the rest of the psyche. Perhaps I "never think of" my father and don't consciously feel anything about him and my childhood interactions with him. But it may be that I do have strong attitudes and emotional reactions toward all this that continue to exert influence on my thought and behavior in various ways, but not via the normal conscious route. I have shut it out from conscious thought and feeling, and so my attitudes to it are forced to express themselves in devious ways. If, through psychotherapy or otherwise, these retaining walls are breached, there may be a sudden rush of thought and feeling into consciousness. The conscious part of me has regained touch with a part of my own life; my reactions to my father can now be integrated with the rest of me, and I can enjoy a greater degree of wholeness. There is now a sharing of life, a mutual participation between that memories-of-and-attitudes-toward-the-father complex and the rest of the psyche.

Finally, a more tenuous source of the concept. Earlier I alluded to the possibility of an exception to the insulation of the lives of different human beings—actual exceptions, not just conceivable ones. I was thinking of what happens when two people share a moving experience, like listening to a performance of a great piece of music. Why is it so much more satisfying to "share" something like this than to enjoy it alone? I find it hard to understand this without supposing that each listener actually experiences, to some extent, the reactions of the other; so that I am not just reacting to the music on my own but am also, to some extent, reacting with your reactions as well. This would account for the fact a shared experience is so much richer. If this is a correct reading of the phenomenon, it is another example of the breakdown of the normal barriers between lives. Perhaps we have an analogous phenomenon in the "identification" of the individual with the group that occurs at political rallies, religious worship, and sports events. Here too, perhaps, there is an interpenetration of reactions, flowing through what are normally impermeable walls, so that each individual shares, to some extent, in the life of the others.

We could also turn to mystical experience as a help in getting a purchase on the notion of life-sharing. Such experience is typically reported as involving a drastic breakdown of barriers, a merging of the self with the One, God, Nature, or whatever. However, this might be an unwelcome ally, since mystics often report a complete identification of self and God, and I am seeking to build up a concept of a *partial* sharing in the life of God. A study of orthodox Christian mystics, who are careful to avoid any suggestion of human-divine identification, might be quite pertinent to our problem. We shall nonetheless have to forgo that in this essay.

Here are a couple of additional points about life-sharing. First, an advantage of the term 'life' for what is shared is that it does not restrict us to a sharing of consciousness or of conscious psychological states and processes. This is not to say that there will not be conscious reverberations for the individual, but it will not necessarily be limited to what the individual is conscious of. I may be in contact with the divine life, and the latter may be actively involved in the work of sanctification, in ways I am not aware of. Second, it may well be that the sharing is fuller, or different in some other way, for different aspects of life. I will just mention a few possibilities. The constant admonitions of spiritual directors not to put much stock in feelings which are evanescent and unstable, and which may or may not be present when the spirit is at work, suggest that feelings are an epiphenomenon of the basic part of the sharing, rather than constituting its essence. On the other hand, the abundant testimony to feeling "filled with the Spirit" suggests that feelings and other experiences may be what is most readily and completely shared.[20] The sharing of attitudes, tendencies, and values may require much more time for consummation. Finally certain cognitive elements—beliefs, ways of looking at things, putting the divine scheme of salvation at the center of one's construal of the world—may be readily taken on by the individual from the Spirit at a time when little progress has been made in the transformation of character.

Thus far I have, at most, lent some color to the idea of a literal sharing of the divine life with the believer, and much remains to be done to fill out the details. But the task remaining for this essay is to indicate how the work of sanctification might be accomplished through God's sharing His life with us. The first point to make is that this model is by no means exclusive of the other two. If the Holy Spirit is within me by fiat; and He may seek to influence me by exhortation and loving encouragement. These moves will be made from a more "internal position" by virtue of the sharing, but they would still exemplify what is made central in the other models.[21] But even if sharing is compatible tion" by virtue of the sharing, but they would still exemplify what is made central in the other models.[21] But even if sharing is compatible

[20]On the other hand, one might suppose that such feelings are our reactions to, rather than part of, what is shared. That would certainly follow from the thesis that feelings are not involved in the divine life.

[21]I want to disavow any intention to try to place limits on God's action in our lives. I am suspicious of attempts to arrive at unrestrictedly universal conclusions as to how God achieves a certain effect, and still more suspicious of claims as to how God *must* carry out sanctification or any other divine operation. I don't feel that we are capable of that degree of insight into the possibilities for, or actualities of, God's activity. I am only seeking to lay out certain modes of operation that, so far as we can see, are real possibilities and, in addition, to suggest that some of these modes are more strongly suggested than others by the data at our disposal.

with the other means of sanctification, my present concern is to explore the distinctive implications of sharing for the work of sanctification; I want to show how, by virtue of sharing His life with us, God *thereby* provides us with resources for growth in the Christian life.

Let's recall that our specific interest is in character development, rather than, e.g., the experience and knowledge of God. We want to consider how a participation in the divine life might alter the nature and/or strength of tendencies, attitudes, desires, habits, and emotional proclivities. Now just what possibilities there are for this depends on how we tie up some of the threads hitherto left dangling. Consider an attitude of love toward all of creation, or, more modestly, toward certain people with whom I come into contact. Are we to think of my sharing that divine attitude as sufficient for my *having* that attitude in the same fully incorporated fashion in which I have all my other attitudes? Or are we to think of the sharing in itself as consisting in some relation in which I stand to that attitude which falls short of full-blooded possession, albeit a relation that comes closer to full possession than a mere awareness of the attitude. On the former alternative the sharing model turns into a particular version of the fiat model, for presumably divine volitions play a crucial role in all these models. On the sharing model, in particular, it will be by divine fiat that I share whatever I share of the divine life. It is not as if participation in the divine life is at my beck and call. But then if the (partial) sharing of God's love itself constitutes my having that attitude of love, this is just a particular way in which God alters my motivational structure by fiat. This version of the fiat model will escape the curse of externality that haunts other versions; if God produces in me by fiat a loving attitude, by way of willing that, to some extent, the barriers should be broken down between His life and mine, this could hardly be deemed an *external* operation on His part. However, there will still be no room left for a human response to divine grace in the engendering of my attitude. That is not to say that no room is left for human voluntary activity at any stage. It can still be up to me whether, or to what extent, I do what the infused habits and attitudes tend to lead me to do; it can be up to me whether these tendencies are encouraged, strengthened, and extended by my further thoughts and actions. Nevertheless, so far as the crucial changes in tendencies and attitudes are concerned it will still be a matter of divine fiat alone.

Thus in order to explore the possibility of a place for human cooperation in character development on the sharing model, we will have to consider the idea that my sharing of divine love, in itself, amounts to something less than my fully taking on this attitude, while at the same time amounting to something that can be a push or a tendency in that direction. How might that be? The weakest internalization of divine love that could lay claim to being a *sharing* in that love, in a way that goes beyond the mere exemplification of a common feature, would be an immediate awareness of that love, the kind of awareness that one has of one's own feelings, attitudes, and tendencies. This would, indeed, be a sort of breakdown of the walls that separate different lives, a breakdown of barriers to experiential accessibility. Normally I can't be aware of your thoughts, feelings, and sentiments in the same direct and unmediated way in which I am aware of my own. If I could, then the walls that separate our lives would have been breached in a very significant respect, and I could be said, in an important sense, to share in your (conscious) life. This breach would be of a cognitive nature, in the first instance, but it could have conative implications. If God has permitted me to be aware (to some extent) of His loving tendencies in the same direct way that I am aware of my own, that means that they are "available" to me as models in a maximally direct and vivid fashion. I now have a sense of what it is, what it feels like, to love others in this fashion. I can model my attitudes, not just on external manifestations of love, but on the inner springs of those manifestations. And by psychological processes the exact nature of which I won't try to delineate, processes that I very well might be able to facilitate or hinder by my own choices and my own effort, this may lead to similar loving tendencies in me, where these latter tendencies would be mine in the fullest sense. On this picture of the matter, the divine contribution is largely cognitive, the presentation in a specially vivid and intimate way of a role model; the actual changes in the individual's own motivational structure come from responses, voluntary and involuntary, to these models.

I believe that the preceding constitutes a possible model of (at least some of) the work of sanctification, a model that deserves further exploration. But now that we have come this far, a further step beckons. Immediate cognitive accessibility is not the last stage on the road to conative assimilation that falls short of installation by divine fiat. If I can be directly aware of divine love without thereby taking it on as my own, why can't I have *some* tendency toward loving in that way without my being fully disposed to love in that way whenever the opportunity arises. Tendencies can enjoy all degrees of integration into the dominant motivational structure. I can have passing fancies or yens that, without active encouragement on my part, will never blossom into effective action tendencies. I can have idle wishes to take a voyage around the world, or to chuck it all and live on a yacht, or to take up the cello. These are genuine conative tendencies, not just purely cognitive awareness of possibilities. I do have some tendency to do these things (or to take steps in the direction of doing them). But those tendencies are so weak, or so effectively opposed by stronger interests or systems of interests, that unless I take active steps to encourage them and to dismantle the opposition there is no significant chance that they will influence my behavior. Why shouldn't we think of participation in the divine life as consisting, in part, of the introduction into my conative system of initially weak, isolated, and fragile tendencies like those just mentioned, as well as consisting, in part, of my immediate awareness of God's tendencies of the same sorts? This would be a foot in the conative as well as in the cognitive door; it would be a foothold, a beachhead from which the progressive conquest of the individual's motivational system could get a start. This would be a decisive act on the part of God without which, let us say, the individual has no chance of sanctification. Without the infusion of these initially weak and isolated tendencies there would be nothing to effectively oppose the status quo, the domination of the person by sinful self-centeredness and self-aggrandizement. But there is plenty left for the individual to do, by way of building up the motivational system from the rudimentary beginning supplied by God. At this point the mechanical metaphor might well give way to the organic metaphors used so effectively in the New Testament. We have been talking about a particular way in which God might sow a seed the further fate of which depends on what the recipients do with it. One is put in mind not only of the parable of the sower, but of the striking images in the Fourth Gospel of "water springing up into eternal life" and of the "true bread come down from heaven". It may well be that in its concern to give glory to God and to put a check to sinful pride and presumption, the Christian theological tradition has been too ready to attribute all the work of sanctification to divine activity and to neglect the roles we all, in practice, realize that we ourselves have. The model I have just been suggesting holds out the promise of according both partners their due share, while yet recognizing the necessity and the crucial initiatory role of divine grace.

In conclusion, I will summarize the advantages of the sharing model. First, as just intimated, it makes an important place in sanctification for human response and human effort, while at the same time recognizing the divine initiative as absolutely crucial.[22] Second, unlike the other two models it recognizes a distinctive and fundamental sort of internality in the process of sanctification, a mode of internality that goes beyond any

---

[22]This is in contrast to the fiat model, which attributes the whole proceeding to God; the advantage over the interpersonal model will be brought out next.

interpersonal intimacy, however close, and that goes beyond the internality God necessarily enjoys with respect to all of creation. Furthermore it indicates how this mode of internality is (or can be) essentially involved in the divine work of sanctification. And because it makes this mode of internality central to the process of sanctification it reveals the goal of sanctification to be not just moral improvement, however extensive, but rather a full communion with God, the fullest possible sharing in the divine nature, with respect to which moral development is both a necessary prerequisite and an essential component. Finally, the sharing model permits a satisfactory interpretation of regeneration. To be born again is to come to share in the divine nature. Given our development of this latter notion, regeneration is thereby represented both as a decisive divine initiative that fundamentally transforms the human condition, and as something that in itself leaves the individual with a lot of work to do before she is ready for full communion with God.[23]

[23]This essay has profited from comments by Charles Taliaferro, Robert Adams, and David Burrell.

Some Suggestions for
Divine Command Theorists

I

The basic idea behind a divine command theory of ethics is that what I morally ought or ought not to do is determined by what God commands me to do or avoid. This, of course, gets spelled out in different ways by different theorists. In this essay I shall not try to establish a divine command theory in any form or even argue directly for such a theory, but I shall make some suggestions as to the way in which the theory can be made as strong as possible. More specifically I shall (1) consider how the theory could be made invulnerable to two familiar objections and (2) consider what form the theory should take so as not to fall victim to a Euthyphro-like dilemma. This will involve determining what views of God and human morality we must take in order to enjoy these immunities.

The sort of divine command theory from which I begin is the one presented in Robert M. Adams' paper, "Divine Command Metaethics Modified Again".[1] This is not a view as to what words like 'right' and 'ought' mean. Nor is it a view as to what our concepts of moral obligation, rightness, and wrongness amount to. It is rather the claim that divine commands are constitutive of the moral status of actions. As Adams puts it, "ethical wrongness *is* (i.e., is identical with) the property

From *Christian Theism and the Problems of Philosophy*, ed. Michael Beaty (Notre Dame, Ind.: University of Notre Dame Press, 1989). Reprinted by permission of University of Notre Dame Press.

[1] *Journal of Religious Ethics*, 7, no. 1 (1979).

of being contrary to the commands of a loving God".[2] Hence the view is immune to the objection that many persons don't mean 'is contrary to a command of God' by 'is morally wrong'; just as the view that water *is* H_2O is immune to the objection that many people do not mean 'H_2O' by 'water'. I intend my discussion to be applicable to any version of this "objective constitution" sort. It could just as well be an "ultimate *criterion* of moral obligation" view[3] or a view as to that on which moral obligation *supervenes*. I will understand 'constitutive' to range over all these variants. Thus I can state the basic idea in the following way.

1. Divine commands are constitutive of moral obligation.

There is, of course, a variety of terms that could be used to specify what divine commands are held to constitute. These include 'right', 'wrong', 'ought', 'obligation', and 'duty'. For reasons that will emerge in the course of the essay, I prefer to concentrate on '(morally) ought'. I have used the term 'moral *obligation*' in 1) because it makes possible a more succinct formulation, but whenever in the sequel I speak of moral obligation I do not, unless the reader is warned to the contrary, mean to be trading on any maximally distinctive features of the meaning of that term. I will rather be understanding 'S has a moral obligation to do A' simply as an alternative formulation for 'S morally ought to do A'. I shall often omit the qualifier 'morally' where the context makes it clear what is intended.

Should we think of each particular obligation of a particular agent in a particular situation as constituted by a separate divine command, or should we think of general divine commands, like the Ten Commandments, as constituting general obligations, from which particular obligations follow? No doubt, God does command particular people to do particular things in particular situations; but this is presumably the exception rather than the rule. Therefore in this essay I will have my eye on the idea that general divine commands are constitutive of general obligations or, if you like, of the truth or validity of general principles of obligation.

II

Now for my Euthyphro-like dilemma. The original dilemma in the *Euthyphro* had to do with whether an act is pious because it is loved

---

[2]P. 76.

[3]So long as the "criterion" for the application of a term is not determined by the meaning of the term.

by the gods or is loved by the gods because it is pious. The analogue that is most directly relevant to a divine command ethics is the following. Which of the following should we accept?

II. We ought to, e.g., love one another because God commands us to do so.
III. God commands us to love one another because that is what is what we ought to do.

The divine command theorist apparently embraces the first horn and rejects the second. Of course, the dilemma is often thought to pose a fatal problem for theists generally and not just for divine command theorists. For it is commonly supposed that both horns are unacceptable, and that, since the theist must choose one or the other, this implies the unacceptability of theism. However, I shall be contending that both horns, suitably interpreted, are quite acceptable, and that if the divine command theorist follows my suggestions he can grasp both horns as I interpret them.

The two classic objections to divine command ethics (to the acceptance of the first horn of the dilemma) that I shall be considering are the following.

First: This makes divine commands, and hence, morality, arbitrary. Anything that God should decide to command would *thereby* be obligatory. If God should command us to inflict pain on each other gratuitously we would thereby be obliged to do so. More specifically, the theory renders divine commands arbitrary because it blocks off any moral reason for them. God can't command us to do A because that is what is morally right; for it doesn't become morally right until He commands it.

Second: It leaves us without any adequate way of construing the goodness of God. No doubt, it leaves us free to take God to be *metaphysically* good, realizing the fullness of being and all that; but it forecloses any conception of God as *morally* good, as exemplifying the sort of goodness that is cashed out in being loving, just, and merciful. For since the standards of moral goodness are set by divine commands, to say that God is morally good is just to say that He obeys His own commands. And even if it makes sense to think of God as obeying commands that He has given Himself, that is not at all what we have in mind in thinking of God as morally good. We aren't just thinking that God practices what He preaches, whatever that may be.

These objections are intimately interrelated. If we could answer the second by showing how the theory leaves room for an acceptable account of divine goodness, we could answer the first. For if God is good in the right way, there will be nothing arbitrary about His commands. On the contrary His goodness will ensure that He issues those commands for the best. Hence I will initially concentrate on the second objection.

In the most general terms it is clear what the divine command theorist's strategy should be. He must fence in the area the moral status of which is constituted by divine commands so that the divine nature and activity fall outside that area. That will leave him free to construe divine moral goodness in some other way than conformity with God's own commands, so that this can be a basis for God's issuing commands to us in one way rather than another. The simplest way of doing this is to make (1) apply only to human (or, more generally, creaturely) obligation. Then something else can constitute divine obligation. This move should be attractive to one who supposes that what gives a divine command its morality-constituting force is solely God's metaphysical status in the scheme of things. God is our creator and sustainer, without Whose continual exercise of creative activity we would lapse into nothingness. If God's commands are morally binding on us solely because He stands in that relation to us, it follows that they are not morally binding on Himself; and so if there are any moral facts involving God they will have to be otherwise constituted. But, apart from objections to thinking of the moral authority of God exclusively in terms of power and status, this view would seem to presuppose that moral obligation is something quite different as applied to God and to human beings. For if it is the same, how could it be constituted so differently in the two cases? And if what it is for God to have an obligation is something quite different from what it is for a human being to have an obligation, how is divine obligation construed? I have no idea.[4]

Hence I shall take a more radical line and deny that obligations attach to God at all. (1) implies that divine moral goodness is a matter of obeying divine commands only if moral *obligation* attaches to God; for only in that case can divine moral goodness be a matter of God's satisfying moral obligations. If the kinds of moral status that are engendered by divine commands are attributable only to creatures, then no puzzles can arise over the constitution of divine morality by divine commands. If this move is to work we will have to develop an account of

---

[4]It would be even less productive to cite differences between the content of divine and human moral goodness. No doubt, there are numerous and important differences. Divine virtues do not include obedience to God, temperance in eating, and refraining from coveting one's neighbor's wife. But as the last sentence in the text indicates, there is an overlap too. And even if there were no overlap in content it would still be possible that that by virtue of which X is morally good is the same for God and for man.

divine moral goodness that does not involve the satisfaction of moral obligations.

But our first task is to defend the claim that moral obligation does not attach to God. Stated more generally, the position is that terms in what we might call the (morally) 'ought' family—'ought', 'required', 'permitted', 'forbidden', 'duty', 'obligation' do not apply to God, that it is impossible for God to have duties or obligations, that it cannot ever be true that God ought to do something or other. How can this view be supported?

The position has been argued for from the premise that God lacks "significant moral freedom". It is assumed that terms of the "morally ought" family apply to a being only if that being has a choice between doing or failing to do what it ought to do. But if God is *essentially* perfectly good, as I shall be assuming in this essay,[5] it is, in the strongest way, impossible for God to fail to do what is right. Therefore it can't be correct to speak of God's duties or of what He ought to do.[6] I am not happy with this line of argument. Although it seems clear that my being determined from the "outside" (e.g., by causal factors that were in place before I was born) prevents my having moral obligations, it is not equally clear that we get the same consequence from a determination that springs from my own nature. Of course in my case it might be argued that my nature in turn was determined to be what it is by factors that existed before I was born. But God's nature is not determined by anything other than Himself, much less anything that existed before He did. Hence it is not at all clear that if God acts from the necessity of His own nature that prevents Him from acting freely in a way that is required for moral obligation.

The support I do want to muster is like that set forth in the previous paragraph in appealing to the essential perfect goodness of God, but it exploits that point in a different and a more direct way, by focusing on the lack of divine opposition to acting for the best, rather than the lack of freedom the previous argument infers from that. If God is essentially perfectly good, then it is metaphysically impossible that God should do anything that is less than supremely good; and this includes the moral good as well as other modes of goodness. If it is morally better to be loving than to be indifferent and morally better to love

---

[5] I shall not argue for this. Indeed, it is no part of my aim here to establish the positions I am recommending to the divine command theorist. I aspire only to exhibit them as plausible, and to show how they strengthen the theory.

[6] See Bruce R. Reichenbach, *Evil and a Good God* (New York: Fordham University Press, 1982), chap. 7; Thomas V. Morris, "Duty and Divine Goodness," *American Philosophical Quarterly*, 21 (July 1984).

everyone than to be agapistically selective, it will be metaphysically impossible for God to display indifference or partiality. I shall now argue that the lack of any possibility of God's doing other than the best prevents the application of terms in the 'ought' family to God.

The intuitive idea here is that it can be said that agents ought to do something, or that they have duties or obligations, only where there is the possibility of an opposition to what these duties require. Obligations *bind* us, *constrain* us to act in ways we otherwise might not act. They *govern* or *regulate* our behavior, *inhibit* some of our tendencies and *reinforce* others. We can say that a person ought to do A only where there is, or could be, some resistance on her part to doing A. But how to support this intuition?

For one thing, we can point to the conditions under which it is appropriate to use these terms. To the extent that we think there is no possibility of S's failing to do A, we don't tell him that he ought to do A, or speak of S's duty or obligation to do A. If an assistant professor in my department not infrequently failed to show up for his classes, it would be quite in order for me, as chairman of the department, to call him into my office and remind him of his obligation to meet his classes regularly. Even if he has so much as given signs of a strong temptation to play hooky, the sermon might have a point. But suppose that he has in fact unfailingly taught his classes and, furthermore, has conscientiously performed all his academic duties, even engaging in acts of supererogation. And, given that, suppose I were to remark to him, when passing in the hall one day, "You ought to meet your classes regularly". That remark would naturally evoke intense puzzlement. "What are you talking about? When haven't I met my classes?" The utter naturalness of that response does strongly suggest that the possibility of deviation is a necessary condition of the applicability of terms in the 'ought' family. The oddness of saying that God ought to love His creatures is just the above writ large. The absurdity is compounded by thinking of God saying to Himself, in stentorian Kantian tones, "Thou ought to exercise providence over Thy creation".

It may, quite reasonably, however, be contended that these considerations have to do only with the conditions of appropriateness for certain kinds of illocutionary acts, and not at all with the truth conditions of ought judgments. Even if there would be no point in my *exhorting* or *enjoining* my colleague to meet his classes, the fact remains (I am assuming) that it is his duty to do so, that he ought to do so, however little possibility there is of failure. Similarly, it may be claimed that although it is inappropriate for us to issue moral *injunctions* or *commands* to God, it is still *true* that God, like any rational agent, *ought* to love other rational agents and treat them with justice. This is just one example of the general point that it may be inappropriate to say something, or to say it with a certain illocutionary force, that is, nevertheless, perfectly true. It is inappropriate and puzzling for me to say that I *know* that I feel sleepy, rather than just reporting that I feel sleepy, just because we all take it for granted that a normal person in a normal condition knows what his feelings are at a given moment. This inappropriateness has been taken, e.g., by Wittgenstein as a reason for denying that 'know' has any application in these cases.[7] But it seems clear to me that the inappropriateness of saying that I know I feel sleepy is simply due to the overwhelming obviousness of the fact that I know it if it is the case, and that this inappropriateness has no tendency to show that I don't or can't know such things. An analogous interpretation of the oddity of 'ought' judgments in the absence of presumption of the possibility of deviation, at least for the human cases, is strongly suggested by the following consideration. A natural way to mark out these cases is to say that they are cases in which there is no reason to think that the person is at all tempted to fail in her duties or obligations, to fail to do what she ought to do. But this presupposes that the person *has* duties and obligations, even though there is no point in reminding her of the fact.[8]

I am prepared to accept this objection to the inappropriateness argument, and even to find the conclusion false as well, at least in its application to human beings. Utter dependability, of the sort of which we are capable, does not cancel obligations but merely ensures their fulfillment. But, I claim, an essentially perfectly good God is another matter. However, we will have to find some other way of supporting that claim. The mere fact that it is out of order for anyone to tell God what He ought to do is not sufficient.

At this point I will turn to the most distinguished of my predecessors in holding this thesis, Immanuel Kant.[9] In the *Foundations of the Metaphysics of Morals* he writes:

---

[7]*Philosophical Investigations*, trans. G. E. M. Anscombe (Oxford: Basil Blackwell, 1953), I, 246.

[8]Of course, if we adopt a noncognitive interpretation of ought judgments, according to which their meaning is exhausted by their role in prescribing, exhorting, enjoining, etc., and according to which they are not used in the making of truth claims, then we will hold that there can be no truths about what one ought to do, independently of the appropriateness of performing acts of enjoining and the like. The applicability of the terms, in that case, hangs solely on the appropriateness of speech acts like exhorting. But our entire discussion presupposes an objectivist account of morality. Otherwise the question to which the divine command theory is an answer, viz., "in what does a moral obligation to do A consist?", would not arise.

[9]There are medieval precedents, and I am indebted to Rega Wood for calling them to my attention. See William of Ockham, *Quest. in II Sent.*, qqs. 15, 19; Duns Scotus, *Opus*

... if the will is not of itself in complete accord with reason (the actual case of men), then the actions which are recognized as objectively necessary are subjectively contingent, and the determination of such a will according to objective laws is constraint.

The conception of an objective principle, so far as it constrains a will, is a command (of reason), and the formula of this command is called an *imperative*.

All imperatives are expressed by an "ought" and thereby indicate the relation of an objective law of reason to a will which is not in its subjective constitution necessarily determined by this law. This relation is that of constraint. Imperatives say that it would be good to do or to refrain from doing something, but they say it to a will which does not always do something simply because it is presented as a good thing to do.

A perfectly good will, therefore, would be equally subject to objective laws (of the good), but it could not be conceived as constrained by them to act in accord with them, because, according to its own subjective constitution, it can be determined to act only through the conception of the good. Thus no imperatives hold for the divine will or, more generally, for a holy will. The 'ought' is here out of place, for the volition of itself is necessarily in unison with the law. Therefore imperatives are only formulas expressing the relation of objective laws of volition in general to the subjective imperfection of the will of this or that rational being, e.g, the human will.[10]

It is clear that despite differences in terminology, and deeper differences in the background ethical and metaphysical scheme, Kant is espousing at least something very close to the thesis currently under discussion. "The 'ought' is here out of place, for the volition of itself is necessarily in unison with the law." Just because God acts for the good by the necessity of His nature, ("only through the conception of the good"), He cannot "be conceived as constrained . . . to act in accord with them" ("objective laws of volition"). But it is not clear that Kant has anything significant to add by way of support. Such support as is proferred is based on the claim "All imperatives are expressed by an 'ought' ". (Actually the argument needs the converse of this, that every 'ought' judgment is, or perhaps has the force of, an imperative. Con-

---

Oxon., IV, d. 46, p. 1, n. 1; Peter Lombard, *Sent.*, I, d. 43, c. unicum. A particularly clear formulation is found in Nathaniel Culverwell, *An Elegant and Learned Discourse of the Light of Nature*, chap. 4; reprinted in *Divine Command Morality: Historical and Contemporary Readings*, ed. Janine Marie Idziak (New York: Edwin Mellen, 1979).

[10]*Foundations of the Metaphysics of Morals*, trans. Lewis White Beck (New York: Liberal Arts, 1959), pp. 29–31. For some contemporary endorsements of this position see A. C. Ewing, *The Definition of Good* (London: Routledge & Kegan Paul, 1948), p. 123; and Geoffrey J. Warnock, *The Object of Morality* (London: Methuen, 1971), p. 14.

sider it done.) Without pausing to go into the question of what Kant means by 'imperative' let's just take the most obvious alternative, viz., that he means 'imperative'. In that case his argument could be spelled out as follows.

1. An ought judgment has the force of an imperative.
2. An imperative can be (properly, meaningfully, . . .) addressed only to one who does not necessarily conform to what it demands (enjoins, . . .).
3. God necessarily conforms to what would be commanded by moral imperatives (necessarily does what it is good to do).
4. Therefore moral imperatives cannot be addressed to God.
5. Therefore ought judgments have no application to God.

But this is just a version of the inappropriateness argument already considered and is subject to the same objection. Even if imperatives are not appropriately addressed to God, it still might be true that God ought to do so-and-so. This objection applies to the above argument by denying the first premise. It is a mistake to think that an ought judgment always or necessarily has the force of an imperative. One could make an ought judgment just to state a fact about someone's obligations.

What now? At this point I will confess that I do not have a knock-down argument for my thesis. In fact I doubt that there is a more fundamental and more obvious feature of moral obligation from which the feature in question, the possibility of deviation, can be derived. All I can hope to do is to indicate the way in which this feature is crucial to obligation. Since I am only concerned to recommend the thesis to the divine command theorist as his best hope of avoiding a horn of the Euthyphro dilemma, all I need do, in any case, is to exhibit the plausibility of the thesis.

Let's look at the matter in the following way. In suggesting that God is perfectly good, morally as well as otherwise, even though He is not subject to obligations, we are presupposing a fundamental distinction between value or goodness, including moral goodness, on the one hand, and the likes of duty, obligation, and ought, on the other. This not only involves the obvious point that the concept of the moral goodness of *agents* and *motives* is a different concept from the concept of an obligation to perform an action. It also includes the claim that the moral goodness of an action must be distinguished from its moral obligatoriness. The fact that it would be, morally, a good thing for me to do A must not be confused with the fact that I morally ought to do A, that it is morally *required* of me, that I am morally blameworthy in case I fail to do it. All that is needed to nail down this distinction is the phenomenon of supererogation, a widely though not universally accepted phenomenon. Let's say that it would morally be a good thing for me to see to it that the children of some remote Siberian village have an opportunity to take piano lessons. Nevertheless, so I claim, I have no obligations, moral or otherwise, to do so; I am not morally blameworthy for not doing it. (If you think I am morally blameworthy for not doing this, pick your favorite example of a morally good but not obligatory action.) Note that Kant, in the passage quoted above, is also presupposing such a distinction. He thinks of objective laws of the good as specifying what it would be (morally) good to do, and as such they are applicable even to a holy will. But these "laws" determine obligations only when addressed "to a will which does not always do something simply because it is presented as a good thing to do".

Given this distinction, it is clear that 'S morally ought to do A' adds something to 'It would be a morally good thing for S to do A'. I am taking it as obvious that the latter is a necessary condition for the former. This being the case, there can be a distinction between them only if the former goes beyond the latter in some way. And what way is that? By posing this issue we can see the strength of our thesis. It provides an intuitively plausible way of specifying at least part of what there is to an obligation to do A other than its being a good thing to do A. Let's spell this out a bit, continuing to think of the distinction, among the things it would be good for me to do, between those I am obligated to do and those I am not.

One thing required for my having an obligation to do A, e.g., to support my family, is that there are general principles, laws, or rules that lay down conditions under which that action is required (and that those conditions are satisfied in my case). Call them "practical rules (principles)". Practical principles are in force, in a nondegenerate way, with respect to a given population of agents only if there is at least a possibility of their playing a governing or regulative function; and this is possible only where there is a possibility of agents in that population violating them. Given that possibility, behavior can be guided, monitored, controlled, corrected, criticized, praised, blamed, punished, or rewarded on the basis of the principles. There will be social mechanisms for inculcating and enforcing the rules, positive and negative sanctions that encourage compliance and discourage violation. Psychologically, the principles will be internalized in higher-level control mechanisms that monitor behavior and behavioral tendencies and bring motivational forces to bear in the direction of compliance and away from violation. There can be something like the Freudian distinction of id, ego, and superego within each agent in the population. I take it that terms like 'ought', 'duty', and 'obligation' acquire a use only against this kind of background, and that their application presupposes that practical principles are playing, or at least can play, a regulative role, socially and/or psychologically. And this is at least an essential part of what is added when we move from saying that it would be a good thing for S to do A to saying that S *ought* to do A.

Instead of arguing, as I have just been doing, that a regulative role of practical principles is presupposed by *particular ought judgments*, I could, as Kant does, exploit the fact that practical principles themselves, and more specifically the subclass that can be called moral principles, are naturally expressed in terms of 'ought', and argue more directly for the inapplicability of *moral principles* to God.[11] Under what conditions does the principle that *one ought to take account of the needs of others* apply to an agent, as well as the evaluative principle that it is a good thing for one to take account of the needs of others? For reasons of the sort we have been giving, it seems that such a principle has force, relative to an agent or group of agents, only where it has, or can have, a role in governing, directing, and guiding the conduct of those agents. Where it is necessary that S will do A, what sense is there in supposing that the general principle, *one ought to do A,* has any application to S? Here there is no foothold for the 'ought'; there is nothing to make the ought principle true rather than or in addition to the evaluative statement plus the specification of what S will necessarily do. That is, the closest we can get to a moral law requiring God to love others is the conjunction of the evaluative statement that it is a good thing for God to love others, plus the statement that God necessarily does so.

Note that these very general considerations as to what it takes for ought statements to be applicable are not limited to the moral ought, but equally apply to, e.g., legal, institutional, and prudential oughts, obligations, etc. It is my legal duty to do A only if there is a law in force in my society that, applied to my case, lays on me a requirement to do A. And laws are in force only if there is at least a possibility that they will be disobeyed; otherwise they have no governing or constraining work to do, i.e., no work to do. I should also make it explicit that I am not purporting to deal in this essay with what makes the difference between moral and nonmoral obligations, duties, oughts, goodness, etc. I am simply assuming that there is such a difference and that we have a secure enough working grasp of it to make this discussion possi-

---

[11]This applies most directly to principles *requiring* actions, but interdictions can be expressed in terms of 'ought not', and permissions in terms of 'not ought not'.

ble. Let me also underline the obvious point that I have not claimed to give a complete account of what it takes for practical principles, whether moral, legal, institutional, or whatever, to be in force de jure as well as de facto, so as to engender real obligations. The account of this will, of course, be different for, e.g., legal and moral obligations. It is the claim of the divine command theorist that moral obligations are engendered by and only by practical principles issued as divine commands. I am not concerned to determine what can be said for this claim. My concern with the divine command theory in this essay extends only to considering what it would take for the theory to answer certain objections. And so I am concerned with only part of what is required for ought statements to apply to S, the part that has to do with the possibility of deviation from what the ought statement requires.

What about 'right' and 'wrong'? Can we say that God acts *rightly* in loving His creatures even if we can't say that He is acting as He *ought*? A. C. Ewing, in the passage referred to in footnote 10, endorses that position. Nothing in this essay hangs on a decision, but I am inclined to think that as 'right' is most centrally used in moral contexts, it is tied to terms of the 'ought' family and borrows its distinctive force from them. In asking what is the right thing for me to do in this situation, I am, I think, typically asking what I ought to do in this situation. Ewing and others hold the view that 'right' in moral contexts means something like 'fitting' or 'appropriate' (in a certain way) and hence does not carry the force of 'required', 'bound', and 'culpable if not' that is distinctive of 'ought' and 'obligation'. I am disinclined to agree, but I can avoid the problem here.

This exhausts what I have to say in support of the view that a necessary condition of the truth of 'S ought to do A' is at least the metaphysical possibility that S does not do A. On this view, moral obligations attach to all human beings, even those so saintly as totally to lack any tendency, in the ordinary sense of that term, to do other than what it is morally good to do. And no moral obligations attach to God, assuming, as we are here, that God is essentially perfectly good. Thus divine commands can be constitutive of moral obligations for those beings who have them without its being the case that God's goodness consists in His obeying His own commands, or, indeed, consists in any relation whatsoever of God to His commands.

Eleonore Stump has urged, in conversation, that if God should break a promise He would be doing something He ought not to do, and that this implies that 'ought' does have application to God. My reply is that if God should do something that is forbidden by a valid and applicable moral principle (and the objection assumes that God's breaking a promise would have that status), this would show that it is possible for Him to act in contravention of moral principles. In that case He would not be essentially perfectly good, and so we would not have the reasons advanced in this essay for supposing that He has no moral obligations. That is, Stump's argument shows only that 'ought' would be applicable to God under certain counterfactual conditions (indeed counterpossible conditions if God is essentially perfectly good), not that 'ought' is applicable to Him as things are.

But God is represented in the Bible and elsewhere as making promises, e.g., to Noah and to Abraham, and as making covenants with Israel, and the very concept of a promise or of a covenant involves engendering obligations. It is contradictory to say "God promised Abraham to give him descendants as numerous as the dust of the earth, but God was not thereby obligated (even prima facie) to give Abraham that many descendants". It is equally self-contradictory to say "God entered into a covenant with Israel to establish them forever in the land of Canaan if they would keep His commandments, but God was not thereby obligated to establish them forever in the land of Canaan if they kept His commandments". So how can God fail to have obligations?

I think this argument does show that if God has no obligations it is not strictly true that He makes promises or covenants. Does my view then imply that all these reports are false? No. We can hold that the Biblical writers were speaking loosely, analogically, or metaphorically in so describing the transactions, just as they were in speaking of God "stretching out His arm" and doing so-and-so. They were choosing the closest human analogue to what God was doing in order to give us a vivid idea of God's action. It would be more strictly accurate to say that God *expressed the intention* to make Abraham's descendants as numerous as the dust of the earth, and that He expressed the intention to establish Israel in the land of Canaan forever if they kept His commandments. Just as we can express intentions without obligating ourselves (provided we don't promise), so it is with God. The difference, of course, is that we can count on an expression of intention from God as we can on a promise from a human being, indeed can count on it much more, because of the utter stability and dependability of God's character and purposes.

III

If there is a conceptual distinction between S's satisfying moral obligations and S's actions being morally good, and if the former is not a conceptually necessary condition for the latter, as the phenomenon of supererogation shows, then there is no difficulty in applying the concept of moral to an agent and his actions even if the concept of moral obligation has no application to that agent. In particular, we can think of God as perfectly good, morally as well as otherwise, even if that moral goodness does not consist in the perfect satisfaction of obligations. To put some flesh on this skeleton we might think of it in the following way. By virtue of practical principles that morally require certain things of us, *we* are morally obligated to act in certain ways; speaking summarily, as the occasion dictates, let us say that we are obligated to act justly, show mercy, and care for the needs of others. Now let's remember Kant's suggestion that an 'ought' statement says "that it would be good to do or to refrain from doing something, but they say it to a will which does not always do something simply because it is presented as a good thing to do". This presupposes that the "same thing" can be said to a will of the other sort, a holy will; i.e., the "same thing", the same type of behavior, can be said to such a will to be a good thing. Extricating ourselves from this Kantian dramaturgy, we can say that the morally good things that we are obligated to do can perfectly well have the status for God of morally good things to do, even though He is not *obliged* to do them.[12] Justice, mercy, and lovingness can be moral virtues for God as well as for man, though in His case without the extra dimension added to our virtues by the fact that exhibiting them involves satisfying our obligations. Some of God's moral goodness can be supervenient on the same behavior or tendencies on which, in us, satisfaction of moral obligations as well as moral goodness is supervenient. It can be morally good, both for God and man, to act with loving concern for others, but only we have the privilege of being morally obliged to act in this way.[13]

Since we can develop a satisfactory conception of the moral goodness of God without thinking of God as having moral obligations, we can also escape the arbitrariness objection to divine command ethics. So far from being arbitrary, God's commands to us are an expression of His perfect goodness. Since He is perfectly good by nature, it is impossible that God should command us to act in ways that are not for the best. What if God should command us to sacrifice everything for the acquisition of power? (We are assuming that this is not for the best.) Would it

---

[12]I am, of course, not suggesting that the content of human and divine morality are exactly the same! I am only pointing out that the absence of divine obligations does not prevent an overlap.

[13]See Morris, "Duty and Divine Goodness," sections III and IV, for another affirmation of this point.

thereby be our moral obligation? Since, on our present assumptions, it is metaphysically impossible for God to command this, the answer to the question depends on how it is best to handle subjunctive conditionals with impossible antecedents. But whatever our logic of subjunctive conditionals, this is not a substantive difficulty just because there is no possibility of the truth of the antecedent.

To help nail down the point, let's consider another form of the arbitrariness objection, that on the divine command theory God could have no reason, or at least no moral reason, for issuing the commands He does issue. Now if it is ruled that the only thing that counts as a moral reason for issuing a command to S to do A is that S morally ought to do A, or has a moral duty or obligation to do A, then God cannot have a moral reason for His commands on a divine command ethics. Since S has a moral obligation to do A only in virtue of God's command to do A, this is not a fact, antecedent to the command, that God could take as a reason for issuing the command. But surely there can be other sorts of moral reasons for commands and injunctions, e.g., that an act would be repaying of a kindness or that it is a morally good thing to behave in a certain way. More generally the moral goodness of doing A, or anything on which that moral goodness supervenes, can be a moral reason for doing A or for requiring someone to do A. Thus if the moral goodness of acts is independent of their obligatoriness, God can have moral reasons for His commands.

IV

Thus the divine command theorist escapes the supposedly fatal consequences of the first horn of the Euthyphro dilemma. But perhaps the maneuvers by which this escape was negotiated result in impalement on the second horn. We evaded the first horn by taking God's moral goodness, including the moral goodness of divine actions, not to be constituted by conformity to moral obligations, and hence not to be constituted by conformity to divine commands, even on this ethical theory.[14] But doesn't that leave us exposed to the second horn? We are not confronted with that horn in the original form, "God commands us to love our neighbor because that is what we ought to do", but with a

14The same considerations will lead to taking divine goodness to be independent of all divine volition. For if God's being good is a matter of His carrying out what He wills (rather than commands), the arbitrariness objection applies in full force. And divine goodness again becomes trivialized as "God carries out His volitions, whatever they are".

closely analogous form, "God commands us to love our neighbor because it is morally good that we should do so". And that possesses the sort of feature deemed repellent to theism just as much as the first form, viz., that it makes the goodness of states of affairs independent of the divine will, thereby subjecting God to valuational facts that are what they are independent of Him. It thereby contradicts the absolute sovereignty of God; it implies that there are realities other than Himself that do not owe their being to His creative activity. If it is true, independently of God's will, that loving communion is a supreme good, and that forgiveness is better than resentment, then God is subject to these truths. He must conform Himself to them and so is not absolutely sovereign.

One way of meeting this objection is to assimilate evaluative principles to logical truths. If evaluative principles are logically necessary, then God's "subjection" to these principles is just a special case of His "subjection" to logical truths, something that is acknowledged on almost all hands.

However, I am going to suggest a more radical response. The difficulty with this horn of the dilemma is generally stated as I just stated it, in terms of a Platonic conception of the objectivity of goodness and other normative and evaluative statuses. If it is an objective fact that X is good, this is because there are objectively true general principles that specify the conditions under which something is good (the features on which goodness supervenes) and S satisfies these conditions. To go back to the *Euthyphro:*

> Soc. Remember that I did not ask you to give me two or three examples of piety, but to explain the general idea which makes all pious things to be pious. . . . Tell me what is the nature of this idea, and then I shall have a standard to which I may look, and by which I may measure actions, whether yours or those of anyone else, and then I shall be able to say that such and such an action is pious, such another impious. [6]

What is ultimate here is the truth of the general principle; any particular example of goodness has that status only because it conforms to the general "Idea".

I want to suggest, by contrast, that we can think of God Himself, the individual being, as the supreme standard of goodness. God plays the role in evaluation that is more usually assigned, by objectivists about value, to Platonic Ideas or principles. Lovingness is good (a good-making feature, that on which goodness supervenes) not because of the

Platonic existence of a general principle, but because God, the supreme standard of goodness, is loving. Goodness supervenes on every feature of God, not because some general principles are true but just because they are features of God. Of course, we can have general principles, e.g., *lovingness is good.* But this principle is not ultimate; it, or the general fact that makes it true, does not enjoy some Platonic ontological status; rather it is true just because the property it specifies as sufficient for goodness is a property of God.

We can distinguish (a) "Platonic" predicates, the criterion for the application of each of which is an "essence" or "Idea" that can be specified in purely general terms, and (b) "particularistic" predicates, the criterion for the application of each of which makes essential reference to one or more individuals. Geometrical terms like 'triangle' have traditionally been taken as paradigms of the former. There are rather different subclasses of the latter. It is plausible to suggest, e.g., that biological kind terms like 'dog' are applied not on the basis of a list of defining properties but on the basis of similarity to certain standard examples. Putnam has extended this idea to natural kind terms generally. Again, there are "family resemblance" terms like 'game' or 'religion', the application of which again seems to rely on standard paradigm cases. A subtype closer to our present concern is the much discussed 'meter'. Let's say that what makes a certain length a meter is its equality to a standard meter-stick kept in Paris. What makes this table a meter in length is not its conformity to a Platonic essence but its conformity to a certain existing individual.[15] Similarly, on the present view what ultimately makes an act of love a good thing is not its conformity to some general principle but its conformity to, or approximation to, God, Who is both the ultimate source of the existence of things and the supreme standard by reference to which they are to be assessed.

Note that on this view we are not debarred from saying what is supremely good about God. It is not that God is good *qua* bare particular or undifferentiated thisness. God is good by virtue of being loving, just, merciful, etc. Where this view differs from its alternative is in the answer to the question, "By virtue of what are these features of God good-making features?". The answer given by this view is: "By virtue of being features of God".

It may help to appreciate the difference of this view from the more

[15]To be sure, it is arbitrary what particular stick was chosen to serve as the standard, while I am not thinking that it is arbitrary whether God or someone else is "chosen" as the supreme standard of goodness. That is a way in which the analogy is not perfect. The example was used because of the respect in which there is an analogy, viz., the role of the individual standard in truth conditions for applications of the term.

usual valuational objectivism if we contrast the ways in which these views will understand God's (perfectly good) activity. On a Platonic view God will "consult" the objective principles of goodness, whether they are "located" in His intellect or in a more authentically Platonic realm, and see to it that His actions conform thereto. On my particularist view God will simply act as He is inclined to act, will simply act in accordance with His character, and that will necessarily be for the best. No preliminary stage of checking the relevant principles is required.

My particularistic suggestion exhibits some instructive similarities and dissimilarities to a recent deployment by Eleonore Stump and Norman Kretzmann of the doctrine of divine simplicity in connection with the Euthyphro dilemma.[16] In terms of the contrast I have been drawing, they use the doctrine of simplicity to show that one can be both Platonistic and particularistic about value. They do not deny that God is perfectly good by virtue of conforming to perfect goodness, but they avoid subjecting God to an independent reality by maintaining, in accordance with the doctrine of simplicity, that God *is* perfect goodness. Thus the supreme standard of goodness is both perfect goodness, the Platonic Idea, and God Himself. As Kretzmann once put it to me in conversation, the really staggering fact is that the Idea of the Good is a person. Since I have difficulties with the doctrine of simplicity I have felt forced to choose between Platonism and particularism; but I agree with Stump and Kretzmann that God can be perfectly good in an eminently nonarbitrary sense without being subject to some independent standard.

I will briefly consider two objections to my valuational particularism. First, it may seem that it is infected with the arbitrariness we have been concerned to avoid. Isn't it arbitrary to take some particular individual, even the supreme individual, as the *standard* of goodness, regardless of whether this individual conforms to general principles of goodness or not? To put it another way, if we want to know what is good about a certain action or human being, or if we want to know why that action or human being is good, does it throw any light on the matter to pick out some other individual being and say that the first is good because it is like the second. That is not advancing the inquiry. But this objection amounts to no more than an expression of Platonist predilections. One may as well ask: "How can it be an answer to the question 'Why is this

---

[16]"Absolute Simplicity," *Faith and Philosophy*, 2 (October 1985), 375–76. For a more extended presentation of the same idea see Norman Kretzmann, "Abraham, Isaac, and Euthyphro: God and the Basis of Morality," in *Hamartia, The Concept of Error in the Western Tradition: Essays in Honor of John M. Crossett*, ed. D. V. Stump, E. Stump, J. A. Arieti, and L. Gerson (New York: Edwin Mellen, 1983).

table a meter long?' to cite its coincidence with the standard meter-stick?" There just are some properties that work that way. My suggestion is that goodness is one of those properties, and it is no objection to this suggestion to aver that it is not.

Here is another response to the objection. Whether we are Platonist or particularist, there will be some stopping place in the search for explanation. An answer to the question "What is good about X?" will cite certain alleged good-making characteristics. We can then ask: "By virtue of what does good supervene on those characteristics?" The answer to that might involve citing the relation of those features to other alleged good-making characteristics. But sooner or later either a general principle or an individual paradigm is cited. Whichever it is, that is the end of the line. (We can, of course, ask why we should suppose that this principle is true or that this individual is a paradigm; but that is a different inquiry.) On both views something is taken as ultimate, behind which we cannot go, in the sense of finding some *explanation* of the fact that it is constitutive of goodness, as contrasted with a defense of the claim that it is constitutive of goodness. I would invite one who finds it arbitrary to invoke God as the supreme standard of goodness to explain why this is more arbitrary than the invocation of a supreme general principle. Perhaps the principle seems self-evidently true to him. But it will not seem so to many others; and it seems self-evident to some that God is the supreme standard. And just as my opponent will explain the opposition to this claims of self-evidence by saying that the opponents have not considered the matter sufficiently, in an impartial frame of mind, or whatever, so the theistic paricularist can maintain that those who do not acknowledge God as the supreme standard are insufficiently acquainted with God or have not sufficiently considered the matter.

Second, it may be objected that, on theistic particularism, in order to have any knowledge of what is good we would have to know quite a bit about God. But many people who know little or nothing about God know quite a bit about what is good. The answer to this is that the view does not have the alleged epistemological implications. It does have some epistemological implications. It implies that knowing about the nature of God puts us in an ideal position to make evaluative judgments. But it does not imply that explicit knowledge of God is the only sound basis for such judgments. The particularist is free to recognize that God has so constructed us and our environment that we are led to form sound value judgments under various circumstances without tracing them back to the ultimate standard. Analogously, we are so constructed and so situated as to be able to form true and useful opinions about water without getting so far as to discern its ultimate chemical or physical constitution, without knowing what makes it water.

As a final note on particularism, I should like to point out its connection with certain familiar themes, both Christian and otherwise. It is a truism of what we might call "evaluational development" (of which moral development is a species) that we more often come to recognize and appreciate good-making properties through acquaintance with specially striking exemplifications than through being explicitly instructed in general principles. We acquire standards in art, music, and literature, through becoming intimately familiar with great works in those media; with that background we are often able to make confident judgments on newly encountered works without being able to formulate general principles on which we are relying. Our effective internalization of moral standards is more often due to our interaction with suitable role models than to reflecting on general moral maxims. The specifically Christian version of this is that we come to learn the supreme value of love, forgiveness, and self-sacrifice by seeing these qualities exemplified in the life of Christ, rather than by an intellectual intuition of Platonic Forms. I do not mean to *identify* these points about our access to the good with the particularist theory as to what it is that makes certain things good. They are clearly distinguishable matters. But I do suggest that a full realization of how much we rely on paradigms in developing and shaping our capacities to recognize goodness will render us disposed to take seriously the suggestion that the supreme standard of goodness is an individual paradigm.

V

This completes my suggestions to the divine command theorist as to how he can avoid the allegedly fatal consequences of both horns of the Euthyphro-like dilemma we have been considering. It only remains to set out explicitly the relationship between the positions I have suggested to escape each of the two horns. That relationship derives from the distinction between value and obligation, more specifically the moral forms thereof. To blunt the first horn I have suggested that we take divine commands to be constitutive only of moral obligation, only of facts of the form 'S morally ought to do A', 'S morally ought not to do B', 'and 'S is morally permitted to do C', leaving value and goodness, moral and otherwise, to be otherwise constituted. When we combine this point with the view that God is not subject to obligations, moral or otherwise, we find that the theory does not saddle us with an inadequate conception of divine moral goodness and hence that it does not represent the basis of human moral obligation as arbitrary. To deal with the second horn, and to fill out the view with an account of goodness and value, we take it that the supreme standard of goodness, including moral goodness, is God Himself, that particular individual, rather than some general principle or Platonic Idea. A creaturely X has value to the extent that it imitates or approximates the divine nature in a way appropriate to its position in creation. This is the most general account of value (as contrasted with obligation) for any sort of value, including the moral goodness of persons, motives, and actions. My visiting a sick friend is a good thing to do because and only because it constitutes an imitation of the divine nature that is appropriate for me and my current situation. But that leaves untouched the question of whether I *ought* to do this, whether it is my *duty* or *obligation*, whether I am *required* or *bound* to do it, whether I would be *culpable, guilty, blameworthy,* or *reprehensible* for failing to do it. This, according to the view here developed, is a matter of whether God has commanded me to do it, or whether my doing it follows from something God as commanded.[17] The divine *nature*, apart from anything God has willed or done, is sufficient to determine what counts as good, including morally good. But we are *obliged, bound,* or *required* to do something only on the basis of a divine command.

This then is my suggestion as to how to recognize a fundamental role for divine commands in morality without being impaled on one or another horn of a Euthyphro-like dilemma. I have not shown, or even argued, that divine commands *are* constitutive of moral obligation; nor have I entered into the question of how they could be. I have merely aspired to develop a view of God, morality, and value that leaves open the possibility that they should play this role.[18]

[17]I don't mean to restrict this "following" to deductive implication. It also includes, e.g., being a reasonable application of some general command issued by God.

[18]Earlier versions of this essay were presented at the Pacific Regional Meetings of the Society of Christian Philosophers, at Cornell University, and at meetings of the Society for Philosophy of Religion. I would like to thank participants in all those sessions for many useful suggestions. Special thanks go to Robert Adams, Jonathan Bennett, Norman Kretzmann, Louis Pojman, John Robertson, Richard Swinburne, Eleonore Stump, Stewart Thau, and Linda Zagzebski.

Index

Actions, 54–62; basic, 55–62, 85;
general concept of, 57–59, 83–85, 94;
human, 55–59, 72, 82–84; intentional
58, 83, 94, 208, 229; nonbasic, 56–62;
plans, 93–94; purposive, 201. *See also*
Agent causation; Behavior; Divine
actions; Divine agency; Divine-human
interaction; Divine replies; Divine
responses
Actual entity, 137–40; infinite, 139–40
Actuality, God as pure, 123, 179, 191.
See also Potentiality
Adams, Marilyn McCord, 163, 165
Adams, Robert M., 206, 253–54
Agent causation, 58–59, 93–94. *See also*
Actions; Divine actions; Divine agency
Analogy, 19, 65, 102
Analytic-synthetic distinction, 57, 82–83
Anselm, St., 142
Aquinas, St. Thomas, 51, 65, 67, 78,
121–24, 127–28, 136, 140–41, 153–
54, 164, 179–81, 183, 199–200, 203,
243, 245
Atemporality of God, 64, 81, 130, 133,
198, 206; and action, 153–60; and
creation, 132–33; and dispositions,
191; and divine-human dialogue,
152–60; intelligibility of, 136–40; and
perfection, 140–42; and problem of
foreknowledge and freedom, 3, 153;
and relativity, 133–36; specious
present as model of, 136–37; and
theological predication, 72–73, 77, 91,
93, 96–100; Whiteheadian actual
entity as model of, 137–40

Audi, Robert, 187, 191
Augustine, St., 199, 243

Behavior, 53, 68–70, 72, 74–76; divine,
52, 76–79, 95. *See also* Actions; Divine
actions
Beliefs, 49, 73–74, 79, 86, 184;
dispositional account of, 191–92;
divine, 76–78, 86–87, 162–63, 166,
168–72, 178–79, 183–86, 190–93;
divine beliefs and free will, 162–63,
166, 168–72; explanation of, 185;
functional account of, 50, 67–69, 70,
88; occurrent account of, 191; as
propositional attitudes, 183. *See also*
Intentional states
Blanshard, Brand, 188
Block, Ned, 69, 99
Boethius, 140
Bonjour, Laurence, 188
Bradley, F. H., 182–83, 188
Braithwaite, R. B., 18
Brandt, Richard B., 50–51
Brentano, Franz, 87
Brunner, Emil, 232

Calvin, Jean, 199
Carnap, Rudolf, 49
Causal laws, 164–65, 169–71, 173, 176,
211–13
Causation: of actions by psychological
factors, 58–60; backwards, 172
Chisholm, Roderick M., 58, 87
Church, 224–28

275

Library of Congress Cataloging-in-Publication Data

Alston, William P.
  Divine nature and human language : essays in philosophical theology /
William P. Alston.
     p. cm.
  Includes index.
  ISBN 0-8014-2258-2 (alk. paper). — ISBN 0-8014-9545-8 (pbk. alk. paper)
  1. Philosophical theology. 2. God. 3. Languages—Religious aspects—
Christianity. I. Title.
BT40.A46 1989   211—dc19   89-898